COLLECTOR'S GUIDE TO
Ideal Dolls

IDENTIFICATION & VALUES

SECOND EDITION

JUDITH IZEN

COLLECTOR BOOKS

A Division of Schroeder Publishing Co., Inc.

The current values in this book should be used only as a guide. They are not intended to set prices, which vary from one section of the country to another. Auction prices as well as dealer prices vary greatly and are affected by condition as well as demand. Neither the author nor the publisher assumes responsibility for any losses that might be incurred as a result of consulting this guide.

Cover Design by Beth Summers
Book Design by Holly C. Long

COLLECTOR BOOKS
P.O. Box 3009
Paducah, Kentucky 42002-3009

Contents

Acknowledgments

It has been my pleasure to compile this second edition of the *Collector's Guide to Ideal Dolls*. I have expanded the Shirley Temple, Toni, Miss Revlon, Little Miss Revlon, Patti Playpal, Tammy, and Crissy sections. Collectors have been most helpful in contributing photos and asking questions that have resulted in this new expanded edition of the Ideal book.

During the research for this book I have talked with many former Ideal employees all who spoke about their happy days at Ideal reminiscing that working there felt like a "family business." Indeed, many still keep in touch through a club and newsletter. This book was written with the help of many of the people who comprised the Ideal Toy Company. Herbert Lawrence, former director of engineering services helped start me on the path; Miriam Gittleson at Ideal several decades has been most generous in sharing her information and archives; Helmuth Moormann at Ideal from 1946 – 83 has shared his extensive knowledge of Ideal's doll production; Hilda Halpern, widow of Sig Halpern the former Production Manager, has also been most gracious. Other Idealites and their spouses have been instrumental in helping my research.

Relatives of Ideal's founder, Morris Michtom, have also been most generous in sharing their memories and photos. I would like to especially thank Anita Child (Abraham M. Katz's daughter) who entrusted me with precious family pictures. I also had the pleasure of interviewing Eleanor Gabriel, David Rosenstein's daughter; Hadassah Michtom, widow of Benjamin Franklin Michtom; Paula Michtom, Mark's widow; Dr. Robert Michtom, Dr. Joseph's son; Betty Katz Weintraub, daughter of Abraham Katz; and Lionel Weintraub, former President of Ideal.

The extended "family" at Ideal who lent me their memories and their catalogs include: Judy Alpert, Arte Alpert, Frank Azarra, Addie Reiley Bagnasco, John Bancale, Julius Cooper, Vincent DeFilippo, Henry Delach, Joseph Diorio, Neil Estern, Nat Gelfand, Carl Gibbony, Joe Ghossen, Joseph Glaudino, William Halperin, Jack Hirschberg, Matthew Hollwedel, Tom Hyde, Abe Kent, Gerald Kirschbaum, Esq., Dick Klein, Dave Koske, Richard Levine, Catherine Lipfert (Bernard Lipfert's daughter-in-law), Bernard Meltzer (Age 92), Al Miller, Hilda Milton, David Niehaus, John Pace, Jean Peet, Rolf Pelikan, Mel Poretz, Max Prupes, Rich Rabkin, Burt Reiner, Oscar Reis, Harry Rothbard, Herb Sands, Leonard Solomon, Jerry Stone, Ben Stopek, Bernie Weiner, Denora Wilcox, Dan Winsor, Alma Wright, and Sam Zimtbaum, also a relative.

At Tyco Industries, Inc.: Jill Ottinger, VP/ Marketing and Product Development (1988), Valerie Williams, Senior Marketing Director, and Robert Lurie, Vice President/Advertising.

I also wish to thank the collectors, dealers, auction houses, and museums who have graciously shared information, dolls, and photos. Marge Meisinger is always most gracious and generous with her Ideal dolls. Don Jensen, newspaperman, also was most kind in sharing information. Diane Buck, doll curator of Wenham Museum, shared several wonderful doll photos. Other kind people who most generously supplied photographs or allowed me to photograph their dolls are: Dorothy Alford, Flora Belle Allen, Patti Anderson, Jan Aranoff, Judy Armitstead, Margaret Baron, Marie Blair, Doris Blocker, John Bonavita, Judy Borges, Maureen Braeden, Millie Caliri, Diane Carpino, Chris and Joe Carrick, Pauline Chantry, B.J. Crane, Kerra Davis, Rita Dubas, Marie Ceil Eastman, Debi Toussaint Edgar, Elsie Fancher, Marcia Fanta, Carol Fetherman, Audrey Fletcher, Beulah Franklin, Nancy Fredericks, Lori Gabel, Debbie Garrett, Susan Giradot, Margaret Groninger, Tricia Gullingsrud, Cheryl Haisch, Susan Haynes, Serena Henderson, Dorothy Hesner, Betty Hopkins, Kerry Israels, Cris Johnson, Betty K. Jones, Iva Mae M. Jones, Mary Kangas, Charlotte Klein, Ruth Leif, Nancy Linder, Beverly Marmon, Pamela Martinec, Patty Massey, Anita Maxwell, McMaster Doll Auctions, John Medeiros, Laura Meisner, Jean Melanson, Cheri Miller, Peggy Millhouse, Susan Mobley, Rebecca Mucchetti, Valerie Myers, Georgia Naylor, Linda Paradis, Edward Pardella, Linda Pearson, Veronica Phillips, Linda Pottle, Karen Puck, Christina Rallo, Robin Randall, Kathy Reed, Victoria Reinert, Terrie Richardson, Evelyn Roudybush, Sylvia Rose, Donna Rygiewicz, Ed Schweizer, Nancy Shomo, Dot Smith, John Sonnier, Frank Sposato, Mary Steucher, Carol Stover, Robert Swerdlow, Marlene Tartaglia, Aida Tejaratchi, Juley Teuscher, Kathleen Tornikoski, Courtesy Ann Wencel, Carol Wetherla, Jessie Williams, Edith Wise, Richard Withington Inc. Auctions, Robin Woods, Rosalie Whyel Museum and its curator, Susan Hedrick, and the Yesteryears Museum, Christy Young, Danny Young, Pam Zampiello, Edna Zeiler.

I also give thanks to my entire family: my wonderful husband, Myles H. Kleper; my great kids, Shulamit Elisheva, Seth Edward, and Naomi Ruth Izen; and my parents, Mel and Shirley Izen, who brought me up in the Juvenile and Toy Trade.

I would be most grateful for any corrections, pictures or additional information about Ideal dolls, especially those not pictured in this book. You may write to: P.O. Box 623, Lexington, MA 02420.

Preface

Every American child born since the beginning of the twentieth century has probably played with an IDEAL Toy Company toy or doll. That's how popular and pervasive Ideal's influence has been on children since 1907. The Ideal Toy Company is one of America's oldest and largest manufacturer of dolls: dolls so popular they became a nation's obsession such as "Shirley Temple," "Betsy Wetsy®," or "Patti Playpal." Ideal's doll production was so proliferate that over 500 different dolls were "brought to life."

This short history will introduce the reader to the genius of the men and women who led the Ideal Toy Company to its great successes. Homage should be paid to those who provided us with so many hours of joy.

Readers will let out short exclamations of joy as they recognize dolls they played with or wished for in their youth.

This book contains all known dolls produced by Ideal, illustrated with photos of the dolls and/or their original ads or pictures in the Ideal catalog. Included are dolls, stuffed animals with human faces, and puppets portraying humans. Teddy bears, when they figure prominently in Ideal's history, are also pictured. Toys and figurines are not covered in this book for they would require another complete volume.

Since Ideal dolls were mass-produced, they are still accessible and affordable to those who wish to recapture some of the joy of youth.

About the Author

Judith Izen, a doll historian and toy industry researcher, has degrees from Boston University and Harvard School of Public Health. Her specialization is 1940 – 1960 era dolls. She is the doll columnist for *ToyShop* and has written extensively for *Doll Readers, Doll News,* and *Antiques and Collecting Hobbies* magazines. Ms. Izen is also a lecturer, teacher, and guest curator on collectible dolls.

How To Use This Book

Dolls are listed chronologically by name. The name is followed by the date the doll was first produced: for example, "Mitzi" (1961). When the doll was produced for more than one year, it is listed as "Toni" (1949 – 55). This listing is for a doll produced from the same mold using the same material. Sometimes a doll was produced at a later date using a different material or mold for the head or body. The doll would then also be listed chronologically when she was subsequently produced with the changes noted in italics. For example, "Betsy Wetsy®" first produced in 1937 is listed there and again in 1956 when she was changed or "Bonny Braids," first produced as a baby in 1951 using magic skin and again as a toddler in 1953 manufactured in all vinyl.

Dolls known to have been produced but not pictured are listed in a separate table in chronological order.

In Order to Identify your Doll

First, determine the material of your doll.
General guidelines:

Composition was produced from 1907 – 1949
Magic Skin Latex from 1940 – 1942, 1947 – 1955
Hard plastic from 1942 – 1956
Vinyl from 1950

If you cannot determine the material of your doll, consult the next section "What Is My Doll Made Of?" You may also consult the Table of Ideal Trademarks which may help you find your doll's marks chronologically.

Second, look for your doll in the photo section. If your doll is not there, look in back in the chronological tables of unphotographed dolls.

Several other tables are also included to aid the collector in identifying dolls that were produced several times in different materials (i.e., "Shirley Temple" and "Betsy Wetsy®") or may cause difficulty in identifying (the "Crissy®" family dolls).

Other tables list all known costumes produced ("Miss Revlon," "Little Miss Revlon" and "Little Betsy Wetsy®").

Pricing

Dolls are valued realistically. They are the prices that doll collectors have *paid* for dolls or can reasonably expect to pay for dolls in excellent condition from dealers at doll shows or through the mail. Mint in Box (MIB) dolls are worth from 25% to 100% more than listed price. Dolls in less than excellent condition would be devalued according to their condition. As a general rule, black versions of dolls cost more than the white versions, since fewer were usually produced.

All dolls featured within this book are given current values. Values for each doll pictured are given in that doll's first appearance. The value guide for dolls not pictured begins on page 313.

Sizes of dolls sometimes vary due to manufacturing processes. A doll advertised in the catalog as 16" could measure 15" or 17"; use the closest size when figuring the price. As always, prices are relative, and ultimately a doll is worth the price a buyer is willing to pay.

What Material Is My Doll Made Of?

Composition

What It Looks Like. Surface looks like it has been painted. Most now have small cracks or the paint is peeling or flaking off. Eyes were made of tin or celluloid. Some dolls' eyes made in the 1930s have a white cast to them. Wigs are made of mohair or human hair. Molded hair dolls are painted and have molded curls.

How It is Made. Composition is a mixture of sawdust, glue, and other ingredients such as cornstarch, resin, and wood flour. A machine somewhat like a bread flour mixer mixed the compound of sawdust and glue which was taken to the pressing machines and then pressed into molds separated in two parts – the front and back. (After World War I the mixture was heated before being pressed.) When dried, the two body parts were glued together and sanded down to remove seams. The finishing department then dipped the parts (which were brown in color) into vats of flesh color liquid which were then dried. Cheek color was sprayed on the heads with an air brush. Then artists hand painted the eyebrows, eye lashes, nostrils, and mouth. Eyes were either painted on or celluloid, metal, or glass eyes were inserted into holes cut out of the composition head. A coating of varnish or lacquer was applied to each body part to make it waterproof.

Hints on Preservation. Composition is a organic compound so it will deteriorate. Keep in cool dry place, not in attics or basements.

Magic Skin (Latex Rubber)

What It Looks Like. Doll has a soft body. Usually the color has darkened or hardened around the edges exposed to sunlight. The doll feels soft to the touch and is stuffed with cotton. The head is made of hard plastic.

How It is Made. *Slush Molding.* An aluminum or other metal mold was dipped into latex to form a thin rubber skin. It was then dried and the thickness of its coating was increased by further series of dippings. After the desired thickness was formed, it was vulcanized by means of steam or hot air. After vulcanization, it was stripped from its mold, and its body was stuffed through the neck opening with a material such as kapok. The forms have natural bendable joints. Fingers were filled with a mixture of either powdered hide glue, glycerine, water, and sugar; or other material such as cork particles, divided fibers of cotton, silk, rayon, mineral wool, and natural wool mixed with a binder, such as glue mixed with glycerine or egg albumin.

Hints on Preservation. The outlook is not good for Magic Skin since it is an organic compound that is rapidly deteriorating. Dolls from the 1940s harden and split.

Hard Plastic

What It Looks Like. Hard plastic dolls are hard to the touch, have seams along their side, can be strung, or have walker bodies, and have a wig glued on their head or have molded hair.

How It is Made. The process of Injection Molding started in the early 1940s is still being used, according to John Bancale, Supervisor of Injection Molding (1942 – 1962). First a clay head model is sculpted. A plaster of Paris cast is made of the head, followed by a rubber mold. The rubber mold is then put into a casting machine and liquid copper beryllium is poured around the face. The beryllium takes the shape of the face to make a beryllium cast mold. This beryllium cast mold is then inserted into a mold press. Plastic, either acetate, styrene or butyrate, is heated to about 350°F inside the cylinder tube on one side of machine. Liquid plastic shoots into the mold under high pressure. Then the mold is cooled. The process produces a head in two halves that are cemented together.

Outlook For Preservation. Since hard plastic is inert, it is not biodegradable. But it will oxidize and change color when exposed to ultraviolet light. Keep these dolls away from sunlight and air. The material is thermoplastic and can be melted down and recycled. The hard plastic dolls made by injection molding from acetate also dry out (an example are the "Toni" dolls). This material is similar to eyeglass frames which dry out and eventually break. Keep these dolls protected from the atmosphere in a glass case.

Rotational Molded Vinyl

What It Looks Like. Vinyl can be hard or soft to the touch and flexible, depending on how much plasticizer was added. For example, Tammy's (1962) body and legs are blow molded vinyl, and her head and arms, which are much softer and more flexible, are rotational molded vinyl.

How It is Made. Ideal started experimenting in double slush molding by 1951. Doll heads were sculpted in clay, and then a wax model was made. The wax model was placed in a tank of sulfuric acid and copper sulfate on metal rods. The rods would rotate in the solution, and copper would adhere to the wax through an electrical charge. When copper had built up to a sixteenth or eighth of an inch, the molds were taken out and put into ovens. Wax would drip out when heated, and the copper mold would be a perfect image of the original wax model inside. These copper molds would be mounted on a platform and filled with vinyl in viscous (liquid) form, then cooked in an oven at 600 degrees, while being rotated in a gyroscopic effect so the liquid would be thrown against the mold causing the vinyl to adhere to the inside of copper mold. This "skin" would then have the consistency of a latex glove. Molds would then be cooled in a water bath, and the covers removed and parts would be pulled out with tongs. (Thanks to David Niehaus, manager of Ideal's Prototype Model Shop, for this information.)

Outlook For Preservation. Vinyl dolls from the 1950s rapidly change color, and they will eventually become harder and crack as the plasticizer migrates out. Plasticizers are used with synthetic resins to make the vinyl softer and more flexible. Because of this process, the clothing is affected as the doll picks up the dyes from the clothes and even from the packaging. Even rubber bands will affect the vinyl as the sulfa from the rubber bands attacks the vinyl.

The only solution is to keep the dolls you have out of the sun (and other ultraviolet light) and away from the air. Ideal engineer Herbert Lawrence recommends putting the dolls in a plastic bag since polyethelene is inert, and it will not interact with the vinyl. Dolls are as sensitive as people and are even affected by the ozone in the air.

Blow-Molded Vinyl

What It Looks Like. Blow-molded vinyl dolls are usually large and hollow, with arms attached by flanges or strung as in the case of "Patti Playpal." These dolls produce a hard, hollow sound when tapped and have seams.

How It is Made. Polyethylene pellets are melted in an extruder, which extrudes a tube down between an open mold. When the tube extends the full length of the mold, it closes, air is blown inside the tube at 90 PSI causing the soft plastic tube to take the shape of the mold. The plastic is cooled, the mold is opened, and the part is removed. Excess material where the mold pinched the tube is trimmed with a knife. This material is thermoplastic and can be recycled.

Outlook For Preservation. The good news is that blow-molded dolls made from polyethylene, such as "Patti Playpal," will last forever. This is the same product that is clogging our dumpsites and environment, since it doesn't disintegrate into its component parts. What is good for doll collectors is unfortunately bad news for environmentalists.

The Beginning of Ideal Dolls
(1907 – 1929)

IDEAL Toy Corporation, one of America's largest and oldest manufacturers of dolls and toys, produced high quality dolls for over 80 years. Each decade of this century saw an extremely popular Ideal doll. Doll collectors, depending on their age, may remember playing with such Ideal dolls as "Flossie Flirt" from the 1920s, "Shirley Temple" and "Betsy Wetsy®" from the 1930s, "Toni" from the 1940s, "Miss Revlon" from the 1950s, "Patti Playpal" from the 1960s, or "Crissy®" from the 1970s. Many of the Ideal dolls are now very desirable to doll collectors and, since they were mass-produced, affordable.

Always an innovator, Ideal used new technology to produce their dolls. Ideal dolls come in materials ranging from cloth, celluloid, composition, hard rubber, latex "magic skin," hard plastic, injection-molded vinyl, rotation-molded vinyl, to blow-molded vinyl. Ideal is responsible for many of the technological breakthroughs in doll manufacturing and holds dozens of patents for innovations such as flirty eyes (eyes that roll from side to side), "mama" voices, "magic skin" latex rubber, and blow-molded vinyl dolls (e.g.,"Patti Playpal").

Ideal was also a forerunner in licensing — tying in with comic strip characters, merchandisers, and movie stars in promoting their dolls. The company started when Morris Michtom named a stuffed bear after President Theodore Roosevelt and called it the "Teddy Bear." Ideal was the first American dollmaker to tie in with a cartoon character — the 1907 comic "Yellow Kid." Their first tie-in with a merchandiser was the "Uneeda Kid" of the National Biscuit Company in 1914. Ideal was the first to strike it big licensing a movie star when they obtained the rights to produce a "Shirley Temple" doll in 1934.

Ideal's Beginning

Morris Michtom, a Jewish immigrant from the Vilna province in Lithuania who had some training as a mechanic, came to the United States in 1889 at age 20. He and his wife, Rose Katz Michtom, began producing stuffed bears and other animals above his candy shop at 312 Tompkins Street in the Brownsville section of Brooklyn in 1903. Mr. Michtom named his stuffed bears Teddy Bears after the famous incident when Theodore Roosevelt refused to shoot a bear cub during a hunting expedition during a 1902 border dispute between Missis-sippi and Louisiana. A cartoonist for the *Washington Star*, Clifton Berryman, drew a picture of the incident and named the bears "Teddy's Bear." Supposedly, Mr. Michtom obtained permission from President Roosevelt to use his name for the stuffed bears. In company legend a letter existed in which President Roosevelt gave Mr. Michtom permission; however, this letter cannot be located. Michtom's Teddy Bear was made of brown plush with moving arms and legs and had shoe-button eyes. The teddys and other animals sold very well, and Mr. Michtom decided to go into toymaking full-time with a loan from Butler Brothers, the big toy wholesaler of the time.

Morris Michtom started manufacturing Teddy Bears in 1906 with two people in a small shop in Brooklyn. Ideal's first ad in *Playthings* (the magazine of the toy trade) appeared in 1906. This is the year Mr. Michtom himself is quoted as saying he began making "hi-grade unbreakable dolls" (*Playthings*, 1922). The Ideal Novelty Company officially began January 10, 1907, when Mr. Michtom went into partnership with Mr. Aaron Cone, and they expanded their production to a 50' x 50' loft. "The Yellow Kid," a comic-strip character, was Ideal's first character doll produced in 1907. The Yellow Kid by Richard Felton Outcault appeared in the *New York Sunday Journal's* comic strip "Hogan's Alley" and the Hearst papers. The Yellow Kid was a bald and faintly oriental looking baby with big ears and dressed in a yellow floursack nightgown. This doll was Ideal's first of many to make use of the popularity of cartoon characters to sell dolls.

1908 was a hard year financially for the company, but they endured. In 1909 Ideal started to make plush bears, cats, and rabbits with celluloid heads and masks at their factory at 311 Christopher Street in Brooklyn. In their ads they claimed they were the "largest bear manufacturers in the country." In the middle of 1909 Mr. Michtom brought out a composition head doll of his own formulation. In 1910 they made some improvements in their composition doll head. Mr. Michtom is quoted as saying (*Playthings*, 1928) that "I started to think of producing an unbreakable doll head, believing it to be a necessity to the toy world. I knew how miserable a little girl can be when she breaks her bisque doll head. I had a little girl myself at the time (editor's note: Emily) who broke her bisque doll and nothing could console her. I knew that little girls everywhere had gone through the same tearful experience, and that it would be a happy day for the youngster when she got a new doll that would be hard to break." We can see that the Ideal Company had its roots in a father's love for his daughter.

In 1910 Ideal came out with a doll/animal, "Mr. Hooligan," which had a composition head with painted features on a stuffed plush fur body. Mr. Hooligan is a take-off of a comic strip character by Frederick Burr Opper, "Happy Hooligan," who wore a tin can for a hat. Ideal, along with the E.I. Horseman Company and Amberg Company, pioneered the use of composition in the United States. Composition is a material composed of sawdust and glue with an oil paint or varnish finish. It was hailed as an improvement over the French and German bisque and china doll heads that were so easily broken.

In 1911 Ideal advertisements stated they were "makers of unbreakable dolls and stuffed animals." Their line of boy and girl character dolls was made of composition and was guaranteed to be unbreakable and washable, unlike the bisque imports of the time. Characters included "Dandy Kid," who was all composition and made by the "skeleton process," and "Ty Cobb," the famous baseball player, who had compo head and hands with stuffed cloth body and limbs. Another doll in 1911 was "Baby Mine" which came in both doll form and a muff form. She was a character from the comedy play of the same name by Margaret Mayo. Baby Mine came in 28 designs and, depending on the size and quality of clothing, cost 25 cents to $1.50.

In 1912 the partnership between Mr. Michtom and Mr. Cone, which lasted five years, was legally dissolved, and Mr. Michtom changed the name of the company to Ideal Novelty & Toy Co. The company was re-organized, and Mr. Isaac A. Rommer became the secretary-treasurer. Mr. Rommer was responsible for the innovations and doll inventions marketed by Ideal.

Ideal was always a family business. In 1912 Morris Michtom took in a nephew, Abraham Katz, who stayed with Ideal over 60 years, and became co-chairman of the board with Morris's son, Benjamin Franklin Michtom, who joined Ideal in 1923. Another son, Joseph, and a son-in-law, David Rosenstein, also joined the company. As the company grew, it kept the atmosphere and quality of a family business.

Morris Michtom's goal was to produce a good quality play doll for the average child — one a child could love and play with without worrying about breakage. Dolls produced in the 1906 – 1914 time period were made of composition heads and hands with cloth bodies. The dolls were dressed in various costumes. The character dolls were "Captain Jinks," who wore a khaki uniform trimmed in red and represented a well-known character of the time; "Baseball Boy," who wore a baseball uniform and cap and carried a little bat; "Naughty Marietta" and "Jack Horner" representing nursery rhyme characters; "Russian Boy," who wore a Russian-style tunic and pantaloons; "Arctic

Boy," who wore knit pants, sweater, and cap; "Freddie and Flora," the country cousins wearing overalls, "Sunny Jim" dressed in a cassack and hat; and "Admiral Dot," a character from the Barnum and Bailey Circus wearing a sailor boy costume.

The baby dolls of this era were "Baby Marion," "Tiny Toddler," "Baby Bettie," "Baby Lola," "Baby Paula," "Baby Dada," and "Little Princess" and were dressed in a baby dress or knit outfit and bonnet. In 1914 Ideal came out with "Baby Bunting," which they proclaimed as the first American unbreakable doll. She had sleeping eyes in a painted hair head. Ideal claims to have devised the mechanism in 1914 which makes the doll close its eyes in sleep when laid on its back.

Licenses

Ideal was a forerunner in using licenses of famous celebrities or fictional characters for their dolls. Ideal's first licensee of a trademark was with the Uneeda Biscuit Company for the "Uneeda Kid," who appeared in a yellow raincoat. He held a tiny box of crackers under his bent arm. He was patented December 8, 1914, and was available in three different sizes. The Uneeda Kid was also produced in Canada by the Reliable Doll Company under license to Ideal in 1915. The relationship with the Reliable Doll Company would last many years.

Ideal's dolls were so successful that in 1915 they had over 200 people employed at their Van Sinderen Avenue Brooklyn plant. At that time they had over 150 numbers in their doll family, which meant the same doll came in several different sizes with several variations of wigs and clothes. Ideal was specializing in character dolls such as school children, farmers, Rough Riders, and country cousins. Dolls were named "Buster," "Sanitary Baby," "Prize Baby," "Dolly Varden," "Jenny Wren," "Bronco Bill," "Baby Talc," "Our Pet," "Dottie Dimples," "Tennis Girl," "The Infant," and "Sealect Baby." Morris Michtom is quoted as saying that since the dolls are replicas of what the children see everyday, the American mothers prefer them to the foreign dolls. Also, since the Ideal dolls can withstand wear, the "baby can be allowed to drive nails with them; it [the baby] won't be able to break the doll" (*Brooklyn Eagle*, August 29, 1915).

Doll Designers

Morris Michtom employed doll designers, most notable of whom was Bernard Lipfert, to design the dolls. Mr. Lipfert (also spelled Leipfert) designed many dolls for Ideal starting in 1912 as well as for other American doll companies. He was the premier doll designer and the "grandfather" of hundreds of dolls by his own admission. Michtom's early partner, Mr.

Aaron Cone, designed the character dolls including "Naughty Marietta," "Russian Boy," and "Captain Jinks."

Mr. Michtom had two partners after the breakup with Mr. Cone, Isaac A. Rommer and, later, Sam Hills. Mr. Rommer joined Ideal as a doll designer/inventor in 1912. Mr. Rommer received a U.S. design patent in 1915 for the "Zu-Zu Kid," a clown holding a cookie box, representing the clown from the product "Zu-Zu Ginger Snaps" from the National Biscuit Company. A former Ideal employee Mr. Bernard Meltzer, now 92 years old, who joined the company in 1917 recalls that he helped Mr. Rommer invent the moving eye for dolls. Mr. Meltzer's job was painting the dolls' faces and setting their eyes.

After Mr. Rommer's death, his brother-in-law, Mr. Sam Hills, was left Rommer's share in the company and became a partner with Michtom in the company. Mr. Hills married Bernie Meltzer's sister Bertha, whom he met while both were working at Ideal. Mr. Hills stayed with the company in production until the 1930s.

Materials

Ideal dolls were made of cloth, composition, and hard rubber during the 1907 – 1927 era. In addition, Ideal even made a doll with a celluloid mask on a sponge body (1912, "Water Baby"). Water Baby was touted as the first fully washable doll. The materials used for the dolls went from washable "imitation kid" body on the "Sanitary Baby" (1915), to cotton-stuffed soft-body, to all composition (1916), to cork-stuffed soft-body (1923), and then to rubber (1926). There was always an overlap in production so that some dolls were composed of the new materials while others were still being produced using the older materials.

Ideal's success was due, in part, to the unavailability of German bisque dolls during World War I. But mostly, success was due to the benefits of the new technology of composition. Morris Michtom is quoted as saying the children "couldn't break [the doll] with anything short of a sledgehammer." Testing of the durability of the composition dolls got rather drastic as Mr. Michtom is also quoted as saying they "dropped them eight stories to the street, and the paint was scarcely scratched" (N.Y. Herald, Sept. 12, 1915).

Wigs

Ideal's earliest dolls had painted and molded hair. The dolls had elaborate molded curls in a complicated pattern. Ideal dolls were usually more detailed and had curls all over

their heads, while dolls from other manufacturers didn't have molding of curls on the backs of the dolls' heads but were just flat and painted. The complexity of their molded hair is one way to identify unmarked dolls of this era by Ideal. Ideal dolls later acquired human hair, caracul fur, and mohair. Most dolls were available in two versions, either molded painted hair or wigs. The wigged version cost more money.

Eyes

Appealing eyes are the key to a doll's popularity. Ideal always worked on the technological development of dolls' eyes. The first dolls Ideal produced had painted eyes. Subsequent dolls had stationary (non-moving), winking sleep (open-close), and flirty (moving sideways) eyes during this era. Ideal held patents on moving eyes that did not stick (1915), on flirty eyes that roll and sleep (1925), and on sparkling eyes (1927). Ideal introduced their "imitation glass eyes" in 1915, which they had spent years developing. This "imitation glass eye" was celluloid over tin. The winking sleep eyes could each move independently from the other eye. Ideal sold over 100,000 moving eye dolls in the year 1916 with only 43 returned for eye repairs — a record for durability at the time. Ideal would fix in the factory dolls returned by customers, sometimes even replacing the doll if the damage was severe. In the early 1920s flirty sleep eyes that could move independently came on the scene. Ideal began buying their dolls' eyes from the Margon Corporation, Rahway, New Jersey, in the early 1920s. The president of Margon Corp., Mr. Marcus, and Mr. Michtom worked closely to develop the new doll eye technology.

Litigations

Since Ideal was such an innovator in doll manufacturing, other toymakers copied Ideal's successes. As early as 1911, imitators infringed on Ideal's patents with the "Baby Mine" muff doll. The first patent infringement case was brought against an imitator of the "Uneeda Kid" (1914) called the "Fisher Boy". Ideal won that case, and many more to follow, including a 1918 one against Majestic Doll for sleeping eye dolls. Ideal always vigorously protected their innovations and products through legal channels.

Character Dolls Developed during the 1916 – 1928 era

Following on the success of the "Uneeda Kid," Ideal's next trademark licensee was with National Biscuit Company for their character "Zu-Zu Kid." The doll was dressed in a yellow satin clown suit and a pointy cap and carried a package of Zu-Zu ginger cookies. She was patented in 1916 and was supposed to be Uneeda Kid's "consort." She was not as popular as the Uneeda Kid, however. Ideal's next trademark licensee was the "Cracker Jack" boy owned by the Rueckheim Bros. & Eckstein Candy Company. He came dressed in a blue or white sailor suit in 1917 and carried a dummy package of "Cracker Jack Candy Food."

Also in 1917 Ideal introduced the "Columbia Kids" dressed in patriotic outfits representing the Army or Navy, and a boy and girl dressed in red, white, and blue stars and stripes outfits.

"Liberty Boy" was conceived and developed by Mr. Michtom to help the war effort in 1917. Liberty Boy was used to help sell War Bonds. He is dressed as a doughboy, is all composition, and is fully jointed. He wears a khaki colored composition suit and boots and a felt military hat with cord. His hand is raised in salute. He was a big success for Ideal and unusual in the doll world, since he depicts an adult male. One entire floor in the factory was devoted to his manufacture.

In 1917 there were over 200 numbers in the Ideal line including baby dolls, boy dolls, girl dolls, dolls in knit sweaters, jackets and caps, and dolls with or without wigs. An Ad in *Playthings* magazine in 1917 says they had 78 different characters with 150 numbers dressed in a variety of styles. Dolls were made with sleeping eyes and had soft bodies, cork-stuffed bodies, double inside steel jointed bodies, or fully spring-jointed all composition bodies. In 1918 there were no names for the dolls, just numbers.

A strike in 1919 slowed down Ideal's doll production. Ideal manufactured over 78 different character doll heads in 1920. They had over 150 doll numbers in the line that walked, talked, and slept. In 1922 their full line had over 200 numbers. In 1923 Ideal introduced two dolls in colorful Egyptian costumes, the "Nile Queen" and "Egyptian Princess." They also had cork-stuffed patented walkers in the line.

Baby Dolls Developed in 1916 – 1928

Ideal was always trying to enhance their dolls' appeal to children by applying new technology to their dollmaking. In 1916 Ideal came out with "Compo Baby," an all composition baby doll who could stand unsupported. She came in five sizes and sold for about $1.00. Ideal's Sleeping Eye dolls in 1917 were made of either fully spring-jointed, all composition bodies or double inside steel joints, cork-stuffed bodies. They had composition heads with or without wigs, and came in five sizes, dressed or undressed. In 1918 babies and toddlers came in six sizes from 12" to 24". Ideal's slogan in this era was "When we do it, we do it right," which referred to the quality and the popularity of the Ideal dolls.

A composition walking doll was patented in 1921. She walked, talked, cried, and slept without the benefit of springs. "Miss Rosy Cheeks" is an example of an Ideal walking doll. To show off the magic of their walking dolls, Ideal had an electric demonstrator for stores to put in their windows. What a sight that must have been to see four dolls all walking! The dolls retailed from $1.50 to $7.00.

Mr. Abe Katz, Morris Michtom's nephew, had been with the company off and on since almost the beginning. He had the idea to put Ideal in the premium business in 1920. Ideal got magazines (such as *Needlecraft*, *The Farmer's Wife*, and *Hearth and Home*) to offer Ideal dolls as premiums for magazine subscriptions. This brilliant marketing move put Ideal on its feet financially.

1922 saw a new generation of Mama dolls, who called "mama" plus "papa" in real human voices. These dolls not only spoke, they sat, they walked, and they slept. They cried "mama" when tilted one way and "papa" when tilted the other. They were available in sizes from 13" to 29" inches.

Ideal also produced "Baby Mine" in 1922 with a solid cloth head and cloth mask, which was very lightweight and made "sanitary" by a secret process. Also this year, "Miss Rainshine" was introduced. She was a two-headed crying and laughing doll dressed in checked rompers and a rainhat.

Ideal produced dolls with three types of bodies in 1923: cotton-stuffed soft body dolls, cork-stuffed position babies, and cork-stuffed straight limb dolls with the patented walking construction. Their clothes were made of many fabrics including organdy, dotted Swiss, poplins, ginghams, crepes, and satins.

In 1923 "Soozie Smiles," a two-headed doll with both a crying and smiling face, was advertised as having "made the Queen laugh" during her Christmas shopping tour of London (*London Daily Graphic*, Dec. 11, 1923).

A big hit for Ideal was the "Flossie Flirt" doll released in 1924. She was Ideal's first doll with flirty eyes (eyes that rolled sideways). These flirty sleep eyes were made of gray tin with a celluloid covering. They also opened when the doll was upright and closed when she was prone. Flossie also said "mama" and walked. She had a cloth body and composition head. She came in three sizes (18", 20", 22") and retailed for $5.00 and up. Flossie's companion was "Beau Brummel," who came with wig or painted hair. By 1925 Flossie Flirt came in seven sizes, had 100 costumes, and was available with either fancy mohair wigs or painted hair. Flossie was kept up-to-date with the latest technology. In 1926 she acquired rubber arms and had a new name, "Vanity Flossie." In 1932 Flossie was produced with rubber legs. Flossie is an example of Ideal's use of new technology to enhance the doll's appeal to children.

Ideal added a new dimension to dolldom in 1924 — music. "Sally Singer" was a 20" sleep-eyed doll with a wig, who not only said "mama" but also had a Swiss music box with several tunes inside.

An innovation was "Hush-A-Bye Baby" (1925) with a one-piece solid composition head, who closed her eyes when rocked to sleep and kept them closed until she was placed upright by her little owner. She looked like a newborn and was wrapped in a blanket and pillow. Hush-A-Bye Baby acquired rubber arms and some models even had rubber legs in 1926.

Ideal introduced their first doll with what Ideal called "composition rubber" arms: "Suck-A-Thumb" Baby. She came with a pacifier, which she could use when she wasn't sucking her thumb. She had a composition head and sleep eyes. She was 15" tall and was dressed in organdy with lace trimming. Ideal used rubber arms on several of the dolls in their line including "Twinkletoes," who cried when her rubber legs were squeezed (patented in 1927).

Even though Ideal introduced the new material of rubber, they also continued producing dolls using the older materials of composition and cloth. "Bouncing Baby Mae" was an example of the composition and cloth baby dolls produced all through these founding years by Ideal.

Marks

Marks on the dolls during this time period were "Ideal Art Novelty Co." on "Mr. Hooligan"; "IDEAL" in center of a dia-mond shape with "Novelty & Toy Co., Brooklyn, New York" on the outside of the diamond on a 1922 mama doll; "IDEAL" in the center of a diamond shape with "U.S. of A." outside on "Flossie Flirt" in 1924; the diamond shape with "IDEAL" inside and "U.S. Pat. 1621434" on the outside of "Hush-a-Bye Baby" in 1925; or just "IDEAL" in a diamond shape in "Suck-A-Thumb" Baby produced in 1926. Many of the Ideal dolls were unmarked. This could be due to the fact that Ideal also bought parts from other manufacturers who supplied arms, legs, bodies, and even heads when Ideal couldn't meet the demand for their dolls.

Morris Michtom's Successors

Like many American toy companies started in the early 1900s, Ideal reflected the entrepreneurial spirit of one immigrant. The company grew and prospered under Morris Michtom's leadership, providing employment for hundreds and enjoyment to thousands. Michtom saw Ideal become one of the major toy companies in America. The time came for Morris Michtom to step down from active leadership of the company in 1928. He relinquished day-to-day control to his family members and remained on the board of directors.

Ideal's Golden Era
(1928 – 1963)

Ideal Toy Corporation was becoming a significant force in the American Toy Industry. Dolls produced during the 1928 – 1963 period under the stewardship of Morris Michtom's son, Benjamin Franklin Michtom, and his nephew, Abraham Katz, are shining examples of Ideal's "golden era."

Morris Michtom, the founder of the Ideal Toy Company, stepped down as president in 1928. A management team of his relatives took over including his son, Benjamin Franklin Michtom, who was in charge of sales, marketing, and public relations; Abraham Katz, his nephew, who was in charge of doll design and production; and his son-in-law, David Rosenstein, who was in charge of administration. Another son, Dr. Joseph Michtom, a dentist, joined the firm in 1938, upon the death of his father. He was put in charge of the factory. Mr. Sam Hills, Mr. Michtom's partner, sold his shares in the business in the 1930s. Morris Michtom, founder of Ideal, died in 1938, but his business lived on in the capable hands of his family. Ideal's success with the toy-buying public during this era was due to innovative technology, licensing, and promotion.

Abe Katz was the acknowledged "doll genius" honored by doll collector's groups and his peers. He had an intuitive feel and love for dolls. He was always on the lookout for new technology to aid in the manufacturing of the dolls. He was intrigued by foreign manufacturing processes and would bring back bits and pieces of 20 different dolls and try to design a doll integrating these various techniques. Ideal's primary concern was to make the dolls as "lifelike" as possible. Ideal dolls walked, kissed, drank, wet, rolled-over, and cried.

Ideal, always in the forefront in advancing the technology of doll-making, employed many in-house chemists and engineers to further the development of "true-life play." The company holds many patents and was responsible for many innovations in the doll world. Ideal was the first doll manufacturer to use "Magic Skin" latex in 1940 and one of the first to use hard plastic in 1942 for dolls. Innovations such as the grills for the crier box in hard plastic "Saucy Walker" and her walking mechanism (1951), the first 36" blow molded vinyl doll (Patti Playpal, 1959), and improvements in dolls' eyes (such as the flirty eye, 1924) were all products of Ideal's devotion to dollmaking technology.

Ideal always saw the value of producing dolls tied in with famous product names, starting in 1915 with the "Uneeda Kid" from the Uneeda Biscuit Company and continuing in this era with dolls such as "Toni" for Toni Home Permanents; "Miss Curity" for Curity Band Aids from Bauer & Black Co.; "Harriet Hubbard Ayer" for Harriet Hubbard Ayer Cosmetics, a division of Lever Brothers; "Miss Revlon" for Revlon Cosmetics; and "Campbell Kids" for Campbell's Soup. In doing so, they were a forerunner of the current licensing trend in the toy world. These advertising dolls are now sought by both doll collectors and advertising collectors.

Ideal also produced some of the now very collectible "celebrity dolls" of the era, depicting such personalities as Shirley Temple, Deanna Durbin, Judy Garland, and Mary Hartline. "Shirley Temple" was Ideal's first celebrity doll, first produced in 1934, and was such a success that she helped make Ideal the most profitable doll company in America in 1935.

Ideal's first doll depicting royalty was "Princess Beatrix" of the Netherlands, which was produced from 1938 until 1943. She was a composition head and limb baby doll with a soft stuffed body and came in 14", 16", and 22" sizes. Ideal also produced male celebrity dolls such as "Roy Rogers" and "Hopalong Cassidy," two cowboy movie stars in 1949.

Ideal also produced dolls of fictionalized personalities — fairy tale, cartoon, and other characters. Their first fairy tale and fictionalized story dolls were "Peter Pan" and "Wendy" in 1928, then "Snow White" and "Cinderella" from 1938. Their first cartoon character in this era was "Sparkle Plenty," then "Bonny Braids," daughter of Dick Tracy, 1951. Dolls were also made of other fictionalized characters such as "Charlie McCarthy" and "Mortimer Snerd" (1938), creations of ventriloquist Edgar Bergen; "Howdy Doody" (1950) the television marionette; and "Betsy McCall" (1953), the *McCall's* Magazine paperdoll. The Ideal Company was always ethical in securing rights and providing royalties to such celebrities or their owners. They also vigorously protected their licenses and patents against infringements. They brought many suits against knock-off manufacturers. The most famous was against "Lenora Doll" for producing phony Shirley Temple dolls in the late 1930s.

Doll Manufacturing

The Ideal Toy and Novelty Company manufactured their dolls in Brooklyn for almost 30 years. They moved manufacturing out to Long Island City, New York in 1935. Hollis (Queens), New York became home for Ideal in 1948. At its largest, Ideal had over 4,000 people working on three shifts producing dolls and toys at the peak pre-Christmas season in their plant in the New York-New Jersey area. Lionel Weintraub, son-in-law of Mr. Katz, joined Ideal in 1941 and took over as president in 1962.

Materials

An overriding principle of dolls at Ideal was that baby dolls were always soft (i.e., soft vinyl, cloth), toddler dolls were a little harder, and teen dolls were hardest. Mr. Katz was always searching for new materials and gadgets to make the dolls more lifelike and interesting to their young owners. They even sought inventions from outside sources. The machine used to make the flexible knitted wire for the Flexy doll was invented by Floyd O. DeMillar of Warwick, RI. This knitted wire allowed the doll to be posed in many positions and added to the play value of the doll.

Ideal dolls during this "golden" era were made from such diverse processes and materials as composition, rubber (1926), Idenite (hard rubber, "Betsy Wetsy®" head, 1936), wood pulp ("Pinocchio," 1939), Magic Skin rubber latex (1940), injection molded hard plastic, the acetates and buterates (e.g., the "Plassie" head, 1942), rotational molded vinyl made from Geon polyvinyl material from B.F. Goodrich (1949, e.g., "Baby Ruth's" head, 1953), then blow molded vinyl (1957, e.g., "Patti Playpal," 1959).

In any given year, there were dolls made of several materials in the line. For example, in 1939 there were hard rubber, wood pulp, and composition dolls. Ideal's rubber dolls were so popular that Ideal purchased the Admiar Rubber Company in 1932 to keep up with the demand.

Individual dolls themselves were often made of several materials. A baby doll such as "Tickletoes" (1928) had a composition head, rubber limbs, and a kapok-stuffed cloth body. Kapok, a silky-cotton from Indonesia or Equador, was used as stuffing for soft bodies. Another example was a doll produced in the 1950s that had a hard plastic head on a rubberized cloth body with vinyl arms and legs. During the World War II years (1941 – 1946), cloth dolls were reintroduced due to the unavailability of plastic for domestic use.

Whatever the material, dolls had to be sturdy. Mr. Katz was very quality conscious and wanted to make sure the dolls would be good enough to give to his daughters. Quality control testing was rather drastic as Mr. Katz would throw or kick a doll down six flights of stairs to make sure the doll was sturdy.

Ideal on Forefront of Technology

Ideal was always on the forefront of technology in doll production. The evolution of the technology affected the decision of what doll was to be made. Ideal was the first company to use latex rubber for dolls. Abe Katz on a visit to a Sandusky, Ohio, balloon factory discovered the revolutionary synthetic material called latex rubber, which looked and felt like human skin. Ideal had always tried to make its dolls as "lifelike" as possible, and with this new material they developed the "Magic Skin" doll. This latex compound was so malleable that the doll could be placed in lifelike poses which were impossible with previous materials. Due to the war shortage of rubber and plastic, Ideal was deprived of Magic Skin until 1946. Ideal was such a leader in plastics technology that they did essential production work for the Army and Navy during World War II at their factory, and dolls were relegated to less than 50% of production space.

Mr. Katz was always searching for new materials and "gadgets" to make the dolls more lifelike and interesting to their young owners. Herbert Lawrence, director of engineering services at Ideal for 30 years, saw the change from the hard plastics through the introduction of the various methods of making vinyl dolls. Many chemists and engineers were employed full-time to find techniques to make dolls with the new post-war man-made materials such as nylon, vinyl, acrylics, and other plastics. For instance, in the 1950s Mr. Katz went to Europe and saw a blow molding machine. He sent the machine back to the factory but didn't know what he was going to do with it. Mr. Katz had to get training in Boston, Massachusetts, on how to use the equipment. Blow molding was a new technology to the doll industry. That is how Ideal was the first on the market with a 36" doll (the "Patti Playpal"). Up to that time, the plastics technology was not able to produce such a large vinyl doll for a reasonable cost.

Design of a Doll

The creation of a doll from concept to production was a long involved process. Ideas for dolls came from many sources. Mainly, Mr. Katz would generate ideas on his own or from things he saw at the annual toy show in New York or in his travels and would want to incorporate them into his dolls. He would have a meeting in his conference room with all of the creative and sales staff to discuss his ideas. Members of this design team included Julius Weih, head of the machine shop, and Mary T. Maidenbauer (also known as Bauer), Katz's assistant. Then Katz would commission a sculptor to sculpt the doll to see if it met his specifications. The sculpting of the doll's head was his first priority. The design team would give the sculptor bits of pictures of dolls or children and a direction to "make the doll sweet" or some other attribute. The head of production would then design the manufacturing process. In essence, the manufacturing processes dictated the look and feel of the doll.

Over the years, several designers produced the Ideal dolls. Both independent artists and an in-house staff were used. The most famous sculptor was Bernard Lipfert who sculpted the heads of such Ideal dolls as "Shirley Temple," "Deanna Durbin," "Judy Garland," "Betsy Wetsy®," "Sparkle Plenty," "Toni," "Betsy McCall," and many others. One of Lipfert's dolls for Ideal was the 1933 "Snoozie" doll who was a yawning baby in rubber. Lipfert was called the Dean of American Dollmakers and probably sculpted hundreds of dolls for over 300 companies during his 90-year lifetime. He was affiliated with Ideal on a free-lance basis for over 30 years. He worked in plasticine, an oil-based clay that never gets hard. He would sometimes do the first mold of his work in a plaster model. The work was done in his Brooklyn, New York basement, and later in his Westbury, Long Island, home. Then the model or sculpture would be given to an in-house sculptor and moldmaker. His granddaughter, Linda, was the model for the 1948 doll "Baby Coos." He worked for Ideal up through the 1960s, and two of the last dolls he designed were "Pebbles" and "Bam-Bam" from the Flintsone cartoons. He died in 1974 after 10 years of retirement.

Julius Weih was head of the machine shop and got the sculpture work done by artists. He started with Ideal in the 1930s and was in charge of design. Abe Katz would give him a photo of a baby that he liked. Julius would then have the head sculpted in clay. Then Mr. Katz would make comments like "change the tongue" or "this looks good." Julius would then have it changed, then he would help design and cast the plaster of Paris molds. Then liquid copper beryllium would be poured around the face to make a mold. This beryllium mold would be put into the injection molding machine, and liquid acetate would be forced into the mold, thus, forming the head in two parts. Weih worked for Ideal for quite a while and oversaw the sculpture of the 1957 "Jesus Christ Doll," among others.

Another doll designer who worked for Ideal in the 1930s was Joseph Kallus, a New Yorker born in the late 1890s. He had worked with other doll companies, including George Borgfeldt Co. on the Kewpie dolls. The dolls he designed for Ideal included the Flexy series: "Baby Snooks," "Mortimer Snerd," "Soldier," "Sunny Sue," "Sunny Sam," and the "Clown." He also designed the Gulliver's Travels Set for Ideal in 1939, which included characters such as "King Little" and "Gabby," who had ball jointed limbs.

Designers of the 1940s included Baroness von Schenk of Vienna, Mieczyslaw Szrajer of Kalisz, and Trudy Wanderman of New York who designed dolls and stuffed animals such as the Papa and Mama Bunnies.

Vincent DeFilippo was employed by Ideal from 1954 to 1981. He started out in the machine shop as a moldmaker and eventually became the head sculptor at Ideal. When he started as a moldmaker, he would make another set of molds over Mr. Lipfert's work, and then cast it into wax. The wax model then had to be highly polished with exact measurements for the size of the eyes and the plugs and fittings for all the body parts. Then the wax model would be brought up to the roof and go into the copper plating tank to complete the lost wax process. They would then get a metal mold and complete the injection molding process for plastic dolls. His first complete commission from Ideal was "Tearie Dearie" in 1963. DeFilippo was the head sculptor for several dolls Ideal produced in the 1970s, such as "Rub-A-Dub Dolly."

Neil Estern, a sculptor of many significant works of American historical significance including the lifesize sculpture of Mayor LaGuardia in New York, did several dolls for Ideal during the 1960 – 1970s era. He worked on a freelance basis for Ideal in the 1960s, and his first dolls for Ideal were the Patti Playpal doll family including "Peter," "Suzy," "Penny," and "Daddy's Girl," all large (28" and over) life-size dolls. Mr. Katz wanted to use the new technology of blow molding to create a life-size doll that could use children's cast-off clothing. Despite negative reaction from toy buyers at the leading department stores, Katz went ahead with plans for "Patti." Neil Estern and his wife, Anne Estern, a theatrical and costume designer, wanted to do these dolls as life-like as possible reflecting the special nature of childhood. Anne designed Patti's costumes and made her hair natural with bangs as was the fashion of children of the day. Neil made Patti have a more natural expression than dolls previously had with a broader face, trying to capture some of the special magic of childhood.

Other dolls Mr. Estern did for Ideal include the 1960 "Miss Ideal," who twists and turns; the 1960 "Saucy Walker;" and the 1961 "Kissy." It would take him a week and half for a simple head compared to a month and a half to sculpt an entire doll that needed technical assistance from the engineering staff.

In later years, Ideal purchased ideas from Marvin Glass, developer and design man. He developed ideas such as "Giggles" (1967) and the pull arms, which the Ideal staff modified to make "Kissy" (1961).

Sometimes independent designers brought ideas to Ideal, such as the 1951 "Saralee" doll conceived by Sara Lee Creech and sculpted by Sheila Burlingame. Saralee was the first anthropologically correct mass produced "Negro" doll, a doll of great sociological significance championed by Dave Rosenstein at Ideal, and former First Lady Eleanor Roosevelt, head of the NAACP Walter White, and many other leading civil rights proponents of the day.

Inner Workings of Dolls

The technology that went into designing and manufacturing an Ideal doll would create envy in NASA engineers. Much time and effort went into developing unique mechanisms and "gimmicks" that would catch the fancy of young consumers and their mothers. One of the earliest examples is "Twinkletoes" (1927), who would cry when a child would squeeze her rubber leg. Another is "Baby Coos" (1948), who would coo by means of a reed arrangement like that on a clarinet and a hollow head designed like a sounding board.

"Betsy Wetsy®" (1934) was another example of Ideal technology. Betsy Wetsy®, named after Mr. Katz' daughter Bette, could drink liquids, cry, and wet her diaper. Betsy is an example of Ideal technology at its finest. One story told by the company is that in 1934 a woman came to Mr. Michtom with the idea of having a doll drink liquids and after an appropriate time, wet her diaper. However, in early models the liquid turned rancid, causing complaints from parents and kids and a decision was made to provide Betsy with an almost straight channel from mouth to diapers, a somewhat unrealistic but unmessy solution. Betsy Wetsy®'s mechanism for shedding tears was a triangular plastic piece with a ball bearing that when squeezed, made the ball bearing shut off the mouth air and pressure forced water out of the eyes. The piece was glued to three nipples molded into the head.

"Betsy Wetsy®" has endured through various changes as technology improved, acquiring a vinyl body, then a vinyl head. "Dy-dee," produced by Effanbee in 1934, is proclaimed America's first drinking and wetting doll. Effanbee sued Ideal over patent infringement. The story told about the outcome of that suit was that the judge ruled that drinking and wetting is a biological function, and you cannot patent a biological function. Another story told by a relative is that a German woman with the idea for the drinking and wetting doll first approached Morris Michtom with the idea, but he rejected it as a "Pishaka" doll (yiddish for one who urinates). He soon changed his mind when he saw how well Dy-dee was selling, and Betsy Wetsy® has remained a staple in the Ideal line through many changes in her materials from rubber, to hard plastic, to vinyl.

Another innovative doll was "Thumbelina," first produced in 1962, a doll who moved her head when activated. Mr. Hel-

muth Moormann, manager of the tool room and a mechanical designer, developed her mechanism from a music box. He changed the gear ratio and spring to make it longer and to get the doll to move and squirm. The rod went through the neck into a plug. The rod was bent, and as the gear turned, the rod would hit the side of the hole in the plug and transfer the force, and the head would turn.

Variations on a Theme

When Ideal was successful developing a doll character or a doll gimmick, they would reissue it in subsequent years with revisions and changes. An example of this practice was "Tickletoes," first issued in 1928. She had rubber arms and legs plus the cry feature. The next year 1929 there were "Curly Tickletoes" with a caracul wig, "Princess Tickletoes" with a kapok-stuffed body, and "Tickletoes Deluxe" with a hand crocheted wool and silk coat. In 1931 there was "New Tickletoes" with swivel head, new outfits, fur wig, and flirty eyes. Another variation on a theme would be the use in later years of a different material for a doll given the same name as an earlier doll. An example of this was their three-headed doll (the head would rotate on an axis with three faces: smiling, crying, and sleeping) first produced in composition ("Soozie Smiles," 1923) and then produced in vinyl ("Trilby," 1951). Another doll that was reissued using different materials was "Snoozie" (1933), a composition doll, who pouted, puckered, and yawned and was reborn as vinyl "Blessed Event" in 1951. Also "Honeysuckle," first out in rubber in 1932, was reissued and redesigned in vinyl in 1956.

Another variation Ideal would use was to issue both a baby doll version and a toddler doll version of the same doll name. For example, "Shirley Temple" (1934) started as a girl doll whose "Baby Shirley Temple" came out in 1935. "Bonny Braids," issued as a baby in 1951 was followed up as a toddler in 1953.

In addition, Ideal would issue a generic equivalent to a personality doll such as a look-alike Shirley Temple or a look-alike "Toni" that appeared in the same 1951 catalog as the brand-name Toni dolls. The generic equivalent was always cheaper, because Ideal did not have to pay royalties to the brand name owner.

Ideal always had stock numbers in their line such as soft baby dolls in all materials such as composition, and later vinyl, who would just be called "Vinyl baby doll" in their catalogs.

Wigs

Ideal's earliest dolls had painted hair. Wigs then progressed to human hair, caracul fur, mohair, nylon, saran, and finally, a vinyl yarn. The original wigs were sewed on buckram, a stiff material used in hats.

The "Toni" dolls (1949 on) have buckram wigs with nylon hair in assorted hair colors. The original method of wig-making was to take a board with a bunch of nails in it, then take a handful of hair and pull the hair through the nails to smooth it, which was called hackling. Then they would take the buckram cap and on a sewing machine sew, smoothing the hair with their fingers. The cap was then glued onto the doll's head using brown glue the Ideal chemists had developed. This method worked well, because it allowed the little girls to comb the doll's hair. "Saucy Walker" also had a buckram wig. Later, they learned how to sew the hair on one strand at a time directly to vinyl heads.

With vinyl dolls, rooting the hair in the doll's head became commonplace. The original concept was that you bought nylon yarns on a long spool of thread, took a sewing needle, cut the back of it so you made a fork out of it, and then an Ideal employee would push the needle through a vinyl head a few strands at a time. An early example of a nylon rooted hair doll was "Princess Mary" (1955 – 1956). Later they developed a machine that was a bunch of those needles attached to a block of wood. Next, came a modified shoemaker's machine that would actually sew the hair into a vinyl head. Hair was either nylon or saran.

Eyes

Ideal Doll Company bought their doll eyes from Margon Corporation of Rahway, New Jersey, starting in the early 1920s. Another source for the dolls' eyes was Dolac Co. of Brooklyn, New York. Ideal dolls' eyes ranged from stationary, to sleep (open-close), flirty (moving sideways), button eyes, that snapped in with a spring-nut, and stenciled eyes. Ideal held patents on moving eyes that did not stick (1914), winking eyes that moved individually (1915), flirty eyes that roll and sleep (1925), sparkling eyes (1927), and double action glacé eyes with real eyelashes (1934).

Clothing

The dressing of the dolls from the 1930s until the 1970s was Mary Maidenbauer's job. Mary exerted a lot of influence over every phase of doll development. She was Mr. Katz's assistant and officially, head of clothing design. She supervised a group of women who did the designing, including Judy Alpert, who later became head upon Mary's retirement.

Miss Maidenbauer had strong control over the doll clothing and a crew of women sewers in the 1930s – 60s. The doll would be designed with specifications as to color of hair, eyes, dress, and even socks and shoes. However, there was poetic

license with "quality control" at rush production periods. If they didn't have the type of lace specified in stock, another would be used. Specifications as to matching clothes, eyes, and hair would be loosened. So, for example, if they didn't have the green eyes that were supposed to go with a certain dress, they put brown eyes in the doll. To understand the enormity of the output, in 1958 Ideal made more dresses than any other garment manufacturer in the United States — over 15 million dresses a year.

Supplementing the factory sewers were scores of women homesewers. Rose Viola, who lived near the Jamaica Ave. factory, was one among many who would sew together the cut pieces delivered to her and put the labels in the dresses during the 1930 era. She was paid by the gross. Other homesewers used to shirr the pleats in the dresses. This hiring-out practice went on at least up until 1958.

Bette Katz Weintraub remembers when she was a little girl if her mother bought her a dress her father, Abe Katz, liked, he would bring her into the factory and have her stand on the designer's table while Miss Maidenbauer copied it for a doll. Mollye Goldman, who owned International Doll Company, also designed clothing for the "Shirley Temple" doll from 1933 – 1936.

The rush period for Ideal designers was before the Toy Fair in February. Mr. Katz would have a new idea and would want it to be available for the Toy Fair. At one point, Judy Alpert had to design 24 outfits for "Tammy" in a two-week period right before the 1963 Toy Fair in New York.

Ideal clothing was well-designed, but there was no emphasis on selling the clothes separate from the dolls until 1956's "Little Miss Revlon" had at least 40 separate outfits. "Honeysuckle" (1932) was the first Ideal doll that came with a wardrobe. She came in a diaper and had an assortment of clothes to wear. Sears catalogs offered separate dresses for the 14", 16", 20" Ideal dolls, but the market dried up in the 1950s, much to current collectors' chagrin who are trying to find dresses for Toni dolls and others. The dresses made in the United States were so expensive, since they cost nearly as much as a little girl's dress.

Voices

Ideal started using their patented "mama" voice in the 1920s. Improvements included the "papa" voice used in the 1940 Papa-Mama doll in which the doll said "mama" when tilted forward and "papa" when tilted backwards. The Margon company also supplied the "mama" voice boxes that were used inside the Ideal dolls.

Doll Marketing

The marketing of the Ideal dolls was very personal by modern standards for most of Ideal's history. Dolls were produced if Ideal thought they would sell. Buyers for major retail store chains and mail-order houses were an important factor in the decision to produce a doll. Adeline Reilly Bagnasco at Ideal from 1940 – 1977 ending up as national sales manager, emphasizes the role doll buyers from major retail chains had. The buyers would actually come to Ideal and help develop the dolls based on the buyers' needs for aesthetics, price, production ability (volume), and packaging design.

Sears bought the greatest volume of dolls for their stores and catalogs and was, therefore, most influential in terms of decisions of which dolls to produce. An example is the 1951 "Saralee" doll, the first anthropologically correct "Negro" doll, an idea by Miss Saralee Creech. She brought the idea to Sears' Chicago buyer Lothar Kiesow, who then brought the idea to David Rosenstein, then president of Ideal. Other chains influential in the decisions of which dolls to produce were Woolworths, followed by Wards, then later J.C.Penney.

Once a doll was designed, certain features such as special color clothes, hair, or different size head, arms, legs, or eyes (either stationary or moving) would be changed to qualify as an exclusive for a chain store. The stores each wanted a little different version of the doll to advertise. Sears buyers were experts in developing dolls as exclusives that appeared to be the same as dolls on the open market but really were cheaper to make. They did this by having the costumes have 12 seams instead of 20, using less elaborate hairdos, or a different line of clothing. An example of an exclusive doll was Ideal's "Liz" (1961) called "Carol Brent" by Montgomery Ward and 1964's "Patti" of the Tammy family, also a Montgomery Ward exclusive.

Ideal's tradition was mass production for the average child consumer. The dolls were not aimed at the collector's market. However, Ideal was a leader in introducing new concepts and technology. Ideal had such a good reputation and creative design staff the entire New York market would imitate Ideal. Ideal made most of its profits on the larger size dolls. Ideal would be able to get more money for a 20" doll than for a 14" doll. Price points were determined by the inch prior to the promotional dolls of television that came in the late 1960s, according to Herb Sands, former vice president at Ideal. The smaller size dolls were made for Sears and other chain stores to sell at the lower end of the price scale. Ideal tried to fill in all the price points for their dolls.

Market Research

After the initial marketing procedures, Ideal would do a limited production run of a doll. The first 200 dolls off the assembly line were given to the employees to take home to their children. The employee would fill out a questionnaire asking how much the child played with it, whether it was unbreakable, and how it survived play. Ideal would also give the dolls to schools and then observe how the children played with the dolls. Then a decision would be made whether to produce the doll and how big to make the initial run.

Ideal's Promotional Genius

Ben Michtom was the promotional genius. He was the one who went out to Hollywood and negotiated for six months with Shirley Temple's parents on such items as to what color to make the doll's eyes (ultimately hazel) and number of curls (10 – 12 corkscrew curls). Ben loved to tie-in with celebrities and produce glamorous images for his dolls.

The Toni Dolls

Ben Michtom liked Hollywood movie stars to plug his dolls. For example, for "Toni" in 1948 he designed a major merchandising campaign involving June Haver who was appearing in the Twentieth Century-Fox movie, "Oh, You Beautiful Doll," and Du Pont, who made the nylon for the doll's hair. Advertising for Toni appeared in the pressbook for 15,000 motion picture theatre managers, and mailings to department stores and their customers. Events suggested to the movie theatre manager included doll matinees for children in which a Toni doll was given away, a Toni doll display in the movie lobbies, and a special Saturday morning show for little girls and their mothers where the department store's hairdresser demonstrated how to give Toni a permanent.

In 1951 Ben Michtom got 12 famous French designers, Jean Desses, Patou, Worth, Heim, Paquin, Lafaurie, Piquet, Bruyere, Rochas, Carven, Gres, and Maggy Rouff, to design special gowns for the "Toni" dolls. The fashionably adorned dolls then had a special touring exhibit at department stores throughout the country, including Gimbel's in Philadelphia, and received quite a lot of publicity and fanfare. This successful promotion garnered a lot of "prestige" for Michtom and the dolls who were insured for $50,000.

After his successful promotion with French fashion designers, Michtom decided to have American designers do a casual line more appropriate for little girls. He again chose 12 fashion designers, among them Ann Fogarty, Oleg Cassini, Ceil Chapman, Claire McCardell, and Molly Parnuss. These clothes were again displayed around the country in department stores, were never mass-produced, and were just for publicity value, although they were available in pattern form for home sewing.

A third promotion was scheduled for leading clothiers mainly based in Philadelphia to design baby clothes for "Toni," but by then the public's interest had waned and plans for this promotion were discontinued.

Saucy Walker

Mr. Michtom got other movie stars, Piper Laurie and Dorothy Lamour, who appeared in the Sears catalog to promote the "Saucy Walker" dolls in advertising. Saucy was a big success starting in 1951 and spawned several additions to her family: a "boy Saucy Walker" (1952), a "toddler Saucy Walker" (1953) and a "big sister Saucy Walker" (1954). Saucy even reappeared with a vinyl head in 1955 and was completely vinyl and a completely different doll in a larger 28" size in 1960.

Smokey the Bear

Ever the promoter, Mr. Michtom got a law passed by the 82nd United States Congress co-sponsored by Senator Richard Russell of Georgia and Senator Edward Martin of Pennsylvania permitting the U.S. government to effectively "license" Ideal for the "Smokey the Bear" that came out in 1953. 1953 was the 50th anniversary of the invention of the Teddy Bear. Michtom got political luminaries such as 31 governors of the United States, Chief Justice Earl Warren of the Supreme Court, and even the President of the United States himself to pose with Smokey. Kids could send in to Washington and become Junior Forest Rangers and receive a seven-piece kit to help them "Prevent Forest Fires." Chief Justice Earl Warren's statement, made when he was Governor of California, illuminates the scope of the project, "The State Division of Forestry and the U.S. Forest Service are cooperating this year to bring a nationwide program to the young people of California. They are asking every youngster to become a Junior Forest Ranger and to learn about forest fires and how they can be prevented. I urge every boy and girl to join in our forest fire prevention campaign by becoming Junior Forest Rangers." People were not allowed to market Smokey the Bear items without a license or even to appear in public in a Smokey costume, thus, Michtom succeeded in having the Congress of the United States, in effect, exclusively license Ideal to produce and promote his Smokey the Bear doll.

Miss Revlon

Miss Revlon was a sweet success for Mr. Michtom. He had to overcome the objections of Mr. Charles Revson, head of Revlon Cosmetics, to allow Ideal to produce the doll as a tie-in with Revlon cosmetics. Mr. Revson felt the tie-in with a doll would make his product seem less glamorous to adult women.

However, Sandy Buxbaum, Revlon's marketing executive, said they should go ahead with the tie-in since they could get the girls familiar with the Revlon name at a young age, and, thus, be more inclined to use their products when they were older. Mr. Michtom then vowed to produce the "most gorgeous doll of all time" to prove to Mr. Revson that the tie-in was a good idea. The Revlon doll was such a success that it made Revlon half a million dollars in royalties. Mr. Michtom even had his marketing man, Mel Poretz, personally deliver the first royalty check for $79,000 to Mr. Revson as a type of "I told you so."

Labor Relations

Ideal had a good relationship with their employee unions since the strikes in 1916 and 1919 and were known for providing good working conditions and a sense of family business. Dave Rosenstein, a former academic, was president of Ideal in 1953. He also had presided over the National Association of Doll Manufacturers, an industry association. Mr. Rosenstein was the "upfront" man who dealt with the union officers, department store presidents, and other higher level outsiders.

Ideal's Biggest Successes

Among Ideal's biggest doll successes were "Shirley Temple," "Betsy Wetsy®," "Sparkle Plenty," and "Toni" which came out in many versions and was produced over several years. "Saucy Walker," "Patti Playpal" and "Thumbelina" were also very successful.

Dave Koske ran the assembly line at Ideal from 1955 – 1984. He says production of the dolls ran from a low of about 25,000 for some dolls up to over a million for the more successful dolls. Ideal sold over one and a half million Shirley Temple dolls in the 1930s, an unheard of success in the depth of the Depression.

The Shirley Temple Dolls

Ideal's most successful dolls, the "Shirley Temples," sold in the millions. There are several different versions of the doll. The first series in the 1930s were composition dolls (1934 – 1938), a "Baby Shirley Temple" (1935), and a Shirley with short curls "Shirley At 9" (1939). The second series was a rotation molded vinyl produced from 1958 – 1961. A third series in 1973 was 16" vinyl. A fourth set of 8" and 12" vinyls were produced in 1982 and 1983. A porcelain doll appeared in 1983. Finally, a 16" reissue of the 1973 doll appeared in 1984.

Shirley Temple was very much involved with Ideal and received the benefits from the success of the dolls. In her autobiography *Child Star*, Shirley states that the royalties from the dolls were over $120,000 for the period 1934 – 1039, and her mother used to say that their Brentwood home was the home that "dolls built." Ideal sold over $6 million worth of Shirley dolls in the 1930s.

The original Shirley doll in composition was designed by Bernard Lipfert. In order to secure the rights to produce the Shirley Temple doll, Benjamin Michtom flew to Hollywood and negotiated for six months with Shirley's parents and agents. He had to negotiate with Mrs. Temple, who was very specific about what she wanted in a doll. Mr. Michtom had to promise Mrs. Temple that the doll's eyes would be hazel like Shirley's eyes, not brown or blue like all other dolls. There also was a specification of exactly 52 curls, the kind of hair Shirley was famous for. Abe Katz had Ideal's designers make 28 molds of Shirley's face until they were sure that they had captured her likeness. Testing was rather offbeat as they then took the prototype of the doll's head through the streets of Brooklyn until they heard enough children squeal, "That's Shirley." After each of Shirley's movies, Ideal would release a doll dressed in the outfit she wore in the film. An Ideal designer would copy Shirley's outfits from her movie costumes. Shirley came in seven sizes ranging from 11" to 27" in 1935, selling for $3.00 to $30.00 retail. "The Shirley Temple baby" came in six sizes in 1935.

Mr. Katz's daughter, Bette Katz Weintraub, who did consumer relations for Ideal in the 1970s, remembers her father taking her to see Shirley Temple movies and meeting Shirley in person when they both were children. She remembers Shirley Temple as intelligent and well-mannered with a good sense of humor.

In 1958 Shirley Temple Black was the hostess of a children's television show "Shirley Temple's Storybook Hour" where she read fairy tales. Mr. Michtom thought it would be a good idea to reintroduce a Shirley Temple doll to tie-in with the publicity. Ideal had always realized the promotional value of Shirley Temple. Actually earlier in 1948 they had wanted to produce a doll of Shirley Temple's first baby from her marriage to John Agar and market "Shirley Temple Mother and Daughter" dolls, but Shirley would have no part of it. Shirley did, however, lend her support to the 1958 dolls. She was interested in the design process and had final approval of the dolls. The dolls came in four sizes, 12" up to 19," and had many different outfits from her movies and playdresses. Shirley Temple was available for personal appearances to promote the doll. Retailers could contact Ideal to arrange a signing party. Crowds as huge as 50,000 came to see her and have her sign their dolls at department stores across the country. In 1960 Ideal produced a 36" Shirley Temple using the same technology as the "Patti Playpal" dolls, which remains a very desirable doll for collectors.

Shirley Temple visited the Ideal factory twice during the 1958 production run of her doll. Employees were touched that she remembered those who had been there during her previous visit. Several employees recalled an anecdote which illustrates Shirley's sense of humor. At an Ideal party celebrating the success of her doll, Mr. Katz referring to the problems of doll production and design said to her, "Shirley, I spent many sleepless nights making you." Shirley is said to have replied, "So did my mother and father."

In 1973 Ideal produced a 16½" "Shirley Temple" doll sculpted by Neil Estern. In 1980 Ideal designed a Shirley sculpted by Vincent DeFilippo in conjunction with the reissue of the movie *Little Miss Marker*. Ideal never produced this 11½" Shirley doll due to lack of agreement with Shirley Temple Black. However, the doll of the new little star of the movie, Sara Stimson, was produced. The 1983 porcelain Shirley doll was designed by Hank Garfinkle and made by Dollsparts in Long Island City, although it was marketed by Ideal.

Deanna Durbin Dolls

In 1938 as the success of the Shirley Temple dolls was waning, Ideal came out with the "Deanna Durbin" doll. Deanna was a teenage singing star of radio and movies. Ideal proclaimed the Deanna doll to be the first "teenage" doll in doll history. The composition doll was brought out in four sizes, 14" to 25," and wore authentic costumes from her films. The doll was introduced at the same time her Universal movie *That Certain Age* was being released. The costumes were really spectacular and the best Ideal had produced. They included long party dresses, dirndls, bolero jacket outfits, and two-piece suits with berets of matching materials. Many were bright plaids. The attention to detail was very much evident. The shoes were suede with tassels. As new motion pictures were released, Ideal made new costumes available to retailers who were promised a "lucrative follow-up business in outfits" in a news release to the trade. The Deanna doll remains a favorite with collectors today.

Comic Strip Babies

The Ideal Toy and Novelty Company popularized the concept of transforming comic babies into cuddly dolls. One of the first of these was the "Yellow Kid" doll in 1907. Yellow Kid was the rascal baby of "Hogan's Alley" comic strip by Richard Felton Outcault appearing in the *New York Sunday Journal*. After World War II, the comic strips experienced a major "baby boom" with babies born into such strips as Dick Tracy, Joe Palooka, and Li'l Abner. These dolls mirrored the baby boom in the American population, and manufacturers were quick to sense the comic strip babies' popularity and soon produced baby dolls depicting these characters.

Ideal's first post-war comic baby success was the "Sparkle Plenty" doll from Chester Gould's Dick Tracy strip. The Sparkle Plenty doll grossed $6 million and was the fastest selling doll up to that time (1947). In the comics, Sparkle Plenty was the daughter of B.O. Plenty, an unkempt, old criminal, and Gravel Gertie, a banjo player who lived in a gravel pit. The birth of this beautiful daughter with waist length hair and sparkling eyes tripled fan mail to the Dick Tracy comic strip. William McDuffee, the toy manager from Gimbel's Department Store, thought that a doll of the popular comic strip character would need little promotion or advertising and took the idea to the Ideal Toy Company. Ideal, capitalizing on Sparkle Plenty's popularity, designed a doll and began production only 48 days later using the revolutionary new material of "Magic Skin." Magic Skin, developed in 1940 by Ideal, was a latex rubber stuffed with cotton that felt soft to the touch and was washable.

The "Sparkle Plenty" doll has a Celanese cellulose hard plastic head, a Magic Skin latex rubber jointed body, long yellow woolen yarn hair, bright blue sleep eyes with long lashes, and pierced nostrils. She cried or cooed when squeezed. She came dressed in either a cotton flannel sacque and diaper or an outfit with a white collar.

Sparkle Plenty's huge success, partially attributed to her waist length yellow wool hair that could be combed and shampooed, started the trend for comic strip dolls in the toy industry. In 1948 Ideal gave Sparkle a jointed rubber body so she could drink and wet and added a voice that cooed and cried. She also came in a print dress or slacks. She was produced through 1951.

After Sparkle's success, Ideal decided to try again for another winner from the Dick Tracy comic strip. "Bonny Braids" is the doll named for the baby born on May 4, 1951 to Tess Trueheart, the wife of Dick Tracy in the comic strip. When Tess and Dick were married, Chester Gould, the cartoonist, got a call from Ben Michtom saying, "When the baby's born, it's mine." Tess and Dick got married on December 25, 1949. In March Gould dropped hints that a baby was on the way and called Michtom. Michtom said the timing for the doll would be terrible in October because he was already pushing another baby doll called "Blessed Event." In order to make the comic character have the baby when it would be more propitious for the doll trade, Gould had a bomb thrown into Tracy's house and made it seem that Tess lost her baby. Then Gould checked with Michtom to decide exactly when the baby should be born. Luckily, the comic strip baby had a safe, if unconventional, delivery in a police car.

In order to promote the doll, Ben Michtom persuaded the Los Angeles police department (after the New York police turned them down) to do a publicity stunt rushing the doll to the department store since Bonny was born in a police car.

The stunt used to introduce the doll to New York was having Miss Charlotte Klein, a publicity representative for Ideal dressed as a nurse pushing Bonny in a baby carriage up Fifth Avenue to the Central Park Zoo with a banner reading "Nobody But Nobody But Gimbel's has Bonny Braids." As another gimmick, Ideal offered a free doll to the first local baby born named Bonny.

Over 7,000 "Bonny Braids" dolls were being made a day in July, 1951. The doll had washable plastic hair and a Vinylite Magic Skin body. When the stomach was pressed, it emitted a hoarse cry. She had one tooth and carried a tube of Ipana Toothpaste. It is interesting to note that Ideal had always tied-in with commercial products to help promote their dolls ever since their first doll, the "Uneeda Kid" (1914), who promoted Uneeda Crackers. The Ipana tie-in seemed a natural for Bonny's one tooth!

Ideal brought out a toddler version of "Bonny Braids" in 1953. Bonny Braids toddler had a vinyl head and body, Magic Skin arms and legs, and sleep eyes and came dressed in an organdy short or long dress. She came in two sizes, 11½" and 13½". Ideal also produced a "Bonny Braids Walker" in 1953. Bonny Braids Walker had a vinyl head, plastic body, sleep eyes, two saran braids, molded yellow hair, and three upper teeth. She carried a toothbrush, and she walked, sat, and turned her head. She wore a flowered dress and came in two sizes, 14" and 16". Her tag reads "Copyright 1951 the Chicago Tribune." She is an adorable doll, and it is nice to see her two new teeth. Ideal made a record-breaking $7 million in sales from Bonny Braids dolls alone.

During the time Bonny was such a success, Ideal publicist Miss Charlotte Klein hinted that since Joe Palooka had married Ann Howe in their comic strip, they would be having a baby, too. "Mr. Michtom will see to that," quotes Charlotte Klein in the *New Yorker* magazine. That hint soon blossomed into a "living" doll. Ideal produced "Joan Palooka," daughter of Joe Palooka and Ann Howe, in 1953. The Joan Palooka doll has a Vinylite plastic head, molded hair with topknot of yellow saran, stuffed vinyl body, latex Magic Skin arms and legs, and blue sleep eyes. She smelled like baby powder and came with Johnson's Baby Powder and soap. Joan Palooka still sweetly smells like baby powder after all these years.

Another birth for Ideal in 1953 was Li'l Abner's baby boy, "Li'l Honest Abe." Since Ideal and the reading public did not know his name for quite some time after he was born in the comic strip and produced by Ideal, he is also known as "Mysterious Yokum." He was the least expensive comic strip baby doll and not a great success.

Adding to the population explosion was "Little Wingy" from the Dick Tracy comic strip in 1953. She was the "little girl" from the comic strip. She had a vinyl head, plastic body, glued on wig with hair to below the waist, closed mouth, sleep eyes, dimples on cheeks, denim slacks, and a hot pink blouse. Her face was coated with phosphorescent paint to make the doll glow in the dark. She was not a very successful doll for Ideal.

However, Ideal was not done with making dolls from the Dick Tracy strip. One more, "Little Honey Moon," arrived in 1965. She was the daughter of Junior Tracy and Moon Maid. She had a soft vinyl head and limbs, stuffed cotton body, white string hair, painted eyes, blue and silver original costume with removable clear plastic space helmet, and she cried when her stomach was pressed. She was not a success, mainly because the Tracy comic strip was not as popular as in the 1950s.

Ideal's Failures

Although most of Ideal dolls were successful and sold well, there was bound to be a few clunkers in their many years of production. A set of four character dolls produced after the very successful Shirley Temple were "Borah and the Harmonica Rascals" in 1937. The dolls were not a big success to say the least.

Ideal's most unsuccessful doll was the "Christ-child" doll (1956), an 8" doll designed by Julius Weih which just wouldn't sell. It came in a maroon box with gold-leaf trim in the shape of a Bible. It came in both Protestant and Catholic versions with the baby Jesus doll inside. The story goes that Ben Michtom had an audience with the Pope and had gotten the Pope's blessing to make the doll, but the Pope died before he could get anything in writing. He proceeded anyway, but when store toy buyers would not stock the dolls, Ben went over their heads to the presidents of all the big department stores such as Strauss, Broadway, and May Department Stores and pitched the doll personally. Orders came in the millions, but reality set in when the retail customers simply would not buy the doll. Then returns from the stores poured into the factory. The Jesus doll was the only doll Ideal had ever sold on consignment, meaning the stores could return unsold merchandise. With thousands of dolls stockpiled in their warehouse, Ideal finally gave them away to their employees and donated them to charities. Employees even had quotas as to how many they had to give away each week. In one instance, the dolls were even dumped into the ocean at a selling price of a half cent each, and now serve as a natural breakwater near Cape Hatteras off the coast of North Carolina. The Jesus Christ doll fiasco caused great financial hardship to the company and almost caused Ideal's collapse in 1957. The doll, Ideal's bad attempt at mixing religion with dolls, remains a collector's item today.

Dolls We Never Saw from Ideal

Mr. Katz was very doll conscious and was said to have loved dolls. He was often seen holding dolls in his arms and cuddling them like real babies. Mr. Katz felt that 11" dolls were easier for little girls to handle and dress so that is why they didn't come out with an 8" competitor to Ginny in the 1950s, much to the doll collector's loss!

Another doll that was not produced was a "full-figured" adult competitor to Barbie by Mattel which came out in 1958. Mr. Katz didn't want to come out with anything that looked too sexy, because he felt that dolls were basically little angels for little girls. Eventually, they reconsidered and came out with "Mitzi," a modern teenage doll, in 1961 and "Liz," another fashion teenager doll, was advertised and sold in 1962. "Tammy" introduced in 1962 was a somewhat developed "teenager," and although produced for several years, she never attained the massive popularity of Barbie.

Another doll never mass marketed by Ideal during this era was an anatomically correct male doll. There were several attempts to come out with one, but it never seemed to make it to the consumer. One story is that in the early days they made a mold for an anatomically correct male doll. However, one of the machinists thought it was a mistake and rubbed off all the "maleness" because he thought there was a defect in the mold. They only made a few of the dolls, because at that time even the older gentlemen in the shop couldn't believe they were going to do it. Mr. Katz was an honorable man and realized the country (or at least some segments) was not ready for reality in doll play. Later on, an anatomically correct Joey Stivic doll boy doll, Archie Bunker's grandson from the TV show (1976), was marketed for a short while but withdrawn after objections by the Catholic Church and other conservative groups in the country.

Another doll never made during the "golden era" was a doll with a heartbeat. Mr. Helmuth Moormann had developed a doll whose heart could be felt and seen beating. It was designed to be put into the Thumbelina mechanism. Ideal even went so far as to get a patent (a doll called Heart Beat was trademarked in 1951), but Mr. Katz felt that when the doll's heart stopped beating, a child would think the doll was dead, which would be too traumatic for the child. There was always that concern for their little consumers.

Marks

The marks on the Ideal dolls went through several variations. In the late 1920s, "Ideal" in a diamond with either "US of A" or "US Pat 162143" on the outer four corners appeared on the back of dolls. In the 1930s marks were

"IDEAL" in an oblong shape or "I.N. & T. Co." standing for Ideal Novelty and Toy Co., or simply "IDEAL DOLL" in block letters. "Shirley Temple" was marked with her name "SHIRLEY TEMPLE" with and without "COP IN & T Co." at the end. Other personality dolls were marked with their names plus "IDEAL." In the 1940s dolls were marked "IDEAL DOLL/MADE IN U.S.A." Some had the size added such as "18" at the end or beginning of the mark. Some dolls were not marked, especially the composition dolls.

In 1942 the "Plassie" doll carried Ideal's patent number for hard plastic, Pat #2252077, which also appeared on several subsequent dolls (the "Sparkle Plenty" doll and the "Betsy Wetsy®" dolls). In the 1950s, P-90 through P-93 was added for the "Toni" doll bodies. A "W" was added in front of the size such as W – 16 to denote Walker, example the "Saucy Walker" doll (1951). A "V" was added in front of the code number to denote vinyl such as V/91. In the late 1950s the "Patti Playpal" doll series had "IDEAL" in an oval on their back.

Starting in 1960, "IDEAL TOY CORP." appeared on the dolls along with various letters and the size of the doll. Usually a © appeared in front of Ideal. In 1970 the country the doll was manufactured in, such as "HONG KONG," appeared on the head (example "Play 'N Jane," 1971). The patent number for growing hair mechanism appeared on the "Crissy®" family dolls in 1970 (U.S. PAT. 3,162,976, e.g., "Kerry" and "Brandi," 1971 and 1972).

Helmuth Moorman, manager of the tool room, was in charge of deciding how to trademark the dolls. His system starting in 1946 was to trademark a head: "HB" or "H" or "125." An arm was marked "A," a leg "L," and the eye was marked "E." The trademarking system was not the same and not always constant. The trademarking system on the dolls was not the same as the catalog numbering system.

Ideal's Doll Hospital

Ideal always stood by their dolls. When customers would return dolls to Ideal, because they were broken or had lost hair, Ideal would always try to repair them and sell replacement parts. The dolls were repaired in-house by Helmuth Moorman and in later years Tom Hyde would send them out to a New York doll hospital or to Dollsparts in Long Island City.

Ideal Dolls Sold By Other Companies

Ideal also sold their dolls to other doll companies to dress and then market under their own name. Vogue dolls of Medford, Mass., makers of "Ginny," dressed and sold Ideal composition and hard plastic dolls (14", 17") under their label in the late 1940s and early 1950s. An example from the Vogue doll company is "Mary Jane" (1941).

Other doll companies selling Ideal dolls included Arranbee Company, the Madame Alexander Company, Eugenia Doll Co., Effanbee Doll Co., Mary Hoyer Doll Company, and the Sayco Doll Company. Most of these dolls are unmarked, some have an "X" with a circle around it, and some have "Shirley Temple" partially scratched out on the back of the body.

Parts Produced by Other Doll Companies

When demand for a certain doll exceeded Ideal's capacity to manufacture, Ideal used custom molding companies for doll parts. Before Ideal got their injection molding machine up and running in 1942, they bought doll heads manufactured by the Plastic Molded Arts (PMA) Company of Long Island City, NY.

Composition doll parts such as legs and arms were bought from parts manufacturers such as New York Doll Parts, Manhattan.

Dolls such as "Tubsy" and "Thumbelina" (1963) were comprised of parts made by custom molding companies.

Ideal Dolls Produced by Reliable Toy Company

Ideal licensed their dolls to the Reliable Toy Company of Toronto, Canada, founded in 1920 and owned by S.F. Samuels and his brother, Alex. Ideal licensed the right to produce dolls such as "Cuddles," "Smiles," "Tickletoes," and "Shirley Temple" up through Krissy, "Tammy" and Thumbelina to Reliable. Reliable made the Shirley Temple dolls with identical Shirley Temple bodies and heads. Some had an open mouth with four teeth and some were closed-mouth. On the box it says "Canadian Shirley Temple." Ideal owned the patent, and Reliable could use the name of Shirley Temple on the body. The Ideal composition was finer than the Reliable. Ideal had a long close relationship with Reliable. Sam Zimbtbaum, nephew of Mr. Katz and a 30-year employee of Ideal, remembers car trips up to Canada with Mr. Katz's family to visit the Reliable plant and to socialize with the Samuels family.

Television

Ideal was one of the first companies to make use of the revolutionary medium of television to advertise their dolls. Ideal sponsored the Macy's Thanksgiving Day Parade starting in 1954. They were the first to buy up blocks of time on kids' Saturday morning shows to promote their dolls. They also advertised on shows such as those starring Art Linkletter,

Johnny Downs, Bob Crosby, and Sandy Becker in 1957. Ideal was viewed by store toy buyers as a promotional house with dolls that could be sold in the hundreds of thousands due to the influence of television and promotion.

Changes at Ideal

In the late 1960s, Ideal felt great pressure from all the cheap foreign import dolls. Eventually in the 1960s they switched the producing of clothes and parts to foreign shores, but price competition increased. In addition, Mr. Katz was getting on in years and relinquished his leading role in daily matters to his son-in-law Lionel Weintraub, Bette's husband. Mr. Katz retained his seat on the Ideal board of directors. In 1963 Lionel Weintraub became president of Ideal. He went on to run the company for 20 years.

Ms. Miriam Gittelson, a long-time Ideal employee, became head of import/export. The nature of the business was changing with so much production going on in the Far East.

The Ideal "people" who worked at Ideal, many for several decades, still retain their sense of fun and family that being with Ideal evoked. They have a newsletter and still meet yearly at a banquet event in New York and Florida to get together and reminisce and appreciate, as all of us collectors do, the "golden years" of Ideal.

The Mass Merchandising Era
(1962 on)

With Mr. Weintraub's ascendancy to president in 1962, Ideal moved into the new age of a modern corporation. He introduced sophisticated product development techniques and integrated the activities of marketing, research and product development, manufacturing and financial operations. No longer was Ideal run by personalities but by committee. Doll decisions were not fought out over a conference table but were decided by modern marketing methods.

Dolls introduced in this era included "Goody Two Shoes" (a walking doll), "Glamour Misty," the "Miss Clairol Doll," "Giggles," "Captain Action," "Flatsy series," "Beautiful Crissy®," "Diana Ross," "Harmony," "Evel Knievel," "Jody – the Old Fashioned Doll," "Tiffany Taylor," "Dorothy Hamill," and "Whoopsie."

Ideal became a publicly owned corporation in June, 1968, and its stock was traded on the New York Stock Exchange. In 1978 it employed more than 4,000 employees, its sales were over $126 million, and its profits were over $42 million. Its international division coordinated the manufacturing activities of wholly and partially owned companies in Canada, the United Kingdom, Germany, Australia, New Zealand, and Japan.

Ideal was sold to CBS (Columbia Broadcasting System, the entertainment conglomerate) in 1983 for $58 million. CBS added Ideal to its Gabriel toy line and called it "Ideal-Gabriel." CBS owned Ideal for three years then closed the doll division in 1986. Then the plastics division was sold to View-Master, makers of the 3-D viewers, who bought the Ideal trademark and several product lines. Ideal Toy Company was then known as the View-Master Ideal Group and came out with dolls at the 1989 Toy Fair. Tyco Industries, Inc. bought View-Master/Ideal in 1989. Mattel bought the rights to Ideal in 1998.

Design of Dolls

Mr. Abraham Katz, the driving force behind the wonderful dolls Ideal is known for retired in 1968 at age 75. This ended the personality driven uniqueness of Ideal's dolls. Under Lionel Weintraub's direction, a design committee developed a doll. Arle Alpert was vice president of research and development. His wife, Judy Alpert, was director of product development and design in the doll division. Mr. Weintraub would then approve a doll based on the judgment of whether it would sell, was beautiful, and was practical to produce.

Designers and their Dolls

Many doll designers and sculptors worked for Ideal during this era. Ideas for dolls were generated both in-house and by outside toy designers. Mary Maidenbauer, the head of doll clothing design had been with Ideal since the early days, eventually became vice president in 1969. Judy Alpert, at Ideal from 1959 – 1981, eventually became head of the doll clothing division. She worked with the sculptor for the 1973 "Shirley Temple" doll. She designed the clothing for "Snuggles" and "Whoopsie" among others.

Mr. Vincent DeFilippo's first complete commission from Ideal was "Tearie Dearie" in 1963. He had been at Ideal for 30 years. He sculpted many of the dolls during the Weintraub era. Mr. DeFilippo's other dolls for Ideal during the 1970s and 1980s include Baby Baby A Handful of Love, Baby Crissy's head, Baby Dreams, Baby Kiss-A-Boo, Brandi and Andy Gibb, Chew-Chew-Suzy Chew, Derry Daring, Tippy Tumbles and Timmy Tumbles, Jackie, J.J. Armes, Jody, Joey Stivic, Karen, Kissy, Laura and Robin, Magic Hair Crissy, My Bottle Baby, New Rub-a-Dub-Dolly, Newborn Snuggles, Posin' Cricket, Pretty Curls, Rub-a-Dub Dolly, Sara Stimpson, Suntan Tuesday Taylor, Taylor Jones, Tearie Betsy Wetsy, 7" Thumbelina, Tressy, Tuesday Taylor, Tuesday Taylor Beauty Queen and Super Model, Upsy Dazy, and Wake-Up Thumbelina.

Neil Estern, a sculptor who had done statues of famous Americans, including John F. Kennedy and Fiorello LaGuardia, brought realism and naturalism to the dolls he did for Ideal. He designed the "Patti Playpal" doll family (including "Patti", "Suzy", "Penny", and "Peter") in the 1960s. He was on exclusive contract to Ideal for two years in the 1970s and did many dolls on a free-lance basis for them. Dolls he designed included "Miss Ideal" (also called "Terri Twist"), "Saucy Walker" (1960 version), "Daddy's Girl," "Pattite," "Walking Pattite," "Kissy," "Kissy Baby," "Deluxe Kissy," "Thumbelina," "Crying Thumbelina," "Tiny Thumbelina," "Newborn Thumbelina," "In-A-Minute Thumbelina," "Kissin' Thumbelina," "Katie Kachoo," "Giggles," "Baby Giggles," "Tubsy," "Playtime Tubsy," "Tearie Betsy Wetsy®," "Little Lost Baby," the "Flatsy Dolls," and the "Fashion Flatsy dolls," "Betty Big Girl," several of the "Crissy®" dolls including "Beautiful Crissy®," "Velvet," "Talking Crissy®," "Talking Velvet," "Movin' Groovin' Crissy®," "Magic Hair Crissy®," "Movin' Groovin Velvet," "Mia," "Diana Ross," "Little Love," "Bizzie Lizzie," "Real Live Lucy," and others. Some may have the trademark "E" on their heads, legs, and arms.

Erin Libby, a doll sculptor, worked for Ideal in the 1970s and 1980s. She sculpted the heads used in the Snuggles line (1978 – 1981). In 1979 there was a Snuggles on a rocking horse. Ideal also used the Snuggles head for a doll called Kit and Kaboodle (1984 – 1985). This same head was used again for an imitation porcelain-look doll, Whoopsie, in 1984. Erin Libby also sculpted one or two more heads for the Ideal Nursery line after Tyco bought Ideal. She says she was "proud to be part of what I considered a long and impressive history as doll makers."

Another sculptor at Ideal was an Italian named Hugo Ungaro who did several dolls at Ideal and was on the staff for a short period of time. He was an excellent sculptor; however, he was not able to successfully translate his ability into the very special art of making dolls.

Another free-lance sculptor was Ivan Berro who sculpted Suntan Eric (1977).

Marvin Glass, an independent inventor, brought several design concept ideas and special mechanisms to Ideal. Several of his doll ideas were "Kissy" (1961), "Real Live Lucy" (1965), "Tubsy" (1967), "April Showers" (1969), "Lazy Dazy" (1972), and "Tiffany Taylor" (1972). Other artists have designed dolls for Ideal but under agreement could not publicize their efforts.

Manufacturing

Ideal built an additional plant in Secaucus, New Jersey, in the late 1960s. In 1973 another plant was built in Newark, New Jersey. A large proportion of manufacturing went overseas in the late 1960s to Hong Kong and other parts of the Orient, especially its smaller size dolls (such as "Tammy" and "Thumbelina") and then later to the Caribbean.

Ideal also had factories in Germany, France, Canada (in a licensing arrangement with the Reliable Toy Co.), Australia, and Japan to sell to those local markets. Sometimes local tastes influenced manufacturing decisions. For example, when a sample of Tammy's little sister "Pepper" was sent over to be produced in the early 1960s, her freckles were considered an imperfection in Japanese culture, so the Japanese Peppers were manufactured without freckles. Dresses were manufactured (in chronological order) in Japan, Hong Kong, Taiwan, and Macau. Ideal manufactured such a large quantity of doll dresses that its sales volume rivaled those of full-size ready-to-wear clothes companies. In the 1980s, View-Master/Ideal manufactured in China.

Marketing

Ideal was known as a promotion house. They advertised extensively on television, and retailers looked to them for the high volume sellers. Ideal used what is called "distribution planning." They would decide where to allocate a product by individual market based on if it was advertised in that market. They used a common practice in the industry at that time called a "roll-out" campaign. If a customer ordered 1,800 pieces, they would ship only 400, because they wanted the product to move off the shelves. When the retailer would perceive that the item moved quickly, then they would reorder a greater volume of the item, and Ideal would have a hit. Their conservative production quotas didn't meet the demand for such dolls as "Rub-a-Dub Dolly" and "Evel Knievel," and they, thus, increased their product's life span.

Ideal employed salesmen, who worked exclusively for Ideal. They marketed the dolls to department stores, toy stores, wholesalers, and chain stores.

Ideal also sold their dolls to be used by companies as premiums. In the late 1970s, Ideal was limited to a $9.95 price point. In order to compete in the marketplace, they had to find ways to make dolls cheaper.

Television

Ideal, the first toy company to advertise extensively on television, stayed in the forefront of television advertising in Lionel Weintraub's regime. In 1962 they not only had network and spot advertising commercials, but also mounted the largest TV advertising campaign in toy manufacturing history. They sponsored the entire Saturday morning line-up of children's shows on the CBS network. They advertised on "Alvin and the Chipmunks," "Mighty Mouse Playhouse," "Rin Tin Tin," and "Roy Rogers Show." Other shows Ideal advertised on were "Jeff's Collie," "Mr. Magoo," and "Brave Stallion."

In 1964 they sponsored the "Magilla Gorilla" cartoon show with characters Peter Potamus, Mushmouse, Punkin' Puss, Ricochet Rabbit, and Droop-A-Long Coyote.

A controversial episode happened in 1971 when "Bizzie Lizzie," the doll who does housework, became the focus of a picket sponsored by the N.A.A.C.P. at Korvettes in New York. The picket was over the perceived portrayal of a black Bizzie Lizzie as a maid or housekeeper in a television ad. The misunderstanding arose because Bizzie Lizzie, who irons, uses a carpet sweeper, and a feather duster, was made in both white and "Negro" versions, but the white dolls had yet to be produced, and there were only "Negro" Bizzie Lizzies in the stores. The misunderstanding was straightened out, and Ideal's proud record with black dolls was upheld.

This record was further strengthened in 1976 when "Tara," an "ethnically" correct black doll, was advertised using a television commercial with a black cast. This was the first time a commercial featured a black doll with a black cast.

Technology

In the Ideal tradition, technological advances in doll making were encouraged. An example of this technology would be "Crissy®" an 18" doll whose hair grew. Her hair was wound on a spool in her belly and when the knob in her back was moved, her hair grew. Crissy® was introduced by Ideal in 1969. The idea for a growing hair doll came from "Tressy," who was produced by the American Character Doll Company, in 1963. The patent rights for Tressy were purchased by Ideal from the original American Character Company which went bankrupt. Ideal engineers re-designed the mechanism to make her hair grow. Her face and body were designed "in-house." Mr. Herb Lawrence molded a mechanism for Crissy®. Crissy®'s body was blow molded. Crissy® happens to be the doll that Mr. Lionel Weintraub, past president of Ideal, says was his favorite.

In 1976 Ideal came out with "Joey Stivic," an anatomically correct male doll who was Archie Bunker's grandson from the 1976 television show "All in the Family." Sculptor Vincent DeFilippo designed Joey to be uncircumcised, but there were some objections raised. Then they redesigned the doll to be circumcised, and everything was fine. Ideal spent a lot of money on advertising; however, the Catholic Church raised objections, and Ideal stopped manufacturing the dolls, donating those remaining.

"Rub-A-Dub-Dolly," a doll that was completely waterproof, had been thought impossible to make. Ideal engineers even found a way to seal off the thousands of hair root openings, as well as the arm and leg joints.

"Suntan Tuesday Taylor" in 1977 represented another scientific breakthrough. She was the first doll that tanned. The same phototrophic chemical used to darken sunglasses was applied to Tuesday Taylor to allow her and her boyfriend "Eric" and sister "Dodi" to get suntanned.

Joe Glaudino, in charge of sewing operations, developed a new cutting action on hair rooting machines. The synthetic fibers such as saran, acetate, nylon, and the new P.V.C. used for the hair were hard on the cutting plates, causing them to break, so he developed a new stronger cutting plate. In 1981 Ideal had over 100 hair rooting machines in their factories in Haiti and Santo Domingo.

Variations on a Theme

Continuing the tradition of redesigning and using new technology for previously developed dolls, Ideal recycled several dolls from earlier on. "Upsy Dazy" from 1973 was given a new face and clothes and a new name, "Tippy Tumbles" and a friend, "Timmy Tumbles," in 1977. The dolls could stand on their heads, tumble, and do other tricks. "Crissy®," the best selling doll of the late 1960s, was brought back as "Magic Hair Crissy®" in 1977 and given changeable hair accessories.

Dolls Ideal Did Not Make

In 1981 Ideal showed a prototype of a "Loni Anderson" doll in their catalog. She is listed as Number 1272-4. She was an 11½" fashion doll with rooted blonde hair, representing the star of the TV show "WKRP in Cincinnati." However, the response from the buyers was not good, and she was never made. However, one source said that she was made and approximately 5,000 were produced.

The 1980 11½" "Shirley Temple" doll shown in the catalog along with the "Sara Stimson" doll from "Little Miss Marker," was not made. There was several reasons postulated for this. One supposedly was disagreement over the size of her body in relation to her head, among other issues, and Shirley Temple Black did not like the doll. Another reason was that there was a lack of pending orders from buyers resulting in Ideal's decision to remove it from the line before it went into production.

Successes and Failures

The "Evel Knievel" stunt doll on his stunt cycle could be categorized as both a success and failure. He represented the popular stuntman of the time. The doll was a big seller in the late 1970s, and each year there was a slightly different gimmick such as his Stratocycle, Chopper, or Supercycle. However, in 1978 Evel Knievel, the stuntman, was convicted of a crime which brought a marked drop-off in sales. Ideal was left with many dolls in the warehouse.

Another doll that initially sold well, but then showed a rapid demise were the 1982 "Jelly Belly" dolls. The Jelly Belly dolls were patterned after the successful "Strawberry Shortcake" dolls that had been manufactured earlier by a competitor. Jelly Belly babies not only were scented according to the color of their costume (e.g., yellow smelled like lemon drop), but they had a soft squishy material inside their belly to imitate jelly beans. They began selling very well but died rather quickly within one year since the squishy material in their belly dried up and became crackly on the toy shop shelves.

The 1983 porcelain "Shirley Temple" was purported to be designed by Hank Garfinkle. He held autograph signing parties at department stores. He signed his name on the back of these expensive dolls, which sold for $400.00, with felt tip pen. There is some controversy over exactly who designed this version of Shirley Temple. Shirley's wig was made by the A + B Artistic Wig Co.

Remnants of Ideal

Ideal went from what was essentially a family business, in which Bette Katz Weintraub would go in on Saturdays and help pack dolls, to being a large subsidiary of a major corporation. From a company whose focus was producing quality dolls for children to one in which only 16% of sales came from their toys in 1974. Benjamin Franklin Michtom, son of the founder Morris Michtom and chairman of the board, emeritus died in November, 1980. Ideal's net income in 1982 was $18 million. Mark Michtom, grandson of the founder of Ideal, sold the company to CBS, the large entertainment corporation, in 1983 for $58 million. Boyd Brown became president. CBS controlled Ideal for three years, and then sold off inventory, tools, and the Ideal name to View-Master, dismantling the once-proud company. Some of the assets were acquired by Hasbro.

When Ideal was moved by CBS, the dolls in the museum and most of the archival material were thrown away. One of each doll Ideal produced had been in the museum; what a great treat that must have been to see! Ben Michtom had scrapbooks of information such as ads, letters from doll buyers, information on dolls, and clippings about each doll. All the years of Ideal history were unceremoniously tossed out by the new owners, a large conglomerate, who did not have the heart and soul of a "doll person." Due to valiant efforts by some of the old guard employees, who realized the value of the material, some of it, only fragments, was saved. After basically disassembling the company and firing most of the old employees, CBS closed the doll division in 1986. View-Master/Ideal Group, originally a toy company, re-introduced some of the very popular dolls Ideal made famous at the 1989 Toy Fair. Tyco Industries, Inc. bought View-Master/Ideal in 1989 and came out with the Ideal nursery doll line in 1991. The Ideal name and rights to several dolls was bought by Mattel in 1998.

Hopefully, another generation of America's children will have the privilege of playing with the quality dolls of the Ideal Toy Corporation.

A company's products are judged on how well they perform and last. If that is the case, then Ideal Toy Corporation's dolls deserve a special place of honor in the hearts of children and grown-ups everywhere.

Family Photographs

Courtesy Anita Katz Child.

Morris and Rose Michtom, founders of the Ideal Toy Corporation (1932).

Courtesy Anita Katz Child.

Abraham Katz and his family, wife Kathryn, Bette Weintraub, for whom Betsy Wetsy® was named (center), and twins Rita Merrin (left), and Anita Child (right) (1938).

Ideal Dolls
(1907 – 1929)

Cartoon of **Yellow Kid** in the comic strip "Hogan's Alley" by Richard Felton Outcault appearing in the *New York Sunday Journal*. He was the first doll produced by the Ideal Novelty Company in 1907. Bald oriental-looking baby with big ears and dressed in yellow flour sack nightgown. He had a compo head and molded ears and a cloth body. $500.00.

Courtesy Sylvia Rose.

Early Compo Character Doll (ca. 1911) 16" Molded hair, compo shoulder plate head, compo hands, cloth legs, four painted teeth, and blonde hair. Clothes not original. Blue tin sleep eyes. Red dots inside nostrils. Marks: Ideal in diamond with U S of A around outer side of head. $90.00.

Mr. I.H. Bernhard, vice president of Ideal Toy Corp. showing the original Teddy Bear to a little girl. Teddy (ca. 1908) has a small head, deep set shoe button eyes, a long snout, elongated torso, arms, three embroidered claws, and a snout made of material (not embroidered). Jointed arms, leg, and neck. Stuffed with excelsior. Marks: none. $1,000.00

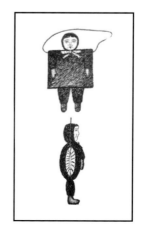

Baby Mine Muff (1911) Design Patent filed by Morris Michtom on Dec. 19, 1910. Patent #41,179. Composition head and stuffed muff forming body with legs and shoes hanging down. $50.00.

Uneeda Kid Design Patent filed Sept. 23, 1914 by Morris Michtom. Patent #46,747.

Girl doll (circa 1913) 12" Composition head, gauntlet hands, molded brown boots on feet, hard stuffed cloth body, jointed neck, arms and legs, yellow painted molded hair, tin sleep eyes, four painted teeth, red dots inside nostrils. She is typical of the Ideal dolls of this era. She looks like "Naughty Marietta." Head marked: IDEAL in a diamond with U S of A on the four outside corners of the diamond. Clothes not original. $90.00.

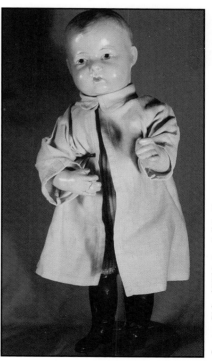

Courtesy Richard Withington Doll Auctions.

Uneeda Kid (1914) 14" or 24" Composition head, gauntlet arms and legs, right arm bent to hold miniature box of Uneeda Biscuits, yellow or brown painted molded hair, blue sleep or painted eyes, closed mouth, jointed, hard stuffed cloth body, black painted molded pants and boots, red dots inside nostrils. Wore rompers under a yellow sateen fisherman's coat and hat. Ideal licensed the image from the National Biscuit Company. Marks: IDEAL in a diamond on back or unmarked; label on cuff of raincoat says "Uneeda Biscuit, pat'd Dec. 8, 1914 MFD. by IDEAL NOVELTY & TOY CO." 14", $250.00; 24", $400.00.

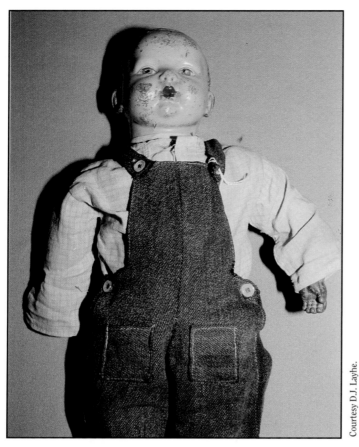

Courtesy D.J. Layhe.

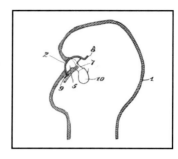

Patent for doll head with eye apertures and weighted eyes, a spring clip resting on the ears. Patent filed by Isaac Rommer, Aug. 10, 1915.

Boy doll (**circa 1915**) Composition head, gauntlet arms, molded boots, cloth body, red dots in nostrils. He is typical of the dolls of that era and has been repainted. Denim overalls not original. Marks: none. $45.00.

"Zu Zu Kid"—15¼ in., concealed hip and shoulder joints, composition hands, yellow sateen suit, allover brown stars, worsted pompons, matched cap, small pkg. "Zu Zus." Each in box.
F7958—⅙ doz. in pkg.....Doz. **$8.75**

Butler Brothers catalog.

Zu-Zu Kid (**1916 – 17**) 15½" Composition molded head and hair, compo hands and feet, cloth body, jointed at hip and shoulders. Girl in yellow sateen with brown stars clown costume with pom-pons and pointed cap, holding a miniature box of Zu-Zu Ginger Snaps, licensed by National Biscuit Co. Original price $0.73. $250.00.

Courtesy John Axe.

Compo Girl Doll (**circa 1918**) 12½" Composition head and hands, molded boots, stuffed cloth body, tin sleep eyes that open and close separately, arms and legs are joined with disks, two painted teeth, red dots in nostrils, painted eyelashes, dimples. Marks: Ideal in diamond with US of A on outer four corners. Dress probably not original. $95.00.

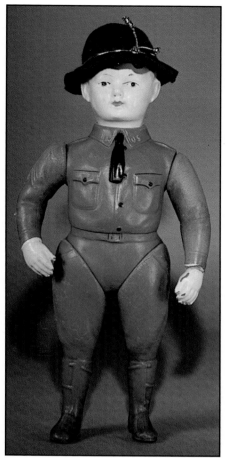

Courtesy Beulah Franklin.

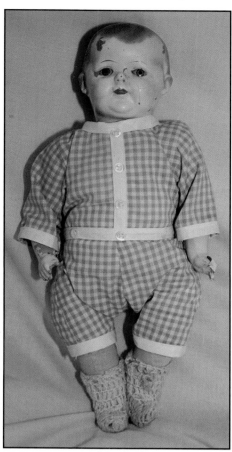

Liberty Boy (1918) 12" All composition, jointed at shoulders, neck, and hips, painted molded hair, and painted blue eyes, khaki painted molded U.S. Army uniform, black painted shoes, felt hat with gold cord, red dots inside nostrils. He was used to aid the WWI Liberty Bonds effort. Sold for $2.33 retail. Trademarked Dec. 27, 1917 #108,179. Marks: IDEAL in diamond shape (on back); U.S. on front collar. $250.00.

Baby Doll (circa 1920) 15" Composition head, gauntlet hands, hard stuffed cloth body and legs, light brown molded painted hair, tin painted sleep eyes, two painted teeth, red dots inside nostrils. Wears original blue check rompers. Typical of the Ideal baby dolls of the 1920s. Head marks: IDEAL in diamond with U S of A on the four outside corners. $90.00.

Ideal Walking Dolls (1920 – 1924) 18" and 20" Composition. Dolls walk naturally when taken by the hand. Patented walking devise, no springs. Patented "mama" voice. Voile dress, embroidery braid and lace trimmed neck and sleeves, lace trimmed petticoat and bloomers. Sewed human hair wig, long curls, real lashes. Original price $1.50 – $7.00. $100.00.

Miss Rosy Cheeks (1923 – 1928) 13" All composition, fully jointed, human hair in brown bob, winking sleep eyes, closed mouth, says "mama," wears organdy dress and bonnet and patent leather shoes. Offered as a premium from the 1923 and 1925 *Needlecraft Magazine*. $100.00.

Courtesy Jessie Williams.

Soozie Smiles – The Surprise Baby (**1923**) 16" (shown) and 17" Two-headed compo doll smiling face and crying face (shown) with tears, painted eyes and hair, red dots inside nostrils, compo lower arms, soft cotton-stuffed body and legs, head turns on flange neck, crying voice when put down, happy "mama" voice when picked up. Wearing blue check gingham rompers, striped socks, and patent leather shoes. Also came in a linene bloomer dress and bonnet. She is the doll that "made the Queen of England laugh." Original cost $2.00 and $3.75. 1924 version had tin sleep eyes on the smiling face. Trademark July 21, 1923 #183,524. Marks: none. $150.00.

Soozie Smiles – The Surprise Baby (**1923**) 16" Two-headed compo doll wears red check romper and white bonnet, showing crying face.

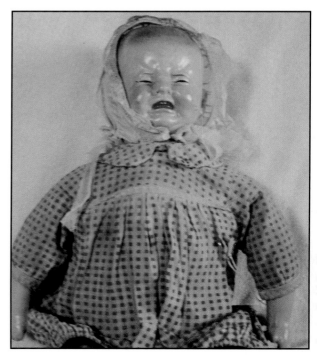

Courtesy Beulah Franklin.

Courtesy Mary Stuecher.

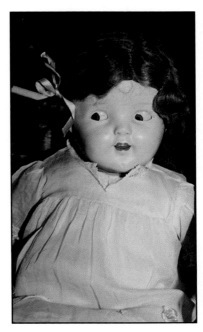

Courtesy Sylvia Rose.

Flossie Flirt (circa 1924) 18" close-up of flirty eyes. Composition head and limbs, cloth body, brown mohair wig, blue tin flirty eyes, open mouth with three upper teeth, red dots inside nostrils. Marks: IDEAL in diamond shape with US of A on the four outside corners.

Flossie Flirt (1924 – 1931) 14" Composition head, gauntlet arms, cloth body and legs, flirty blue sleep eyes, painted lashes, closed rosebud mouth, human hair wig, red dots inside nostrils, original pink voile dress and bonnet, one piece slip/panty with bloomer leg, leather shoes. Trademark December 23, 1924 #207,136. Marks: IDEAL in a diamond with four dots on each side (on head). Seven sizes (14" – 28") available in 1925. $100.00.

Suck-A-Thumb Baby (1926 – 1931) 13", 15" composition head and legs, soft rubber arms, molded hair, comes with pacifier, sleeps, cries, organdy dress, stockings, moccasins, flannel diaper. $2.50 retail. Marks: IDEAL in diamond shape. 13" $85.00, 15" $95.00.

Vanity Flossie (1926 – 1929) 20" Composition head and legs, rubber arms that move up and down, comes with comb and mirror that she can hold in her hand and other accessories, cries, says "mama," flirty eyes, jointed head, organdy cap and dress, short stockings, black shoes. Advertised in 1927 as Flossie Flirt's half-sister. Given as a premium from *Needlecraft Magazine*. Sold in 1929 *Needlecraft* Ad under the name "Gay Flossie Flirt." $195.00.

Needlecraft Magazine.

Baby Mae (**1927 – 1928**) 18" Composition head and legs, cloth stuffed body, mohair or human hair curly wig, sleep eyes, "mama" voice, wears organdy or voile bloomer dress and bonnet, patent leather shoes, and knit socks. 20" called "Bouncing Baby Mae." Offered as a premium. $100.00

Red Peter Pan (**1928**) 16½" (shown) and 18" composition head, compo gauntlet hands, felt stuffed body and limbs, tin sleep eyes, blond molded hair, red felt suit forms body, felt cap, red dots inside nostrils. Offered as a premium. Marks: IDEAL in diamond. $150.00

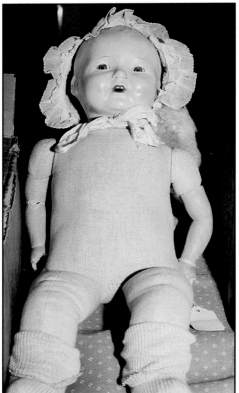

Courtesy Veronica Phillips.

Courtesy Mary Kangas.

Buster Brown (**1929**) 16" Composition head, hands, and legs, cloth body, tin eyes. Represents Richard Felton Outcault's cartoon character. Original price $2.00. Marks: IDEAL in a diamond. $200.00.

Tickletoes (**1928 – 1930**) 17" Compo head, rubber arms, an early model with cloth legs and crier in body, kapok-stuffed cloth body, flirty sleep eyes, open mouth with two painted teeth. Marks: IDEAL in diamond with U S of A on the four outside corners. $125.00.

Tickletoes (1931 – 1939) 15", 17" (shown), 20", 24" Composition head, rubber arms and legs, open mouth, painted teeth, tin "flirty winking sleep" eyes, three voices: cries when each leg is squeezed and has a cry voice when put down, kapok-stuffed cloth body, organdy dress with rubber panties, comes with pacifier which fits in hole in her mouth. Same head as "Baby Smiles." Originally $3.00, $4.00, $5.00, $6.00. Catalog: #163, #253, #369 and #V562. U.S. Patent #1,621,434 & #1,793,335. Marks: IDEAL in diamond with U S of A on the four outside corners. Other marks seen: 82 IDEAL DOLL/ MADE IN USA. 15", $100.00; 17", $125.00; 20", $150.00; 24", $170.00; 17" MIB, $175.00.

Courtesy Sherry Lynne Wilson.

Courtesy Millie Caliri.

Tickletoes (1931 – 1939) Compo head, rubber arms and legs, open mouth with two painted teeth, tin flirty eyes, clothes all original. Marks: Ideal in diamond with US of A on outside corners.

Compo toddler (circa 1930) 14" Compo head and body, jointed arms, legs, and neck, tin flirty sleep eyes, molded hair. Wearing original dress. Yellow bow not original. Marks: IDEAL/ T7. $125.00.

Courtesy Marge Meisinger.

Saucy Sue (1931 – 1934) 14", 18", 21", 24" Composition head and limbs, soft body girl doll wearing short dress, panties, and matching bonnet, says "mama," flirty sleep eyes with lashes, wig. Pat. 1931. Original price $3.30, $5.20, $6.50, $8.00 in 1934 Johnson Smith catalog. $100.00.

Ducky (1932 – 1939) 11", 13" (shown), 15", 17", 19" Composition head, rubber body, arms and legs, separate fingers and toes, tin flirty sleep eyes (11" had painted eyes), two voices, leg squeaked when pressed, open mouth, can be fed her bottle. Also came in suitcase with bottle, diapers and accessories (shown). U.S. Patent #1,876,433, April, 1931. Catalog: #311, #313, #315, #317, #319. Original price $1.35, $1.80, $2.25, $3.40, $4.50. Marks: IDEAL in diamond with PAT. PEND. on lower sides. Ducky Deluxe had rubber head with soft fontanel. 11", $65.00; 13", $75.00; 15", $80.00; 17", $85.00; 19", $90.00.

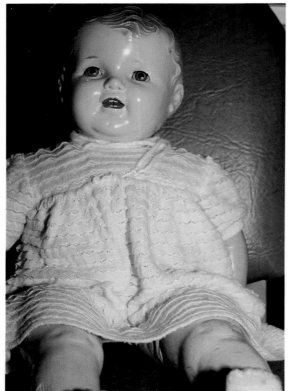

Courtesy Dorothea Thumith.

Cuddles (1928 – 1940) 22" (shown) Composition head, arms, legs, rubber shoulder plate, cloth body. Other version of Cuddles from 1928 – 32 had rubber arms. Glassene eyes, open mouth with two upper and two lower teeth, reddish molded hair, red dot inside each nostril. White dress not original. Marks: I.N. & T.C. $150.00.

Cuddles (1928 – 1940) 14", 16", 19", 20½", 22", 25", 27" Compo head and limbs, others had rubber arms, kapok-stuffed cloth body, molded hair, *tin* blue or brown flirty sleep eyes with long lashes. Some 14" and 16" came with sleep eyes and lashes only. Open mouth with two upper and two lower teeth and tongue, cry voice, organdy dress and bonnet, rubber panties. 20" doll weighs two pounds. Catalog Numbers: #19, #29, 216 ML, #1919, #1220, #1222, #1225, #1227. Original price $1.25, $1.50, $2.00, $3.00, $3.50, $4.00, $5.00, $5.00. Marks: Ideal Doll/Made in U.S.A. (on head). 14", $100.00; 16", $110.00; 19", $125.00; 20½", $135.00; 22", $150.00; 25", $175.00; 27", $200.00

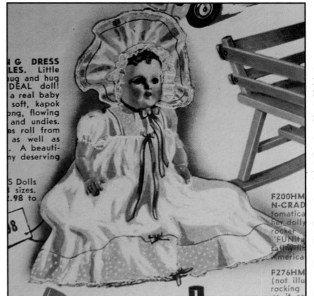

Famous Funn Family service catalog. Courtesy Marge Meisinger.

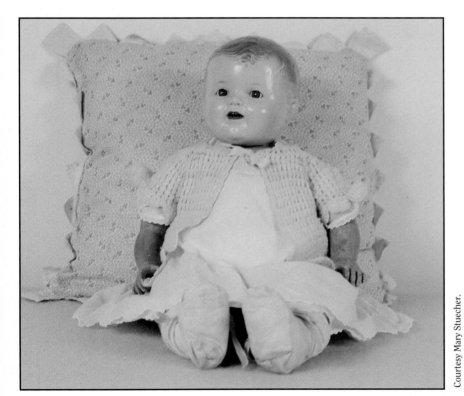

Courtesy Mary Stuecher.

Ad in *Needlecraft* magazine. Courtesy Mary Stuecher.

Sallykins (also known as Cuddles) (1934) 14", 19", 22" (shown), 25" Compo head and legs, rubber shoulder plate, rubber arms, cloth body, flirty blue eyes, open mouth with two upper and two lower teeth, orange color painted hair, wears organdy dress with lace trim (clothes shown not original), a *Needlecraft* premium. Marks: I.N.& T. CO. (on head shown) or IDEAL in diamond, or unmarked. 14", $100.00; 19", $150.00; 22", $150.00; 25", $200.00.

Sallykins (1934) 14" Compo head, has rubber hands, soft kapok-stuffed body, winking and sleeping eyes, "mama" voice, organdy dress.

1938 Sears catalog.

Honeysuckle (1932 – 1938) 11", 12½", 14½", 16½" Hard rubber head, soft "true-flesh" rubber body, flirty sleep eyes with lashes, drinks and wets, voice in each leg. Could purchase 10 pc. layette for each size separately. Could "feel her ribs." Original price: $1.98, $4.98, $5.50, $7.00. Doll came in either wood frame case or cardboard case with layette. Made in 1939 with hard rubber head. $100.00.

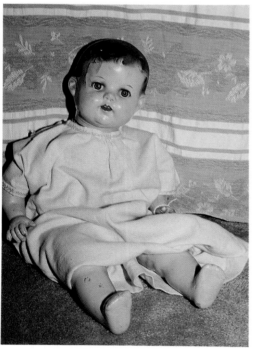

Courtesy Barbara Scully.

Courtesy Ruth Falkinburg's Doll Shop.

Mama Doll (1930s) Compo head and limbs, oilcloth body, brown eyes, two inset upper teeth, red paint inside nostrils, molded painted brown hair, clothes not original. Marks: IDEAL DOLL/MADE IN U.S.A. (on head). $100.00.

Mama Doll (1930s) Composition head, arms, and legs, cloth body, two painted teeth, crier, green/blue sleep eyes with lashes. Clothes not original. Marks: PO/IDEAL DOLLS/MADE IN USA (on head). $85.00.

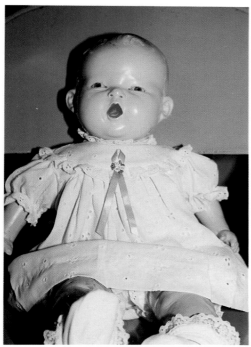

Courtesy Dorothea Thumith.

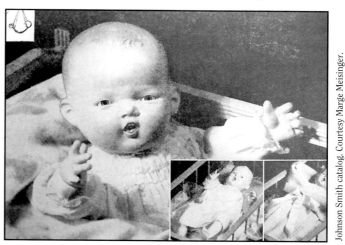

Johnson Smith catalog. Courtesy Marge Meisinger.

Snoozie (1934) Rubber hands and legs, cloth body, open yawning mouth and molded tongue with two upper teeth, three voices, holes in nostrils. Hug her and you can feel soft breath on your cheek!

Snoozie (1933) 14", 16", 18", 20" Compo head, painted hair, rubber hands and feet, kapok-filled peach rubberized cloth body and upper limbs, open yawning mouth and molded tongue, blue-gray or green celluloid over tin winking sleep eyes, painted lashes, painted yellow molded hair, red dots in nostrils and inner corner of eyes, voice in body and each leg, dressed in white batiste smocked baby dress (redressed in photo). Designed by Bernard Lipfert. Original price $3.00, $5.90, $7.30, $9.00. Marks: © B.LIPFERT /Made for Ideal Doll & Toy Corp. 1933 or © by B. Lipfert or IDEAL SNOOZIE/ B.LIPFERT(on head). 14", $125.00; 16", $150.00; 20", $175.00.

Johnson Smith catalog. Courtesy Marge Meisinger.

1934 Johnson Smith catalog. Courtesy Marge Meisinger.

Ginger (1934 – 1937) 16", 18", 20", 23", 26", 21" Compo head and body, ball-jointed rubber arms and compo legs that assume poses, other ones had ball-jointed compo arms, brown or blue flirty sleep glacé eyes with silky eyelashes, human hair wigs in marcel ringlets, crying voice, 21" came with sleeping eyes only, seven different costumes including a chinchilla coat. Catalog Numbers: 9016, 9018, 9020, 9023, 9026, 7021. Original price $3.00, $4.00, $4.50, $5.00, $6.00, $3.00. 16", $150.00; 21", $225.00.

Winnie (1934) 12", 13½", 16", 18" Compo head, arms, legs, and body, molded fingers and toes, hands that clasp, sleep eyes, tongue, teeth, jointed at hips and shoulders, semi-straight legs can sit or stand, voice in each leg, pink or white organdy dress with lace trim, matching bonnet, petticoats, white flannel diaper. Original price $3.30, $4.00, $4.70, $5.30. Some had rubber heads. $125.00.

Shirley Temple

Ideal flyer No. 452.

Shirley Temple Girl Dolls (1934 – 1939) 11", 13½", 15", 16", 17", 18", 20", 22", 25", 27" All compo, hazel eyes, gold mohair wig, open mouth with teeth, movie costumes included Littlest Rebel, Curly Top, Our Little Girl, doll designed by Bernard Lipfert. Original price $1.00 – 30.00. Marks: SHIRLEY TEMPLE/ cop Ideal N & T Co. (on head); SHIRLEY TEMPLE/11(on body) for 11"; 18 for 18", etc. 11", $650.00; 13", $595.00; 15" – 16", $595.00; 17" – 18", $700.00; 20", $800.00; 22", $800.00; 25", $800.00; 27", $900.00.

Ideal brochure.

Morris Michtom with Shirley Temple around 1935.

Courtesy Vernoica Phillips.

Shirley Temple (1934) 18" in pink taffeta dress from "The Little Colonel." Also came in green, yellow or lavender. Organdy dress also available.

Courtesy McMasters Doll Auction.

Shirley Temple (1930s) 18" in pink dress with white leaf print.

Courtesy Modern Doll Convention.

Shirley Temple (1934) All composition, mohair wig, sleep eyes, fully jointed, hazel eyes. In common early pink woven pleated organdy dress with woven NRA dress tag.

Courtesy Iva Mae Jones.

Shirley Temple (1934) 15" in common early woven pleated organdy dress with woven NRA dress tag. Marks: COP. IDEAL N & T Co.(on head); No marks on body. Notice original Shirley Temple box. Box label says "white," box marked "Made In U.S.A. by Ideal Novelty and Toy Company."

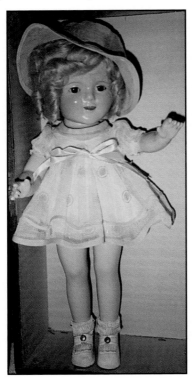

Shirley Temple (1934) 16" in yellow organdy polka-dot "Stand Up and Cheer" with original clothing in trunk. Marks: SHIRLEY TEMPLE (in an arch shape with CO under it on head; SHIRLEY TEMPLE 16 (on body) This variation of "Stand Up and Cheer" had a hat and sunsuit and sold as part of the trunk wardrobe. Trunk sets also came with dolls in 13" and 18" sizes.

Shirley Temple (1934) 16" in "Stand Up and Cheer" with original clothing in trunk. Also came in red or green polka-dots. Also shown is 20" Shirley Temple Baby (1935). 16" Shirley in trunk $1,400.00; Shirley Baby $1,200.00.

Courtesy McMasters Doll Auctions.

Shirley Temple (1934) 20" in "Bright Eyes" outfit which came in variations of plaid. $2,000.00 MIB.

Courtesy McMasters Doll Auctions.

Shirley Temple (1934) 18" in "Bright Eyes" corduroy coat and hat with ermine trim. Replaced wig. Marks: 18/SHIRLEY TEMPLE/COP. IDEAL N & T CO. (on head); SHIRLEY TEMPLE/ 18 (on body).

Courtesy Iva Mae Jones.

Courtesy McMasterss Doll Auctions.

Shirley Temple (1934) 16" in hard-to-find outfit from "Our Little Girl." $495.00.

Courtesy Millie Caliri.

Shirley Temple (1935) in "Our Little Girl" dress with musical notes glued on. Also came in red or royal blue with white notes.

Courtesy Iva Mae Jones.

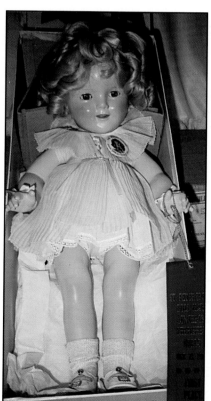

Courtesy Iva Mae Jones.

Shirley Temple (1935) 20" in knife-pleated star cluster dots on blue background organdy dress from "Curly Top." Dress came in several variations, blue or yellow with star bursts. Marks: SHIRLEY TEMPLE/ COP. IDEAL N & T CO. (on head); SHIRLEY TEMPLE 20 X with line drawn through it (on Back).

Shirley Temple (1935) in knife-pleated pink organdy dress from "Curly Top." One of several colors and variations that included red, lavender, or white polka-dots. MIB.

Shirley Temple and the Shirley Temple doll (1935) in pleated dress which has embroidered flowers and glued-on daisy appliqués.

Shirley Temple and the Shirley Temple doll (1935) in striped dress from "Curly Top."

Courtesy Iva Mae Jones.

Courtesy Iva Mae Jones.

Shirley Temple (1935) 18" in red dress from "Curly Top," all original in box. Marks: SHIRLEY TEMPLE/COP. IDEAL N & T CO. (on head); SHIRLEY TEMPLE (on body).

Shirley Temple (1935) 18" white fur coat from "Curly Top." Marks: SHIRLEY TEMPLE/Cop. IDEAL/N & T CO. (on head); SHIRLEY TEMPLE/ 18 (on body).

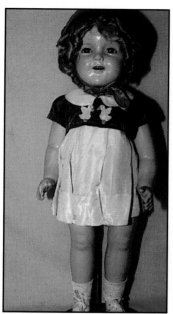

Shirley Temple (1935) 27" in "Curly Top" black velvet top with glued-on duck appliqués and floral embroidery, yellow taffeta skirt. Also available in green and yellow.

Courtesy Veronica Phillips.

Shirley Temple (1935) in outfit from "Littlest Rebel." Also available in yellow. Some outfits came with pantaloons and a gray felt hat.

Courtesy Veronica Phillips.

Shirley Temple (1935) in outfit from "Littlest Rebel," another version in cotton with organdy apron. This dress was also used to promote the movie "Heidi."

Courtesy Anita Maxwell.

Shirley Temple (1936) 18" Wearing "Captain January" outfit. Also came in white. $700.00

Courtesy Richard Withington Auctions.

Courtesy McMasterss Doll Auctions.

Courtesy Rosalie Whyel Museum of Doll Art. Photo by Charles Backus.

Shirley Temple (1936) 18" in sailor dress from "Poor Little Rich Girl," navy piqué with white trim. Also available in light blue and red.

Shirley Temple Texas Ranger (1936) 11" (shown), 17", 27" 13" also seen. All composition. Special souvenir of the Texas Centennial. Original 10-gallon felt hat, vest, chaps, boots, pistol, and holster. Original price $2.95, $4.95, $14.50. Marks: SHIRLEY TEMPLE (on head); SHIRLEY TEMPLE/11 (on back); 1836-TEXAS CENTENNIAL-1936 (on hat band); 11", $850.00; 17", $800.00; 27", $900.00.

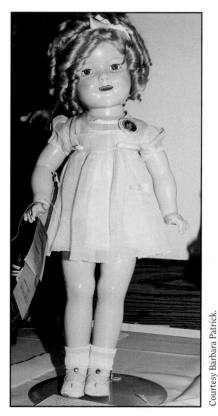

Courtesy Barbara Patrick.

Courtesy Veronica Phillips.

Shirley Temple (1936) 15" Turquoise dress. $595.00.

Shirley Temple (1930s) plaid raincoat that was available as a separate, had matching umbrella and hat. Also available in red.

Courtesy Millie Caliri.

Shirley Temple (1930s) in separate dress. Marks: Cop IDEAL/N 8 R (on head), no marks on body.

Ideal Catalog.

Shirley Temple At Nine (1938) 11", 13", 16", 18", 20", 22", 25", 27" All composition, new hair style mohair wig with curls close to head, parted on side, flirty eyes, open mouth with inserted teeth and tongue. Catalog numbers: #2011, #2013, #2016, #2018, #2020, #2022, #2025, #2027. Original price: $2.50, $3.00, $4.00, $5.00, $6.00, $7.00, $10.00, $12.00.

Ideal Catalog.

Shirley Temple Beauty Kit (1938) With lipstick, blush, tissues. $75.00.

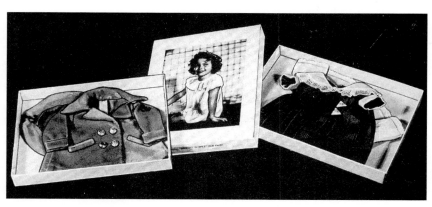

Ideal Catalog.

Shirley Temple Coat and Hat and Dress Sets (1938) Exact duplicates of dresses worn by Shirley in her hit pictures with coats and hats to match. Ranging in price retail from $.89 to $2.00. Coats and hat sets fit from 13" to 27" dolls. Dress fits from 11" to 27" dolls. $100.00.

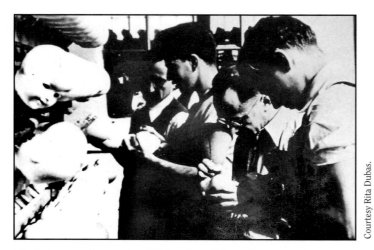

Courtesy Rita Dubas.

Ideal plant workers paint Shirley Temple's eyebrows, eyelashes, and lips at the Ideal factory (circa 1934).

Courtesy Rita Dubas.

Ideal worker curls Shirley Temple's wigs at the Ideal factory (circa 1934).

Courtesy Rita Dubas.

Assembling Shirley Temple's body at the Ideal factory (circa 1934).

Ideal worker puts wigs on dressed Shirley Temples at the Ideal factory (circa 1934).

Courtesy Rita Dubas.

Shirley Temple Baby (**1935**) 16" (shown), 18", 20", 22", 25" Composition head, arms, and lower legs, kapok-stuffed cotton body, cry voice, double-action flirty glacé green eyes, painted hair, two upper and three lower teeth, pink organdy dress, ST label on dress. Marks: SHIRLEY TEMPLE (on head). 16", $600.00; 18", $700.00; 20", $900.00; 22", $1,000.00; 25", $1,500.00.

Shirley Temple Baby (**1935**) 20" in 27" Shirley Temple wicker doll carriage made by the F.A. Whitney Carriage Company of Leominster, Mass., under license from Ideal. Other type of carriage made had wooden body and folding oilcloth hood. Both had oval medallion of Shirley's photo on the side as well as on the four hubcaps. 20" Baby $900.00; carriage $900.00

Shirley Temple Baby (**1935**) 20" in 27" Shirley Temple metal doll carriage made by the F.A. Whitney Carriage Company of Leominster, Mass. Has oval medallion of Shirley's photo on the side as well as on the four hubcaps.

Shirley Temple type (**1934**) 13" All composition, red hair, sleep eyes, open mouth with teeth, dimple in chin, original dress, replaced shoes. Probably Ginger. Marks: IDEAL/MADE (on head); U.S.A./13 (on body). $200.00.

Photo from American Toy Pictorial Catalog. Courtesy Stephen Olin.

Photo from American Toy Pictorial Catalog. Courtesy Stephen Olin.

Suzy also known as the Lifetime or Idenite Doll (1936) 14", 18", 20" Idenite (hard rubber), brown sleep eyes with eyelashes, open mouth with two teeth, curly wig or painted hair, wears batiste dress and bonnet with leatherette snap shoes and socks. Suzy supposedly looks like Shirley Temple but without dimple. Catalog #814, #818, #820. Original price $3.00, $5.00, $6.00. $150.00.

Suzette also known as the Lifetime or Idenite Doll (1936) 12", 14", 16" Idenite (hard rubber), brown sleep eyes with eyelashes, open mouth with two teeth, curly wig or painted hair, wears batiste dress and bonnet, leatherette snap shoes and socks. Younger sister looks like a toddler with curved arms. Catalog #712, #714, #716. Original price $3.00, $4.00, $5.00. $150.00.

Courtesy Diane M. Goff and Bertha Corl.

Courtesy Diane M. Goff and Bertha Corl.

I-De-Lite: The Doll of a Lifetime (1930s) 13" all rubber. Available with brown or blue sleep eyes, molded hair under brunette, blonde or auburn wig, pink, blue, maize, green or white dress. Probably the same as the Idenite doll. Clothes unmarked. Marks: none.

I-De-Lite: The Doll of a Lifetime (1930s) shows box.

I-De-Lite: The Doll of a Lifetime (1930s) shows three sizes of dolls available.

Courtesy Diane M. Goff and Bertha Corl.

Courtesy Mary Stuecher.

Betsy Wetsy® (1937 – 1938) 11" (shown), 13", 15", 17", 19" Hard rubber (Idenite) head, soft rubber body and limbs, blue or brown sleep eyes with lashes or painted eyes, molded hair or mohair wig, lashes, open mouth that drinks, wets, can be bathed, came with bottle, wearing pink organdy dress, pink and white wool booties, flannel diaper, knit undershirt. Original price $2.00 – 6.00. Original box shown. Also came in layettes, trunks, suitcases or with bathinette. IDEAL (on head); IDEAL (on body). New model in 1939. 11", $85.00; 13", $100.00; 15", $125.00; 17", $125.00; 19", $150.00.

Courtesy Sheryl Bauknecht.

Betsy Wetsy (1937 – 1938) 11" Hard plastic (Idenite?) head, rubber body, drink hole in mouth, no hole on bottom. Marks: IDEAL DOLL (on head); IDEAL DOLL (on back).

Ideal Catalog.

Betsy Wetsy® with bathinette and layette (1937). Set, $250.00.

Courtesy Jessie Williams.

Snow White (1938 – 1939)
14", 17½", 19" (shown) Composition head on shoulder plate, compo arms and legs, side glancing painted eyes, red painted bow on molded black hair, soft body, red dress with white bodice that says Snow White on it. Catalog #SN3=19" Original price for 14", $3.00. Marks: IDEAL DOLL on head. Also sold as premium in 1938. 14", $175.00; 17½", $250.00; 19", $300.00.

Ideal Catalog.

Snow White (1938) 17" All composition, molded painted hair and features. Black version is rare. Redressed. $600.00.

Sears Catalog.

Courtesy Marge Meisinger. Photo by Anthony L. Colella.

Snow White (1938) 11½", 13", 14", 18", 22", 27" All composition, jointed at neck, shoulders and hips, black mohair wig, flirty glass eyes with real lashes, open mouth with four teeth, dimple in chin. Catalog numbers: SN014, SN018, SN022, SN024. Shirley Temple mold, dress has bodice of red velvet, skirt of rayon taffeta has pictures of Seven Dwarfs. Taffeta-lined velvet cape. Also black version, all compo, painted black eyes, closed mouth, black hair. Marks: some marked Shirley Temple/18 on back; some unmarked. 11½", $300.00; 13", $325.00; 14", $325.00; 18", $400.00; 22", $425.00; 27", $450.00. 11½" Dopey composition head that turns, stuffed body, cloth hands and feet. $250.00.

Snow White (1938) 16" Cloth body and limbs, mask face with painted side glancing eyes, glued on black human hair wig, dress had red cotton or velvet bodice and organdy or taffeta skirt which reads "Snow White and the Seven Dwarfs," small cape on back of bodice, pantaloons and slip, white shoes and socks. Marks: none. Catalog #SN1 and #SN2 (16") which has velvet cape. Original price, $2.19, $3.25.

Courtesy Martha Mullins.

Happy (**1938**) One of the Seven Dwarfs which include: Doc, Sneezy, Sleepy, Grumpy, Bashful, Dopey. 12" Oilcloth hands and face, fur beard, cloth back of head, felt jacket, shoes and cap, corduroy pants. Tag reads: Authentic Walt Disney Snow White and the Seven Dwarfs. Made in U.S.A. by IDEAL NOVELTY AND TOY CO. Original price $1.50. $165.00.

Dopey, The Ventriloquist doll (**1938**) 20" Composition head and hands with three fingers and thumb, cloth body, arms, and legs, hinged mouth operated by drawstring, molded tongue, painted eyes, large ears, long coat, cotton pants, felt shoes which are part of leg, felt cap with name, can stand alone. Catalog #D53, Original price $3.00 Marks: IDEAL DOLL (on neck). $800.00.

Courtesy William Furnish.

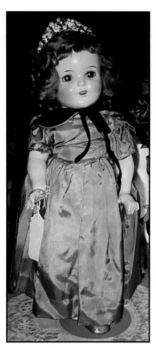

Courtesy Iva Mae Jones.

Courtesy Marge Meisinger. Photo by Carol Stover.

Cinderella (**1938 – 1939**) 13", 16", 18" (shown with red hair), 20", 22", 25", 27" All composition, brown, blonde, or red human hair wig, flirty brown or blue glass sleep eyes with lashes, painted lower lashes, open mouth with six inset teeth and tongue. Formal evening gowns of organdies and rayon taffeta in white, pink, blue, or yellow, came with sparkling rhinestone tiara, silver snap shoes and matching shoulder bag; also came in set of a 13" doll dressed in ski outfit with six costume changes. The 400 series (shown) came dressed in rayon satin evening gown with matching long, satin-lined velvet wrap. Catalog numbers: #01013, #01016, #01018, #01020, #01022, #01025, #01027. Actual box: #3325. Original cost: $3.00, $4.00, $5.00, $6.00, $7.00, $10.00, $13.00. Marks: 18", none on head; SHIRLEY TEMPLE/18 (on body). Also seen: 22" IDEAL (in diamond)/USA (on head), 22 (backwards) IDEAL DOLL/USA (on body). $250.00+.

Cinderella (**1938**) 13½" All composition, red human hair wig, flirty green sleep eyes with lashes, six inset upper teeth, dimple in chin, long yellow gown, tiara, silver snap shoes. Marks: none (on head), SHIRLEY TEMPLE/13 (on body).

Courtesy Robin Randall.

Cinderella (1938) 13½" all composition, hazel flirty eyes, brown human hair wig, six teeth, dimple in chin, pink gown. Marks: none. $250.00

Courtesy Rosalie Whyel Museum of Doll Art. Photo by Charles Backus.

Marama, So-called Hawaiian Shirley Temple (1940) 8", 13" (shown) All composition with glued-on black yarn wig, brown complexion, painted side-glancing eyes, painted teeth. Came in one other size. Ideal marketed the doll as "Marama, the Hurricane Doll." She is meant to portray the Marama doll that Terangi treasured to remind him of his love for the real Marama in the movie "The Hurricane." Marks: 13/Shirley Temple (on head); U.S.A./13 (on body). $800.00.

Courtesy Marge Meisinger Photo by Carol Stover.

Probably Ginger (1937) 27" All composition body, ball jointed arms and legs, brown (shown) or blue glacé flirty sleep eyes with eye shadow, open mouth with inset teeth, human hair wig with marcel ringlets. Marks: IDEAL DOLL/MADE IN U.S.A. (on head); SHIRLEY TEMPLE 27 (numbers are backwards) (on body).

Ideal Catalog.

Courtesy Dyan Murphy

Rubber Story Book Dolls (**1938**) 10" All rubber dolls with movable arms and heads dressed as storybook characters: Queen of Hearts, Mary Had a Little Lamb, Little Bo Peep, Little Miss Muffet, and Mistress Mary Quite Contrary. Outfits have their names on them. Painted hair and features. Costumes same as 16" storybooks. Catalog numbers: 10N/1-10N/5. Original price $1.50. $125.00.

Mistress Mary Quite Contrary, Story Book Dolls (**1938**) 16" All cloth, mask face, washable hands, worsted wool hair, jointed head, kapok-stuffed, dressed as storybook characters: Mary Had a Little Lamb, Little Bo Peep, Little Miss Muffet, Queen of Hearts, Daffy Down Dilly, Little Boy Blue, and Tom, Tom the Piper's Son. Catalog numbers: #N1-#N9. Original price $2.00. Marks: none on body, just on costume. $200.00.

Mistress Mary Quite Contrary (**1938 – 1942**) 14½" and 15½" (shown) All compo, jointed at neck and shoulders, blue glassene sleep eyes with lashes, open mouth with four teeth (14½") or six teeth (15½"). Wearing skirt saying "Mistress Mary Quite Contrary." Marks: U.S.A./16 (on back). Other dolls in Mother Goose series are Miss Muffet, Little Bo Peep, and Mary Had a Little Lamb. $150.00.

Courtesy Sara Feldman.

Mortimer Snerd (1938) 13" Composition head, gauntlet hands, flexy doll with flexible wire tubing for arms and legs, painted features, wooden torso and feet, brown felt jacket and herringbone knit pants. Edgar Bergen's dummy, designed by Joseph Kallus. Catalog number #S3. Original price, $1.19. Marks: IDEAL DOLL/ MADE IN USA (on neck) $200.00.

Baby Snooks (1938) 13" Composition head, gauntlet hands, flexy doll with flexible wire tubing for arms and legs, molded painted light brown hair, painted blue eyes, open/closed mouth with painted lower teeth wooden torso and feet, cloth dress and matching pants. Fannie Brice character designed by Joseph Kallus, Catalog number #S4. Original price, $1.19. Marks: IDEAL DOLL/Made in U.S.A. (on head). $200.00.

Courtesy Wenham Museum. Photo by Diane Buck.

Courtesy Beulah Franklin.

Courtesy Veronica Phillips.

Courtesy Veronica Phillips.

Black Flexy (1938 – 1942) 13" Composition head and hands, flexible wire arms and legs, wooden torso and feet, painted black molded features, felt suspenders, and herringbone pants. Marks: IDEAL DOLL (on head). $225.00.

Soldier Flexy (1938) 13" Compo head and hands, flexible wire arms and legs, painted features, wooden torso and feet, dressed in khaki soldier's uniform. Marks: IDEAL DOLL (on head). $200.00.

Sunny Sam Flexy (1938) 13" Compo head and hands, flexible wire arms and legs, painted molded bob style hair, wooden torso, large black painted feet, and cloth clothes. Sunny Sam head is the same used on Soldier Flexy. Catalog #S1. Original price $1.19. Marks: IDEAL DOLL (on head). Also shows Sunny Sue. $200.00.

Sunny Sue Flexy (1938) 13" Compo head and hands, flexible wire arms and legs, painted molded bob style hair, wooden torso, large black painted feet, and cloth clothes. Girl wears flowered long blouse with rick-rack and pants. Catalog #S2. Original price, $1.19. Marks: IDEAL DOLL (on head). $200.00.

Clown Flexy (1938) 13" Compo head and hands, flexible wire arms and legs, wooden torso and feet, painted molded hair, clown outfit (missing hat). Looks like Mortimer Snerd painted as a clown. Catalog number #S5. Original price, $1.00. Marks: IDEAL DOLL/ MADE IN USA (on head). $200.00.

Ideal Catalog.

Queen of the Ice (**1938 – 1943**) 13", 16", 18", 20" All compo fully jointed, blonde mohair curls, sleep eyes, open-closed mouth, inset teeth, ice skating dress with zipper, coat, hat with pom-pon and skates, Catalog numbers: #6013, #6016, #6018, #6020. Original price: $3.00, $4.00, $5.00, $6.00. $150.00.

Ideal Catalog.

Cross Patch (**1938**) 16" All composition, painted side glancing eyes, molded hair, pug noses, puckered lips, and puffed cheeks. Wearing Sunday outfits or patched overalls, hat. Catalog number: C.P. asstd. Original price $3.00. $125.00.

Ideal Catalog.

Courtesy Pam Zampiello.

Baby Beautiful (**1938**) 16", 18", 20", 22", 27" Composition head and limbs, stuffed cotton body, painted molded hair, flirty sleep eyes and lashes, cries when put down to sleep, organdy dress and bonnet, or long gown and bonnet. 25" and 27" came with chest plate on body and full composition arms in 1947. Catalog numbers: #1516, #1518, #1520, #1522, #1527. Original price: $3.00, $4.00, $5.00, $6.00, $8.00. $175.00.

Princess Beatrix (**1938 – 1943**) 14", 16", 22", 26" (shown) Composition head and limbs, soft kapok-stuffed cloth body, flirty glass-like sleep eyes, painted molded hair, fingers molded in fists, rosebud mouth, originally dressed in baby organdy dress and bonnet or long organdy gown and bonnet, in sweater and organdy gown and bonnet or in pajamas, 14" size had only sleep eyes with lashes. Represents Princess Beatrix of the Netherlands. Patented 1938. Catalog numbers #1714, #1716, #1722. Original prices: $2.50, $3.00, $5.00. Marks: "IDEAL DOLL." $200.00.

Toddlin Sue (**1938**) 14", 17", 20", 23" Composition, jointed head, arms and legs, sleep eyes, painted hair version. Catalog #14TD, #17TD, #20TD, #23TD. Also came with wig, dress and coat. Catalog #14TDW, 17TC@W, 20TCW, 23TCW.

Ideal Catalog.

Courtesy McMasters Doll Auctions.

Courtesy McMasterss Doll Auctions.

Deanna Durbin (1938 – 1941) 15", 18", 21" (shown), 24", 25" All composition, fully jointed, very dark brown human hair wig, brown sleep eyes with lashes, dark eyeshadow, open mouth with six inset teeth and felt tongue. Came dressed in costumes from her movies, party dresses, or school dresses. Teen-age movie star doll. Autographed picture and name pin came with each doll. 1939 Catalog numbers: #9015, #9018, #9021, #9025. Original prices: $3.00, $4.00, $5.00, $7.00. Only the 21" and 25" were produced in 1938. A 15" walker has been seen with a twist waist. Marks: DEANNA DURBIN/IDEAL DOLL (on head); IDEAL DOLL/21 (on body). 15", $400.00; 18", $450.00; 21", $520.00; 24", $650.00; 25", $650.00; MIB 20", $1,300.00.

Deanna Durbin (1938) 24" all composition, dark brown human hair wig, wearing wool jumper and dotted swiss blouse, purse is made of jumper material and strap is made of blouse material. Marks: DEANNA DURBIN/IDEAL DOLL (on head); IDEAL DOLL/25 (on back).

Courtesy Cathie Clark.

Deanna Durbin (1938) 15" all composition, dark brown human hair wig, shown with box.

Courtesy Sharon Jahraus.

Deanna Durbin (1938) 20" in frequently found floral print long gown. $800.00.

Courtesy Christine Trudeau.

Gulliver's Travels (1939) 21" composition with black mohair wig, painted brown eyes, a Deanna Durbin doll dressed in Gulliver's Travels outfit. From Paramount Pictures, Inc. movie. Original price $6.00. Marks: Deanna Durbin/Ideal Doll (on head). $800.00. Shown with **Gabby Doll**, 11" Composition head and body, segmented wood limbs, painted clothes, designed by Joseph L. Kallus. Original price $1.00. Marks: "Gabby"/© by Paramount Pictures Inc, 1939/MADE BY IDEAL NOVELTY & TOY CO.INC" on tag in front of body. $250.00.

Prince David and Princess Glory from Gulliver's Travels (1939) 11" all composition doll, mohair wigs, painted eyes, same doll as Coquette. From the Paramount Pictures, Inc. movie. Shown with the Deanna Durbin doll dressed as Gulliver. $300.00.

Courtesy McMasters Doll Auctions.

Courtesy McMasters Doll Auctions.

King Little from Gulliver's Travels (1939) 13" composition head and body, segmented wood limbs strung with elastic, painted side glancing eyes, mustache, molded painted clothes – red, yellow, and gray costume with cloth train, wooden triangular shape crown. Designed by Joseph L. Kallus. Original price $1.00. Marks: IDEAL DOLL/©P.P.P.I./MADE IN USA (on body); King Little© by Paramount Pictures Inc. 1939/ Made by Ideal Novelty & Toy Co. Inc. (on label on chest). Shown with Gabby doll missing hat. $350.00.

Pinocchio (1939) 8", 11" (shown), 20" compo head and patented wood pulp segment body construction, painted features and clothes, yellow felt cap. Walt Disney creation. Original price: $.50, $l.00, $5.00. Also in flexy construction at $1.50. Marks: PINOCCHIO/Des.© by Walt Disney/Made by Ideal Novelty & Toy Co (on front); ©W.D.P./Ideal Doll/Made in USA (on back). 8" $200.00; 11", $250.00; 20", $350.00.
Jiminy Cricket (1939) 8" Compo head and patented wood pulp segmented body. Marks: JIMINY CRICKET/DES & BY WALT DISNEY/MADE BY IDEAL NOVELTY & TOY CO. (on foot). $300.00.

Courtesy Linda Pottle

Ferdinand the Bull (**1939**) All compo. Trademarks: ©W.D. Ent./Ideal Novelty & Toy Co./Made in USA with firefly imprint on rump. $85.00.

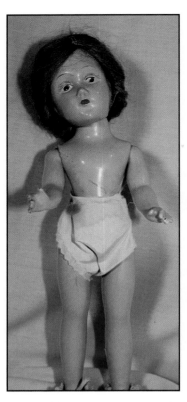

Coquette (**1939**) 11" All composition, jointed arms, legs, and neck, dark blonde wig in curls, painted blue eyes. Catalog #11/240. Original price $2.00. Came in a long or short dress. Same doll used as Princess Glory in the Gulliver's Travels series. $125.00.

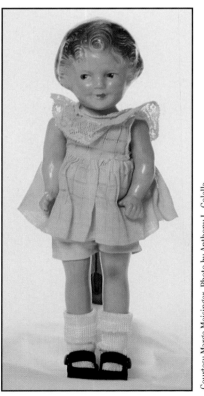

Courtesy Marge Meisinger. Photo by Anthony L. Colella.

Coquette (**1939**) 9" All composition, jointed arms, legs, and neck. Painted molded hair, painted blue side glancing eyes. Catalog #9. Original price $0.80. Came dressed in long gown, also available with a carrying case with a layette and other outfit. This doll has previously been incorrectly called a Shirley Temple. Marks: (backwards 9)/IDEAL/DOLL (on back). $100.00.

Photo by Anthony L. Colella. Courtesy Marge Meisinger.

Bride (**1939 – 1944**) 15" All compo, blonde (shown), red, and dark brown mohair wig, sleep eyes, four inset upper teeth, bridal gown, flowers not original. Shown with original box. Marks: X in circle (on head); blotted out Shirley Temple (on back). $150.00.

Ideal Catalog.

Mayfair (**1939**) 15", 18", 21", 25" All compo, jointed body with one arm bent at elbow, can bend and twist at the waist, sleep eyes, real hair wig. Same Body-twist doll used by Mary Hoyer. Catalog #7715, #7718, #7721, #7725. Original price: $3.00, $4.00, $5.00, $7.00. $150.00.

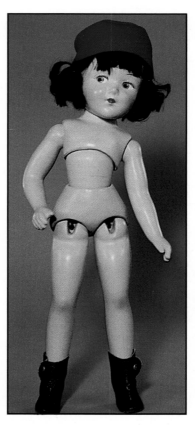

Russian Boy (1939) 13" all composition, painted blue eyes, black mohair wig. Uses same type body as Mayfair doll, jointed at waist and chest. Strung so legs can be moved sideways. Marks: IDEAL DOLL/U.S.A. (on head), 13 on back. $100.00.

Russian Boy (1930s) 13" all composition, showing jointed body type used for Mayfair doll. $100.00

Ideal Dolls
(1940 – 1950)

Courtesy McMasters Doll Auctions.

Judy Garland as Dorothy from *The Wizard of Oz* **(1939 –
1940)** 13", 15½" (shown), 18" All composition, fully jointed,
glued on auburn brown (shown), dark brown or black human
hair wig in braids, brown glass sleep eyes with lashes, open
mouth with tongue and six teeth. Sculpted by Bernard Lipfert,
dressed as Dorothy from the *Wizard of Oz* in blue or red-
checked rayon jumper dress. Original price: $3.00 – 5.00.
Marks: (for 15½" shown) 15/IDEAL DOLL/Made in U.S.A. (on
head); U.S.A./16 (on body). Cowardly Lion is not by Ideal. 13",
$1,300.00; 15½", $1,500.00; 18", $1,800.00.

1941 Spiegel catalog. Courtesy Marge Meisinger.

Judy Garland and Deanna Durbin (1941) Judy is 18" and 21", all
composition, Deanna is 15" and 21", all composition.

Courtesy Rosalie Whyel Museum of Doll Art. Photo by Charles Backus.

Judy Garland teen (1940 – 1942) 15" and 21" (shown) All composition, original outfit from "Strike Up the Band," brown or
auburn human hair wig, green or brown glassene sleep eyes,
open mouth with four inset teeth, felt tongue, dress of pink
organdy with red and blue flowers. The doll came in other costumes from the 1941 movie "Babes on Broadway." Designed by
Bernard Lipfert. Original price for 21" is $9.90. Several promo-
tions were used to sell her including free photos of Judy holding
the doll when purchased. Body was from Deanna Durbin mold
but has a rounder face than Deanna Durbin. Marks: MADE IN
USA (on head); IDEAL DOLL/(a backwards 21) (on body). Tag
reads Judy Garland/A Metro Goldwyn Mayer/ STAR/in/"Little Nel-
lie/ Kelly." Original pin reads JUDY GARLAND/A METRO GOLD-
WYN MAYER STAR. 15", $450.00; 21", $500.00.

Toddlers (1940) 17" and 20" all composition, chubby body, fully jointed, wig, glass sleep eyes and lashes, open mouth with inset upper teeth, chubby face has dimples, wearing blue flannel coat, organdy dress with hat. Original price: $2.90, $3.65. $150.00.

Poppa-Mamma Doll (1940 – 1942) 14", 16", 19", 22" composition head and limbs, cotton-filled cloth body, tilt forward she says "mama," tilt her backwards she says "papa," brown glass-like sleep eyes and lashes, dressed in bonnet and dress, and white moccasins. Original price $2.00 – 7.00. Marks: IDEAL DOLL/MADE IN USA. 14", $125.00; 22", $175.00.

Soldier Doll (early 1940s) 13" all compo head and body. Same head as Soldier Flexy doll. Marks: 13 (on head). $150.00.

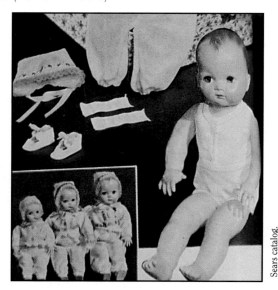

Sears catalog.

Courtesy Jessie Williams.

Magic Skin Baby Doll (**1940**) 14", 16", 18", 20", hard plastic head, latex one-piece molded body and legs, jointed arms, separate fingers, sleep eyes, molded painted hair, jointed shoulders and hips. Lightweight: 20" weighs 1 lb. Came either undressed with layette in a box, elaborately dressed, or deluxe in a suitcase. Pink romper with pink and blue strawberry bonnet with pink bow. Catalog numbers (from 1947: 9AR, 9BR, 9CR, 9DR. Original price: $5.98, $7.98, $10.98, $12.00. Marks: 18/IDEAL DOLL/MADE IN U.S.A. (on head). Produced again in 1946 – 1949. $125.00.

Magic Skin Baby (**1941**) 13", 15" (shown), 17", 20" Hard plastic head, stuffed one-piece latex body, only arms jointed. Sleep eyes, molded hair. Notice how latex has darkened.

Magic Skin Baby Doll (**1940**) Patent applied for by Abraham M. Katz of the Ideal Toy Co.

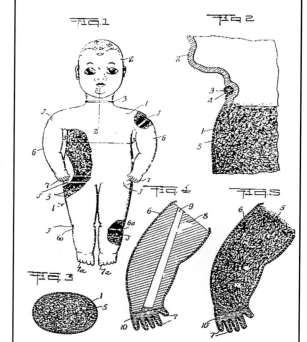

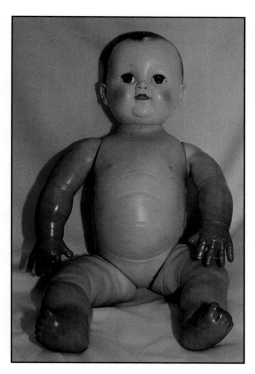

Baby with Magic Skin (**1940s**) 14", 16", 18" (shown), 20"
Hard plastic head, stuffed latex body, jointed arms and legs,
separate fingers, molded hair, hazel sleep eyes, open/closed
mouth, holes in nostrils. Marks: 18/IDEAL DOLL/MADE IN
U.S.A. (on head). $55.00.

Ideal photo.

Ad from *Toys & Novelties Magazine.*

Pigtails (also called Pigtail Sally) (**1941**) 13", 14",
16", 18", 20" All composition, wig in braids with ribbons, fully jointed, glass sleep eyes and lashes, wears
print dress with white pinafore, white shoes and
socks, and babushka. Original price: $2.25, $2.90,
$3.65, $4.45. $150.00.

Bunny Dolls (**1941**) 14" or 18" Mask face stuffed bunnies, stuffed cloth body, yarn bangs, ears of pile rayon,
squeak voice. One has terry cloth body and is dressed
in printed organdy dress; one has percale body and
dress. Ribbon bows at hands and feet. Original price:
$1.00, $2.00. $40.00.

1941 Spiegel catalog.

Courtesy Susan Haynes.

Betty Jane (also known as Mary Jane or "Miss America") (1940 – 1943) 15", 16", 18", 20", 22" All composition girl doll, fully jointed, mohair wig in braids, sleep eyes with lashes, open mouth with teeth, cotton print dress with organdy pinafore, straw hat. Mary Jane had pink & white checked dress and straw bonnet (advertised in Spiegel 1941). Original price: $3.45, $4.45, $5.45. Marks: 16": U S A/16 (on body); 18": IDEAL 18 (on head). 15", $185.00; 16", $200.00; 18", $250.00; 20", $275.00; 22", $300.00.

Mary Jane (1941) This Betty Jane Doll is an example of an Ideal doll sold and dressed by another company, in this case Vogue Doll.

Ideal photo.

Betty Big Girl (1941) Mask face, stuffed cloth body, dressed in pants or dresses. Large size. $55.00.

Courtesy Nancy Uttech.

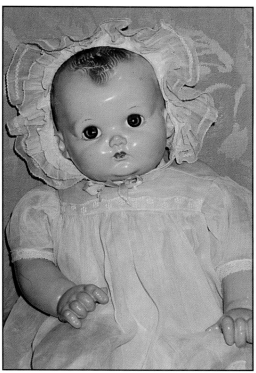

Courtesy Nancy Uttech.

Plassie (**1942**) 16" (shown), 19", 22", 24" Hard plastic head on composition shoulder plate, composition limbs, stuffed pink cloth body, blue or brown sleep eyes with lashes, painted molded hair. Original dress. Head tilts and turns. Marks: IDEAL DOLL/MADE IN USA/PAT.NO. 225 2077 (on head). 16", $125.00; 19", $135.00; 22", $150.00; 24", $165.00.

Plassie (**1942**) 22" hard plastic head on composition shoulder plate tilts and turns, composition limbs, stuffed cloth body, brown sleep eyes with lashes, original dress, cry voice, closed mouth. Doll could be bought separately or with layette sets. Original price: $5.95 – $15.00. Marks: IDEAL DOLL/MADE IN USA/PAT.NO. 225 2077 (on head).

Sears catalog.

Sears catalog.

Plassie (**1946**) 16", 19", 22" hard plastic head (16" and 19" on shoulder plate so can tilt), Magic Skin rubber arms and legs, cloth body. Sleep eyes. Cries when you squeeze her legs. Sheer cotton dress and bonnet. Cotton slip, panties, rayon socks, imitation leather shoes.

Plassie (**1946**) 14" with baby legs, 15" with straight legs. All plastic, molded painted hair, tilt and turn head, sleep eyes, wears sunsuits, rayon socks, and leatherette shoes. Retail $5.79.

Courtesy Jessie Williams.

Hard Plastic Transitional Baby Doll (1940s) Hard plastic shoulder plate head, oil cloth body, composition arms and legs. A transitional doll. $50.00.

JOLLY
Junior Miss
JUMBO SIZE SOFT
STUFFED DOLL.
Retails for $15.00
(Life Size)

100% ALL WOOL
WASHABLE
Terrier
Retails for $3 to $10

Ad from *Toys and Novelties Magazine*.

Mary
AND HER
Lamb

Retails
for
$6.95

Ad from *Toys and Novelties Magazine*.

Junior Miss (also called Pin-up Girl) (1943 – 1947) 40" All cloth soft stuffed doll, mask face with blonde wool braids, wearing pants, dress, or skirt and sweater, and beret. Had elastic on bottom of feet so child could dance with her. Size of a four-year-old child. Catalog number #1691-15, original price $15.00. $55.00.

Mary and her Lamb (1944) Cloth-stuffed doll with mask face, yellow yarn hair, wearing short dress with organdy apron, bonnet, white shoes and socks, carries a little stuffed lamb. Original price $6.95. $55.00.

Toys and Novelties Magazine.

Bit of Heaven (1945 – 1947) Mask face, cloth stuffed angel doll with wings, closed painted eyes, comes with cord to hang over baby's crib. U.S. Design Patent #140969. Catalog number #1730-3. Original price $3.50. $30.00.

"Girl Doll" (1947) 18", 20", 22" All composition jointed girl doll. Mohair wig, glacé sleep eyes with lashes, open mouth with inset upper teeth, wears red straw hat and red short dress. 1947 Catalog numbers: G9620, G9622, G9624. Original price $8.65, $9.70, $10.80. A "moderately" priced doll. $125.00.

Ideal Catalog.

Ideal's Bridal Party Dolls (1944 – 1947) 15" Flower Girl, 22" Bridesmaid and 22" Bride. All composition, fully jointed, wig, glacé sleep eyes, and lashes. Flower Girl wears colored rayon taffeta gown, rayon underwear, white socks and formal shoes, carries basket of flowers, catalog #GD9615. Original price $7.50. Bridesmaid wears colored rayon taffeta gown and short veil, rayon underwear, white socks, and gold formal sandals, carries bouquet of flowers, catalog #GBM9622. Original price $18.00. Bride wears white rayon satin gown and veil, rayon underwear, white socks and white formal sandals, carries bouquet of flowers, catalog #GB9622. Original price $22.50. $250.00+.

Courtesy Sherry Lynn Wilson.

Curly Hair Baby Beautiful (1947) 18", 20", 22", 24" (shown), 25", 27" Composition head, arms, and legs, cotton-stuffed body, mohair wig, green glacé sleep eyes with lashes, clothes all original, crier. Reissued doll from 1938. 25" and 27" doll came with chest plate on body and full composition arms. Catalog #BW964, #BW965, #BW966, #BW967, #BW968, #BW969. Original price $8.65, $9.70, $10.80, $13.50, $16.20, $21.60. Marks: IDEAL. $200.00.

Courtesy Wenham Museum. Photo by Diane Buck.

Courtesy Larry Doucet.

Sparkle Plenty (1947) Magic Skin in rare jumpsuit outfit. Cries when squeezed. Dolls came in original cartoon type box shown.

Sparkle Plenty (1947 – 1950) 14", 16", 18", 20" Hard plastic head, Magic Skin latex rubber jointed body, yellow wool yarn hair, bright blue sleep eyes with long lashes, pierced nostrils, cries or coos when squeezed, dressed in cotton wrapper and diaper or outfit with white collar. Character from Dick Tracy comic strip – daughter of B.O. Plenty and Gravel Gertie. 14" and 18" produced in 1951 with voice, dressed in print dress or slack suit. Catalog number: #0144 and #0184. Original price $6.00 to $12.00. Marks: Made in USA, Pat 272 (on head) #2232077. Her wrist tag reads, "Baby Sparkle Plenty Doll, The World's Most Famous Baby" by permission of the *Chicago Tribune News* Syndicate. 14", $150.00.

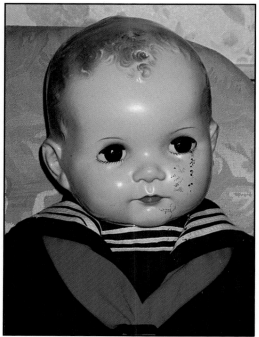

Courtesy Nancy Uttech.

Brother Coos (1940s) 24" Composition head and limbs, cloth body. Makes a cooing sound. Marks: IDEAL DOLL CO./ Pat.#225 2077 (on head).

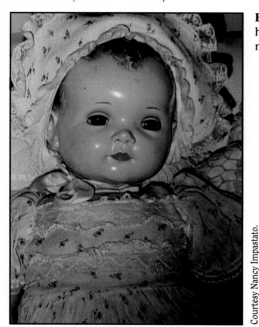

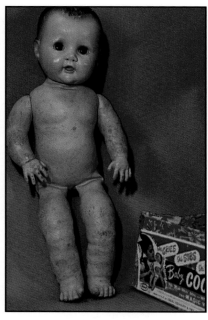

Baby Coos (1940s) Hard plastic head, Magic Skin body, holes in nostrils, wearing flower print dress.

Courtesy Nancy Impastato.

Baby Coos (1940s) 14" Hard plastic head, Magic Skin body, hole in nostrils, shown with box. Makes a cooing sound when body is pressed.

Playthings Magazine.

Baby Coos Brother & Sister (1948 – 1952) 14", 16", 18", 20", 22", 27", 30" Life size, hard plastic head, stuffed Magic Skin body filled with foam rubber stuffing, jointed arms, lucite sleep eyes, real eyelashes, molded painted hair. Sobs if you pat the body too hard, cries when spanked, squeals if pinched, coos when hugged. She is dressed in corduroy skirt, Basque-style shirt, beret. He is wearing cordoroy pants, Basque shirt and beret. Layette of lace trimmed white organdy dress and bonnet, cotton slip, socks, shoes, and plastic 10-piece tea set. Designed by Bernard Lipfert. Dressed in sunsuit in 1951. Catalog #BC1 and #BC8. Original price $6.95 up to $25.00. Marks: IDEAL DOLL/MADE IN USA or 16 IDEAL DOLL, MADE IN U.S.A.(on head). 14", $55.00; 30", $100.00.

Hard Plastic Doll with Mohair Wig and Toni Body

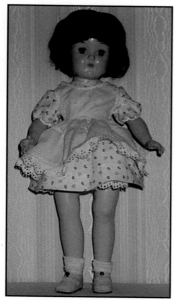

Courtesy Patrice Simonelli.

Hard Plastic Doll (late 1940s – early 1950s) 15", 17", 19" (shown) All hard plastic with mohair wig, Toni head and body. Marks: "P-92/ IDEAL TOY CO./ MADE IN THE U.S.A." P-91 also seen with mohair wig. 15", $250.00; 17", $275.00' 19", $300.00.

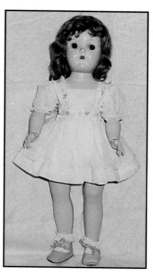

Courtesy Mary Davis.

Hard Plastic Doll (late 1940s – early 1950s) 19" All hard plastic with mohair wig, Toni head and body. Marks: P-92/ IDEAL TOY CO./ MADE IN THE U.S.A. Original pink dress with blue, pink, and white embroidered flowers on the lace.

Courtesy John Sonnier.

Hard Plastic Doll (late 1940s – early 1950s) Hard plastic doll with Toni body and mohair wig in long beige gown.

Courtesy Willa Cunningham.

Hard Plastic Doll (late 1940s – early 1950s) 19" All hard plastic with mohair wig and Toni head and body. Marks: P-92/ IDEAL TOY CO./ MADE IN THE U.S.A. (on head); IDEAL DOLL/P-19 (on back). Original blue dress complete with hang tang and price tag of $6.98.

14" (P-90) Toni Dolls

Courtesy Eleanor Baker. Photograph by Gary Faulkner.

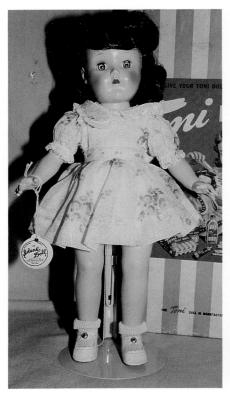

Toni (1949 – 1953) 14" (shown), 16", 19", 21", 22½", All hard plastic, jointed body, Dupont nylon glued-on wig; wig colors are platinum blonde, yellow blonde, red, light brown, dark brown. Eyes were blue with rare brown ones seen. Tie-in with Toni Cosmetic Company and 20th Century Fox Picture Studio. Came with kit containing curlers, shampoo creme, and play wave solution of sugar and water. Designed by Bernard Lipfert. Pictured: Platinum blonde with red skirt, yellow blouse, braid trim, red leatherette snap shoes, box, play wave set. Catalog numbers: #1140, #1160, #1190, #1210. Original price: $10.00, $12.00, $15.00, $18.00. Marks: IDEAL DOLL/MADE IN U.S.A.(on head). 14" doll: P-90/ IDEAL DOLL/ MADE IN U.S.A. (on head); IDEAL DOLL/P-90 (on body). 14"(P-90), $200.00; 16"(P91), $250.00; 19"(P92), $275.00; 21"(P93), $300.00; 22½"(P94), $800.00.

Toni (1949) 14" Brunette with original wrist tag shown with box. Marks: P-90. First Tonis had the rolled bangs

Toni (1949 – 1953) 14" brunette with red jumper with embroidered flowers and white blouse, showing variation in this Heidi-type outfit. Marks: IDEAL DOLL/P-90 (on body).

Courtesy Jeannie Nespoli.

Toni (1949) 14" Blonde in nylon V-front plaid jumper with whit blouse. Mint with box showing all her lotion, play wave, comb, and directions. Marks: IDEAL DOLL/P-90 (on body).

Courtesy Cris Johnson.

Toni (1949) 14" Black hair (a hard-to-find color) in nylon V-front plaid jumper with white blouse in interesting color variation. Marks: IDEAL DOLL/P-90 (on body).

Courtesy Ann Tardie.

Toni (1949) 14" Strawberry blonde in cotton V-front plaid jumper with white blouse, notice oilcloth shoes. Marks: IDEAL DOLL/P-90 (on body). Tag sewn on back of dress: "Genuine Toni Doll with NYLON wig made by Ideal (in oval) Toy Corporation."

Courtesy Susan Mobley.

Toni (1949) 14" Blonde Toni with green eyes. In red plaid dress variation. Marks: IDEAL DOLL/P-90 (on body).

Toni (1949) 14" Auburn hair in waffle cotton dress with faux jacket style. Marks: IDEAL DOLL/P-90 (on body).

Courtesy Jeannie Nespoli.

Toni (1949) 14" Platinum blonde in blue dress with faux jacket. Marks: IDEAL DOLL/P-90 (on body).

Courtesy Mary Davis

Toni (1949) 14" Black hair in green jumper with red rick-rack jumper and white blouse. Mint in box with rare black shoes. Marks: IDEAL DOLL/P-90 (on body).

Courtesy McMasterss Doll Auctions.

Toni (1949) 14" Light blonde in pink dress, rare brown eyes, mint in box still wearing her hair net. Marks: IDEAL DOLL/P-90 (on body). $450.00.

Courtesy Mary Davis

Toni (1952) 14" Light brunette in pleated turquoise nylon party dress. Shown with her box and original brochure and tags. Marks: IDEAL DOLL/P-90 (on body).

Courtesy Jeannie Nespoli.

Toni (1949) 14" Platinum blonde in mustard color dress with mustard and green flowers. Marks: IDEAL DOLL/P-90 (on body).

Courtesy Ann Tardie.

Toni (1949) 14" Platinum blonde in green and navy striped dress. Notice later box with photo of child and doll larger. Marks: IDEAL DOLL/P-90 (on body). Tag sewn on back of dress: "Genuine Toni Doll with NYLON wig made by Ideal (in oval) Toy Corporation."

Courtesy Beverly Marmon.

Toni (1949) 14" Red head in white polka dot dress, with blue ribbon and rick-rack and pink flowers. Navy oilcloth shoes. Marks: P-90 (on body).

Courtesy Susan Mobley.

Toni (1949) 14" Platinum Toni in tagged dress with turquoise skirt and pink top. Marks: IDEAL DOLL/P-90 (on body).

Courtesy Louise Dodgion.

Courtesy Louise Dodgion.

Toni (1949) 14" Platinum blonde in red print dress with white pinafore. Unusual light red hair (orange) with blue dress with overlay of red dotted white organdy, replaced flowers. Blonde hair still in hairnet in navy red and white dress with butterfly sleeves also seen on Betsy Wetsy. Marks: IDEAL DOLL/P-90 (on body). Socks and shoes not original.

Toni (1949) 14" Black hair doll with organdy figured blouse, light blue pinafore overdress with chevron design and pink ribbon around waist. Marks: IDEAL DOLL/P-90 (on body).

Courtesy Susan Mobley.

Courtesy Betty K. Jones.

Toni (1949) 14" Champagne blonde in Heidi type dress. Marks: IDEAL DOLL/P-90 (on body).

Toni (1949) 14" Dark brunette in light blue dress with white organdy bib front with pink ribbon and embroidery. Marks: IDEAL DOLL/P-90 (on body).

Toni (1949) 14" Yellow blonde in gray and white check dress shown with box.

Courtesy Patricia Irving.

Toni (1949) 14" Honey blonde in an unusual print dress the same as seen on Plassie (1950s). Marks: IDEAL DOLL/P-90 (on body).

Courtesy Jan and Derek Clanton.

Courtesy Louise Dodgion.

Toni (1949) 14" Blonde bride in embossed white nylon dress, lined top slip attached with stiffening piece up from bottom, white leatherette snap shoes, tagged, veil possibly cut. Marks: P-91/IDEAL DOLL/MADE IN U.S.A. (on head); IDEAL DOLL/P-90 (on body).

16" (P-91) Toni Dolls

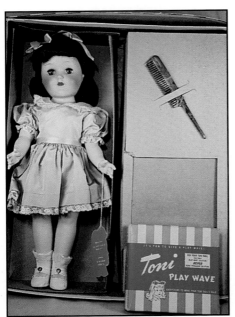

Courtesy Ann Tardie.

Courtesy Mary Davis.

Toni (1949) 16" Black hair, wearing blue nylon dress. These earlier dolls had rolled hair and oilcloth shoes. Marks: IDEAL DOLL/P-91(on body).

Toni (1949) 16" Platinum blonde hair in blue dress with collar, white ribbon around waist. Dress also came in green. Shown in her box. Marks: IDEAL DOLL/P-91(on body).

Courtesy Louise Dodgion.

Courtesy Wenham Museum. Photo by Diane Buck.

Toni (1949) 16" Blonde in dress with pink cotton top, jacket, and belt, buttons in back. Top, belt, skirt, and slip top are attached. Hat has an open crown. Shoes have a flower design. Replaced socks. Marks: IDEAL DOLL/P-91(on body).

Toni (1949) 16" Platinum blonde wearing blue nylon dress with pink and blue thread and white lace.

Courtesy Susan Mobley.

Toni (1949) 16" Lemon blonde in red and white striped dress with navy bib front. Marks: IDEAL DOLL/P-91(on body).

Courtesy Susan Mobley.

Toni (1949) 16" Hair in original set with dried flowers and pinned with short bobby pins. Original untagged dress with unusual gold/brown braid. White lace trim not original. Marks: IDEAL DOLL/P-91(on body).

Toni (1949) 16" Golden blonde pink nylon dress with white organdy bib front with embroidered flowers, mint in box. Marks: IDEAL DOLL/P-91(on body).

Courtesy Paula Brown.

Toni (1949) 16" Original upswept hairdo and gown with rhinestones. Marks: IDEAL DOLL/P-91(on body).

Courtesy Janet Klosterman

Toni (1949) 16" Bride in white rayon gown, bridal veil, slip, undies, shoes, and socks. She also came complete with a Toni Play Wave kit with curlers, shampoo, play wave solution, rubber bands, tissues, and directions." (according to catalog). She is pictured in the 1951 catalog holding a bouquet, but the catalog blurb does not mention it. Marks: IDEAL DOLL/P-91(on body).

Toni (1949) Dress for P-91 doll showing original tag in back. Some dresses had tags, some had no tags.

Comparison of Toni P-91 faces. Doll on left is older; notice paler face color. Came with the oilcloth shoes. Later doll on right has rounder chin and lower shinier face.

19" (P-92) Toni Dolls

Courtesy Pam Keith. Photo by Gary Faulkner.

Toni (**1950s**) 19" Black hair in plaid jumper, white blouse with box, wave kit, and wrist tag. Marks: P-92/IDEAL DOLL/MADE IN U.S.A. (on head); IDEAL DOLL/P-19 (on body).

Courtesy Chree Kysar.

Toni (**1950s**) 19" Platinum blonde in box. Marks: P-92.

Courtesy Jeanne Melanson.

Toni (**1949**) 19" Blonde in pink cotton dress with blue embroidery; notice blue plastic shoes. Marks: IDEAL DOLL/P-92 (on body).

Courtesy Louise Dodgion.

Toni (1949) 19" Brunette with center part, wearing green dress with organdy pinafore trimmed in red. Marks: IDEAL DOLL/P-92(on body). Shoes and socks not original.

Courtesy Chree Kysar.

Toni (1950s) 19" Blonde in tagged bridal outfit. Marks: P-92.

21" (P-93) Toni Dolls

Courtesy Mary Davis.

Toni (1949) 21" Blonde in common red and white dress showing hang tags. Marks: IDEAL DOLL/P-93 (on body).

Courtesy Chree Kysar.

Toni (1950s) 21" Red hair, print dress. Marks: P-93.

Courtesy McMasterss Doll Auctions.

Toni (1949) 21" Light blonde in lime green dress. Mint In Box. Marks: IDEAL DOLL/P-93 (on body). $750.00.

Courtesy Jeannie Nespoli.

Toni (1949) 21" Brunette in pink print dress with hot pink apron. Marks: IDEAL DOLL/P-93 (on body).

Courtesy Mary Davis.

Toni (1949) 21" Platinum blonde in baby blue and pink dress. Replaced socks. Marks: IDEAL DOLL/P-93 (on body).

Courtesy Mary Davis.

Toni (1949) 21" Brunette bride (P-93), tagged dress, veil replaced, necklace not original. Marks: IDEAL DOLL/P-93 (on body).

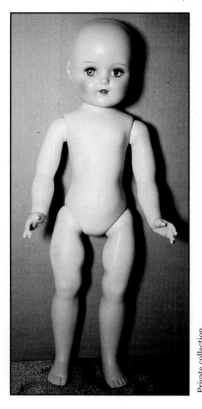

Private collection.

Toni (1949) 21" P-93 doll direct from the factory from the collection of an Ideal employee, showing body construction.

22½" (P-94) Toni Dolls

Courtesy Chree Kysar.

Courtesy Chree Kysar.

Toni (1950s) 22½" Brunette, a very rare doll. Marks: IDEAL DOLL P-94 (on back). $900.00.

Toni (1950s) 22½" Close-up. Notice neck jointed at bottom of neck. Marks: P-94.

Toni Dolls – Walkers

Courtesy Pam Keith. Photo by Gary Faulkner.

Toni Walker (**1954 – 1956**) 14½" (shown), 16½", 19½", 21½" Celanese acetate hard plastic, Dupont nylon hair, pinned on legs. Came with Toni play wave kit, called sub-deb, teen, princess, queen size. 14½" blonde with flowered dress with white pinafore, wrist tag, box, wave kit, black plastic shoes. Catalog numbers: #1141, #1161, #1191, #1211. Original price: $10.00, $12.00, $15.00, $18.00. Marks: 14": P-90 W/IDEAL DOLL (on head); IDEAL DOLL/90W (on body) also seen 14": IDEAL DOLL/ P-90 W (on head); IDEAL DOLL/ P-90 W (on back); for 16": IDEAL DOLL/ P-91 (on head); IDEAL DOLL/16 (on back). 14½", $200.00; 16½", $250.00; 19½", $275.00; 21½", $300.00.

Courtesy Mary Davis.

Toni Walkers (**1954 – 1956**) 14½" and 19½" As she walks, her head turns from side to side; doll can even walk backward.

Toni Walker (**1954 – 1956**) 16½" Reddish brunette in blue and pink print dress with nylon sheer organdy apron. Shown in her box with original walker tag. Marks: IDEAL DOLL/P-91(on body).

Courtesy Sharon Jahraus.

Courtesy Sharon Jahraus.

Toni Walker (1954 – 1956) 16½" Red hair with green eyes. Mint with her wrist tags. Still wearing hairnet. Marks: IDEAL DOLL/16 (on back).

Toni Walker (1954 – 1956) 19½" Toni Walker tagged dress. Hair bow and bow on dress not original. Marks: IDEAL DOLL/P-92W (on body).

Toni Brochure available at stores, showing movie star June Haver curling her Toni doll's hair.

Toni Brochure available at stores, showing hair-dos and contents of play wave set including curlers, lotion, play wave, papers, rubber bands, and rat tail comb.

Ideal publication Courtesy Mel Poretz.

Gimbel's display of Toni dolls in toy department. Notice beauty parlor in the showcase (**1951**).

Courtesy Miriam Gittleson.

Tonis wearing American Designers' Fashions with Hadassah Michtom and child relative (in front) and from left: Abe Katz, Dave Rosenstein, fashion models dressed in replicas of Toni fashions, and Ben Michtom (**1951**).

Ideal Publicity Photo courtesy Mel Poretz.

Tonis (1951) in unique French Designer Clothing designed by (from top left): Jean Desses, Lefaurie, Gres, Piguet, Rochas, Bruyere, Rouff, Heim, Carven, Worth, Patou, Paquin.

Ideal Publicity Photo courtesy Mel Poretz.

Benjamin Franklin Michtom (center), Patty Ann Jackson (left) star of the stage version of "Gentlemen Prefer Blondes," and Marguerite Piazza (right), Metropolitan Opera star, admire the Rouff and Piguet designed Toni Fashions.

Ideal publicity photo courtesy Mel Poretz.

Kathi Norris, TV star, poses with the Paris designed Toni dolls wearing dresses by Jacques Heim (on left) and Worth (on right).

Dolls with Toni Body and Head

Sara Ann

Courtesy Jeanne Melanson.

Courtesy Cathie Clark.

Sara Ann (1951) 15" and 24" All hard plastic Toni look-alike doll, blonde Saran wig; uses Toni body, sleep eyes, jointed head, arms, and legs. 24" is a rare size. Marks: 15": P-90/IDEAL DOLL/MADE IN USA (on head); IDEAL DOLL/P-90 (on body). 24": P-4/IDEAL DOLL/MADE IN U.S.A. (on head); IDEAL DOLL/P-4 or P-94 (on back). 15", $175.00; 24", $500.00.

All Plastic Girl Doll with Saran Wig (also known as Sara Ann) (1951) 15" (shown), 17", 19", 21" All hard plastic Toni look-alike doll, thinner hard plastic than Toni, Sara Ann for "Saran hair", has blonde or brown (shown) Saran wig; uses Toni body mold, sleep eyes, jointed head, arms, and legs; comes with curlers, wears dress, hat, and snap shoes. Same as Toni doll except less expensive since Ideal did not have to pay royalties for the Toni name. Catalog numbers: #1507, #1707, #1907, #1207. Marks: 15": P-90/IDEAL DOLL/MADE IN USA (on head); IDEAL DOLL/P-90 (on body). 21": P3/IDEAL DOLL/MADE IN U.S.A. (on head), IDEAL DOLL/P3 or P93 (on back).15", $175.00; 21", $275.00.

Courtesy Carol Fetherman.

Sara Ann (1951) 24" Hard plastic wearing lavender nylon dress with saran wig, uses Toni body. Marks: P-4/IDEAL DOLL/MADE IN U.S.A. (on head); IDEAL DOLL/P-94 (on back).

Mary Hartline

Courtesy Ann Wencel. Photo by Carol Stover.

Courtesy McMasters Doll Auctions.

Mary Hartline (1952) 22½" Hard plastic. Wearing red satin-like costume with her name on it. Notice doll's head which is jointed at the base of the neck. P-94 body. Marks: IDEAL DOLL (on head) IDEAL DOLL/P-94 (on back). $700.00.

Mary Hartline "The Pretty Princess of TV" (1952) 16" (shown) and 22½" Hard plastic fully jointed, blonde nylon wig, blue sleep eyes with lashes, black eyeshadow over and under eye. Original box and Rayve hairstyling set. Red, white, or green drum majorette costume and baton and twirling instructions. From ABC-TV show "Super Circus." Catalog #1260 and #1270. Original price $11.98 and $19.98. Marks: 16": P-91/ IDEAL DOLL/MADE IN U.S.A. (on head), IDEAL DOLL/P-91 OR IDEAL 16 (on body). 22½": IDEAL DOLL(on head); IDEAL DOLL/P-94 (on body). Walker doll made in 1953. A later version also had a vinyl head. 16", $350.00, 22½", $325.00. MIB, $700.00.

Courtesy Ann Wencel. Photo by Carol Stover.

Mary Hartline (1952) 16" showing red and blue cotton costume colors, also available in teal. Marks: P-91/IDEAL DOLL/MADE IN U.S.A. (on head) IDEAL DOLL 16 or P-91 (on back).

Courtesy Ann Wencel. Photo by Carol Stover.

Ideal factory (**1952**). Notice **Mary Hartline** and **Magic Flesh Vinyl Head Doll** in background.

Mary Hartline (1954) 16" vinyl head, hard plastic walker body, rooted platinum blonde hair, white costume variation. Hard to find doll. Marks: V/91 (on head); Ideal 16 (on body). $300.00

Courtesy Anita Child.

Courtesy Ann Tardie

Mary Hartline (**1952**) in person shown with Abe Katz's two grandsons Andrew Merin (left) and Richard Weintraub (right) holding the **Mary Hartline** dolls.

Mary Hartline (**1952**) 7½" Hard plastic, jointed neck and arms, blonde nylon wig, blue or yellow sleep eyes, painted lashes, molded white boots, in box. Catalog #1250. Original price $1.98. Marks: IDEAL (in script on back). $85.00.

Miss Curity

Courtesy Peggy Millhouse.

Miss Curity (**1953**) 14½" Hard plastic, saran wig, sleep eyes with black eyeshadow, nurse's outfit, navy cape, and white cap, had Bauer & Black Curity first aid kit and book. Also came with curlers. Uses Toni body. Pat. 1951. Catalog #2800. Original price $11.98. Marks: P-90/IDEAL DOLL, MADE IN U.S.A. (on head). 14½", $300.00.

Courtesy McMasters Doll Auctions.

Miss Curity (**1953**) 14½" Hard plastic, saran wig, sleep eyes with black eyeshadow over and sometimes under the eye, nurse's outfit with navy cape and white cap. Bauer & Black Curity first aid kit and book. Also came with curlers. Uses Toni body. Marks: P-90/IDEAL DOLL/MADE IN U.S.A. MIB $650.00.

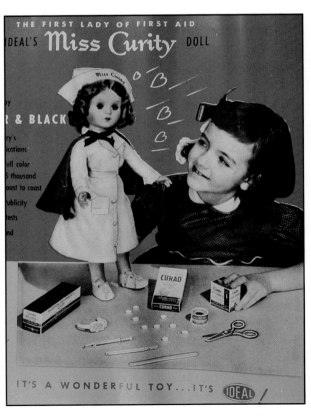

Ideal Catalog.

Miss Curity (**1953**) Notice brown hair color on doll.

Dolls With Toni Body
Betsy McCall

Courtesy Karen Puck.

Betsy McCall (1952 – 1953) 14" Soft vinyl head, hard plastic body. Marks: McCALL CORP.® (on head), IDEAL DOLL/IDEAL DOLL/P-90 (on back). 14", $300.00; 20", $350.00.

Courtesy McMasters Doll Auctions.

Betsy McCall (1952 – 1954) 14" Vinyl head, hard plastic Toni Walker body. Marks: McCall Corp (on head)/IDEAL DOLL/P-90 (on back). MIB $400.00.

Courtesy Rebecca Mucchetti.

Betsy McCall (1952 – 1953) 14" Soft vinyl head made of Bakelite vinyl resins, hard plastic Toni body, glued-on dark brown saran wig. 14" size is a walker and has brown sleep eyes. 20" has flirty eyes. Seven different outfits sold separately. Designed by Bernard Lipfert from the copyrighted *McCall Magazine's* paper doll. Catalog #1360. Original price $7.98. Pat. 1952. Marks: McCALL CORP.® (on head), IDEAL DOLL/P-90 (on back). Came with McCall patterns.

Ideal Factory (**1952**). Sewing **Betsy McCall** clothes.

Betsy McCall (**1952 – 1953**) Ideal ad showing patterns
available for sewing matching child's and doll's dresses.

Harriet Hubbard Ayer

Courtesy Millie Caliri.

Courtesy McMasters Doll Auctions.

Harriet Hubbard Ayer (**1953**) 7½", 14", 16" (shown), 19", 21" Soft vinyl head made from Geon™ paste resin stuffed with cotton, hard plastic body, glued-on wig or rooted hair. Striped apron outfit most common. Came with eight-piece H.H. Ayer cosmetic kit, beauty table, and booklet. Catalog: 14", #2900, 21", #2903. Original price 7½", $1.98; 14", $11.98; 16", $12.98. Marks: MK 16/IDEAL DOLL (on head); IDEAL DOLL/P-91 (on body). 14", $150.00, 16", $175.00, 18", $250.00.

Harriet Hubbard Ayer (**1953**) Ideal's Doll of Beauty. It took three years of experiments to find the geon paste resin material for the head that could withstand application of make-up and subsequent cleaning. Harriet has the hard plastic Toni body. Harriet Hubbard Ayer was a division of Lever Brothers. MIB, $450.00.

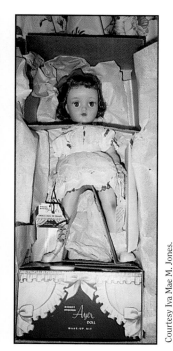

Courtesy Iva Mae M. Jones.

Harriet Hubbard Ayer (**1953**) 16" Vinyl head, Toni body. MIB doll.

Courtesy Anita Child.

Abraham M. Katz at the luncheon where he received a citation of Notable Achievement and Honorary Life Membership from Sandra Thomas, president of the National Doll and Toy Collectors Club, Inc. April, **1953**. Shown on left, Mrs. Thomas with a Greiner Doll and Mr. Katz with the **Harriet Hubbard Ayer** "Doll of Beauty."

Dolls With Toni Walker Body

Princess Mary

Courtesy Cathie Clark.

Courtesy John Axe.

Princess Mary (1953 – 1956) 16" (shown), 19", 21" Stuffed vinyl head, hard plastic Toni Walker body, rooted saran hair, blue sleep eyes, walker, wears rayon dress with attached slip, came with plastic curlers. Catalog numbers: #1625, #1925, #2125. Marks: IDEAL DOLL/V-87(on head) also seen IDEAL DOLL/V-91 (on head); IDEAL DOLL/16 (on back). 16", $200.00; 19", $225.00; 21", $250.00.

Princess Mary (1953 – 1956) 16" Stuffed vinyl head, hard plastic walker body. Rooted saran hair, yellow rayon dress with attached slip. Replaced socks. Marks: IDEAL DOLL/V91 (head). P-91 body.

Princess Mary (1953) 14" Vinyl head, unusual hard plastic nonwalker body. Shown with box. 14", $200.00.

Courtesy Betty K. Jones.

Princess Mary (1953 – 1956) 19" Stuffed vinyl head, hard plastic Toni Walker body wearing evening gown, came with plastic curlers. Shown with 16" and 7½" **Mary Hartline (1951)**.

Princess Mary (1953 – 1956) 21" Vinyl head, hard plastic Toni Walker body in long pink gown. Marks: P-93.

Courtesy John Sonnier.

Courtesy Kerry Israels.

Princess Mary (1953 – 1956) 19" Vinyl head, hard plastic Toni Walker body.

Other Dolls with Toni Body

Ruth (1953) 17", 19" (shown), 21" Vinyl head, plastic jointed body, long straight saran hair in ponytail inserted into head, sleep eyes and lashes, dressed in party dress, came with curlers. Marks: IDEAL DOLL/V-92 (on head), IDEAL DOLL/P-19 (on body). Rosy color on knees. Original dress, replaced shoes and socks. Catalog #1705, #1905, #1205. 17", $125.00; 19", $150.00; 21", $175.00.

Ideal Catalog.

Walking Girl Doll (1955) 25" Vinyl head and body, arms and legs are jointed so they can bend at elbows and knees, rooted saran hair, sleep eyes, organdy dress, slip, panties, socks, and vinyl shoes. Catalog #2050. $125.00.

Courtesy Nancy Shomo.

Ideal's Walking Bride Doll (1955 – 1956) 14" (shown) or 19" Vinyl head, plastic walker body, rooted saran hair with flowers in hair. Wears bridal gown and veil, socks, holds bouquet of flowers, turns head from side to side when walks. Slip attached to dress. Comes with plastic curlers. Catalog #1427. Red blush on knees. Marks: IDEAL DOLL/W90 (on head); IDEAL DOLL/90W (on body). Shoes marked: IDEAL TOY CORP. 14" $125.00; 19", $150.00.

Ideal's Walking Bride Doll (1955 – 1956) 14" or 19" (shown) Vinyl head, plastic walker body, rooted saran hair, wears nylon tulle bridal gown and veil, still has netting on hair, holds bouquet of flowers, turns head from side to side when walks. Comes with plastic curlers. Catalog #1427. Marks: IDEAL DOLL/V92 (on head); IDEAL DOLL/19 (on body). Shoes Marked: IDEAL DOLL/19. 14", $125.00, 19", $150.00.

Hopalong Cassidy (1949 – 1950) (left) 20" and 24" Vinyl head, cloth body, giant size doll. Head made from Vinylite resins. Cost $6 and $8 retail. 20", $200.00, $24", $225.00.

Hopalong Cassidy doll (1949 – 1950) 18", 21", 23", 25", 27" "Vinylite" soft vinyl head and hands, head stuffed with cotton, life-like resemblance, molded painted gray hair, painted blue eyes, soft one-piece body, dressed in black cowboy outfit with black corduroy pants, black leatherette boots, guns and holster, and black felt hat. Catalog 23", #1513-8, 25", #HC7, 27", #1513-10. Original price: 23", $8.00, and 27", $10.00. Marks: Hopalong Cassidy (on buckle). Could get Topper as a rocking horse for $12.00. **Judy Splinters (1950).** 18", 22", 36" "Vinylite" vinyl head, ventriloquist doll, cloth body, jointed arms and legs, turns head, open/closed mouth with molded tongue, painted eyes, yarn-like pigtails, dressed in broadcloth romper dress and bolero jacket, wears clothes of four-year-old child. From TV show created by Shirley Dinsdale. Catalog #JS-1, #0057, #0058. Original price $25.00. Marks: IDEAL DOLL (on head). Two **Blessed Event** Dolls also shown.

Tickletoes (1950) 15", 19", 24" (shown) Hard plastic head and shoulder plate, latex arms and legs stuffed with cotton, cloth body, molded hair or mohair wig, open mouth with teeth and tongue (except 15"), glassene sleep eyes, lashes, cry voice. Marks: 16/IDEAL DOLL/MADE IN USA (on head); or P2000/ IDEAL DOLL (on head). 15", $150.00; 19", $175.00; 24", $200.00.

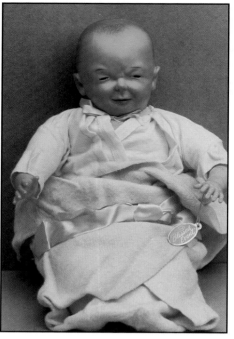

Courtesy Wenham Museum. Photo by Diane Buck.

Blessed Event (1950) Benjamin Franklin Michtom and stewardess showing the elaborate publicity stunt used to introduce the doll involving having a woman "give birth" to the doll in a hospital, taking her in an ambulance to the plane, and finally bringing her to a department store where she is "adopted."

Blessed Event (also called Kiss Me) (1950) 19" and 21" (shown) Soft vinyl head and lower limbs, stuffed oilcloth body with plunger in back to make doll cry or pout. Realistic newborn face, open mouth with molded tongue, pouts, puckers and opens mouth to cry, press plunger in back to change expression, wears cotton kimono and soft blanket. Catalog numbers: #0216 and #0236. Original price: $11.98 and $14.98. Marks: 3/IDEAL DOLL/Patent Pending. 18", $80.00; 21", $100.00.

Courtesy Judi Radley. Photo by Ray Radley.

Ideal Catalog.

Talking Tot (also called Talkytot) (1950) 22" Hard plastic head, cloth and vinyl, holes in body, key wind talker, voice box marked Shilling in back, molded or wig glued over molded hair, laughs when lying down, cries other times. Talky Tot trademarked Oct. 3, 1950, #585,168. Unmarked. $100.00.

Boopsie (1950 – 55) 8" All plastic jointed doll with side glancing sleep eyes, painted molded hair, wearing diaper. Packaged in cellophane bag. Catalog #3120. Original price $0.99. $25.00.

Courtesy Richard Withington Auctions.

Howdy Doody (1950 – 1952) 18" (shown), 20", and 24" Hard plastic head, ventriloquist doll, mouth operated by pull string on back of neck, soft stuffed cloth body and limbs, with vinyl hands. Original price $2.98. Marks: IDEAL (on head). 18", $250.00; 20", $275.00; 24", $300.00.

Courtesy Sherry Lynne Wilson

Hard Plastic Baby Doll (circa 1950) 24" Hard plastic head, lower arms and legs, cloth body, mohair wig, open mouth with two teeth, green sleep eyes with lashes, crier, original outfit. Marks: P-400/IDEAL DOLL/MADE IN USA. $125.00.

Courtesy Robin Randall.

Deluxe Baby Beautiful with saran wig (1951) 17", 19", 21", 23", 25" Hard plastic head, vinyl arms and legs, cloth cotton filled body. Sleep eyes and lashes, saran wig came with plastic curlers. Organdy dress, frilly bonnet, slips, undies, socks and shoes. Catalog Numbers: #2167, #2187, #2207, #2237, #2257. Deluxe Baby Beautiful with molded hair came in same sizes. Catalog Numbers: #2160, #2180, #2200, #2230, #2250. Marks: P-100/IDEAL DOLL/MADE IN U.S.A. (on head). $150.00. MIB $300.00.

Ideal Catalog.

Howdy Doody (1953 – 1955) 20½" and 25" Hard plastic head, all cloth body ventriloquist doll. Clothing is part of body. Also available in 1955 was a talking Howdy Doody doll and a doll with a vinyl face.

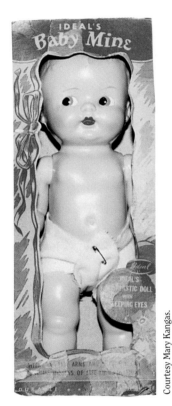

Courtesy Mary Kangas.

Baby Mine (also known as Thrift Kit Dolls)(1950) 11" Plastic dolls showing the Bucilla Thrift Kits that one could buy separately to sew Cowboy, Little Nurse, Roller Skating Dress, Sailor Boy.

Courtesy Beverly Marmon.

Ideal Catalog.

Lolly (also known as Tiny Girl) (1951 – 1955) 9½" Hard plastic walker, jointed arms, sleep eyes, molded painted hair. Legs have same hip joints used on Saucy Walker. Catalog #3126. Original price 98¢. Marks: IDEAL DOLL/9 (on head and body). $30.00.

Baby Mine (also known as Thrift Kit doll) (1951 – 1954) 11" All plastic fully jointed doll. Blue painted side glancing eyes, four painted upper lashes, molded painted hair. Wears panties, packaged in acetate window box. Catalog #PBJ100 and #3110. Marks: IDEAL DOLL (on back). $35.00.

Snookie Doll (1951 – 1955) 10" Vinyl head with molded hair, Magic Skin body. Holes in ears. Painted side glancing blue eyes. Came dressed in diaper and bathrobe. Coos when squeezed. Clothes probably not original. Pat. 1951. Catalog #0091, retail price $1.00. Marks: IDEAL DOLL (on head). $35.00.

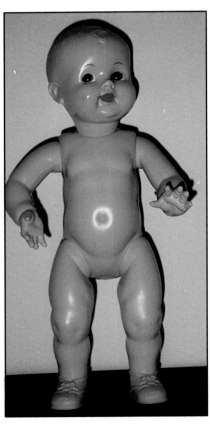

Courtesy Bonnie Kuziak.

Handy Annie (1951) 15½" Hard plastic, sleep eyes, jointed wrists, neck, arms and hips, molded hair, painted side glancing eyes. Catalog #3137. Replaced shoes, came dressed in diaper and shoes. $45.00.

Pete and Repete (Snookie Twins) (1951 – 1955) 10" and 12" Vinyl Idealite head, one-piece Magic Skin body, coos when squeezed, twins dressed in blanket and diaper. 12" has movable arms. Catalog #0092. Original price for 12", $6.95. Marks: IDEAL DOLL. Dressed in crocheted boy and girl outfits in 1955. 10", $40.00, 12", $45.00.

Pete and Repete (1951) showing box.

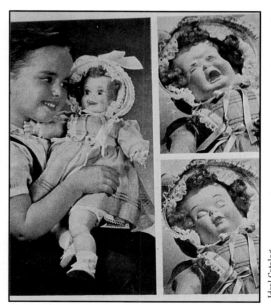

Trilby (1951) 18¾" Vinylite brand resin vinyl face and limbs, three-faced doll. Knob on top of head turns to show smiling, sleeping, and crying faces. Peach color cloth body, squeaks when pressed, blonde curly hair attached to bonnet, blue eye shadow, wears blue dress and bonnet. Pat. 1951. Mark: none, except for tag on wrist. $100.00.

Trilby (1951) showing her three faces.

Saralee

Courtesy Peggy Millhouse.

Saralee (1951 – 1953) 17" Vinyl head and limbs, stuffed cotton body, molded hair, brown sleep eyes with lashes or painted eyes, cries when tilted, organdy dress, cotton slip. Pat. 1952. Anthropologically correct "Negro" baby doll. Catalog #2300. Original price $7.50. Marks: C or G 17/IDEAL DOLL(on head). $200.00.

At Mrs. Roosevelt's reception for **Saralee** are Lester Granger, president of the National Urban League; David Rosenstein, president of Ideal Toy Corporation; Mrs. Eleanor Roosevelt, former First Lady; Dr. Ralph J. Bunche, Nobel Prize winner; Benjamin Franklin Michtom, board chairman Ideal Toy Corporation; and Abraham Katz, treasurer, Ideal Toy Corporation **(1951)**.

Courtesy Miriam Gittleson.

Examining model heads, which were never produced, for the **Saralee** line sculpted by Mrs. Sheila Burlingame are: Sara Lee Creech, Maxeda von Hesse, Walter White (president of the NAACP), Mrs. Eleanor Roosevelt, and Dr. Ralph Bunche. **(1951)**.

Bonny Braids

Courtesy Dorothy Alford. Photo by Gary Faulkner.

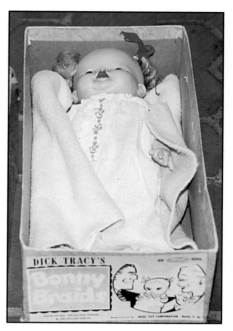

Bonny Braids (1951 – 1953) 14" vinyl head and Magic Skin latex body.

Bonny Braids Baby (1951 – 1953) 11½" and 14" (shown) Vinylite brand vinyl head, jointed arms, Magic Skin latex rubber one-piece body, open molded mouth with one tooth, painted yellow hair with two yellow saran pigtails on each side, painted blue eyes, coos when squeezed, wears long white gown and pink bed jacket, came with toothbrush and tube of Ipana toothpaste. Catalog #00010. Original price $6.98. Comic strip daughter of Dick Tracy & Tess Trueheart. Tagged dress and wrist tag. Marks: ©1951/Chi. Tribune/IDEAL DOLL/ U.S.A. (on neck). 1953 version dressed in organdy dress and has 3½" saran braids. Another 1953 version had vinyl body, sleep eyes, and walked. 11½", $175.00; 14", $200.00.

Bonny Braids (1951 – 1953) 14" Vinyl head and Magic Skin latex body in her blanket.

Courtesy Charlotte Klein.

Bonny Braids (1951 – 1953) Ideal publicity photo showing Miss Charlotte Klein, publicist for Ideal, dressed in nurse's uniform walking Bonny Braids in Central Park, New York, for a promotion for Gimbel's Department Store.

Ideal publicity photo showing Ideal officials meeting with Chester Gould, creator of Dick Tracy comic strip featuring Bonny Braids.

Courtesy Wenham Museum. Photo by Diane Buck.

Courtesy McMasters Doll Auctions.

Bonny Braids (1953 – 1955) 13½" Vinyl head, plastic walker body. Showing her box she came in. $195.00; MIB, $300.00.

Bonny Braids Walker (1953) 13½" Vinyl head, plastic body, turns her head when she walks, open/closed mouth with painted teeth, blue sleep eyes, yellow painted hair with two saran braids, dressed in flowered short dress. Catalog #2004. Advertised as "Now One-Year-Old Bonny Can Walk." Marks: COPR. 1951/CHICAGO TRIBUNE/IDEAL DOLL (on head); IDEAL DOLL/14 (on body). Toddler also came in a non-walking version with same head but different bodies. $150.00.

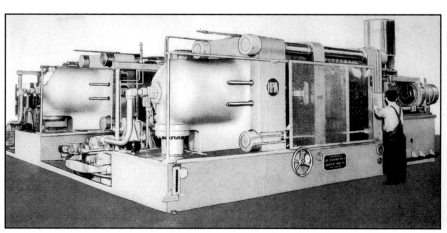

Ideal brochure.

Injection Molding Machine (1951). Used to make hard plastic dolls.

Saucy Walker

Saucy Walker (1951 – 1955) 16" and 22" (shown) All hard plastic (Hercules Acetate). Walks and turns head from side to side when arm is held. Flirty blue eyes, crier, two inset top teeth, holes in body for cry mechanism. Blonde, tosca, brunette, or red saran braided hair wig with bangs. Came with plastic curlers. Shows original box. Catalog #2007. Original price $15.98. Marks: IDEAL DOLL/W22 (on neck and back). No marks on clothing. Rare black Saucys have been seen. 22", $195.00; MIB, $350.00.

Courtesy Linda Paradis.

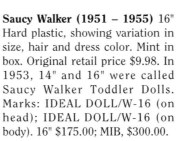

Saucy Walker (1951 – 1955) 16" Hard plastic, showing variation in size, hair and dress color. Mint in box. Original retail price $9.98. In 1953, 14" and 16" were called Saucy Walker Toddler Dolls. Marks: IDEAL DOLL/W-16 (on head); IDEAL DOLL/W-16 (on body). 16" $175.00; MIB, $300.00.

Courtesy Iva Mae M. Jones.

Saucy Walker (1951 – 1955) 22" Hard plastic. Marks: IDEAL DOLL/W-16 (on head); IDEAL DOLL/W-16 (on body).

Courtesy Diane Carpino.

Saucy Walker (1951 – 1955) 22" Hard plastic.

Courtesy Pauline Chantry.

Courtesy Cheryl A. Haisch.

Saucy Walker (1951 – 1955) 16" Hard plastic in printed cotton dress. Model #2006. Box #113/998.

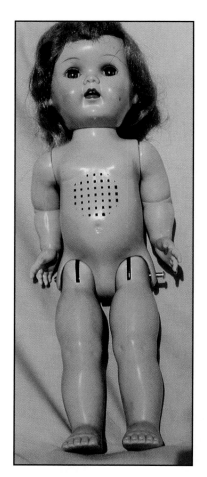

Saucy Walker (1951 – 1955) 16" Showing the crying and walker mechanism. Author's childhood doll.

Ideal ad.

Saucy Walker (1952).

At the Ideal factory dressing Saucy Walker (**1951**).

Courtesy Miriam Gittleson.

Courtesy Sally Minear. Photo by Evelyn Roudybush.

Saucy Walker Toddler (**1953**) 14" (shown) and 16". In 1953 14" and 16" were called Saucy Walker Toddler dolls. Original clothes. Catalog #2005 and #2006. $150.00.

Courtesy Nancy Shomo.

Saucy Walker Boy (**1953**) 22" All hard plastic (Hercules Acetate), same as Saucy Walker except wears boy's outfit and has saran wig with boy's hairstyle. Missing matching cap. Marks: IDEAL DOLL (on head); IDEAL DOLL (on body). Catalog #2008. $250.00.

Courtesy Marge Meisinger.

Saucy Walker "Big Sister" (**1954**) 25" Hard plastic walker, saran wig, flirty sleep eyes. Original price $19.95, given as premium from *Chicago Daily Tribune*. $300.00.

Courtesy Linda Pottle.

Ideal ad.

Saucy Walker Big Sister (**1955**) 25" Close-up, original burgundy coat. Flirty eyes, open mouth with two inset teeth, saran hair. Marks: IDEAL DOLL (on neck and back).

Saucy Walker (**1955 – 1956**) 14", 16", 19", 21" Vinyl head, hard plastic body, rooted saran hair, comes with Toni Play Wave Kit. Catalog #1141, #1161, #1191, #1211. 14", $135.00; 16", $150.00; 19", $170.00; 21", $190.00.

Courtesy Nancy Shomo.

Courtesy Nancy Shomo.

Saucy Walker (**1955 – 1956**) 14", 16" (shown), 19", 21" Vinyl head, hard plastic walker body, flirty eyes, crier, rooted saran hair. Marks: IDEAL DOLL/VP 17 (on head); IDEAL DOLL/W 16 (on body).

Saucy Walker (**1955 – 1956**). 14", 16" (shown), 19", 21" Vinyl head, hard plastic walker body, flirty eyes, crier, rooted saran hair. one-piece undies, slip attached to skirt of dress. Marks: IDEAL DOLL/VP17 (on head); IDEAL DOLL/W 16 (on body).

Courtesy Kerry Israels.

Hugee Girl (1952) 15" Vinyl head with oilcloth body, blue sleep eyes, open/closed mouth, molded curly hair. Marks: IDEAL DOLL/BC 16 (on head). $150.00.

Courtesy Wenham Museum. Photo by Diane Buck.

Joan Palooka (1953) 14" Vinylite plastic head, stuffed latex Magic Skin body, jointed Magic Skin arms and legs, yellow molded hair with topknot of yellow saran, blue painted eyes, open/closed mouth. Cartoon character daughter of Joe Palooka. Smells like baby powder, came with Johnson's Baby Powder and soap. Catalog #0014. Original price $6.98. Marks: ©1952/HAM FISHER/IDEAL DOLL (on head). $85.00.

Courtesy Susan Giradot.

Mysterious Yokum (1953) Li'l Abner's new baby boy, Li'l Honest Abe. Plastic head and body, Magic Skin latex arms and legs, painted eyes, molded hair with a forelock, wearing overalls with one suspender crossed over his chest, knit cap, and socks. Original price $2.98. $80.00.

Courtesy Nancy Schwartz.

Little Wingy (1953) 13" Vinyl head stuffed with cotton, plastic walker body, glued-on below the waist length saran wig, closed mouth, blue sleep eyes, dimples on cheeks. Face coated with phosphorescent paint to make doll glow in the dark. Little girl from Dick Tracy comic strip. Marks: CPR 1953 CHICAGO TRIBUNE IDEAL DOLL (on head); IDEAL/14 (on body). $200.00.

Ideal brochure.

Talkytot (1953) 25" Cloth doll with mask face and gold wool hair, dressed in plaid dress and hat, hand crank makes doll say phrases like "Rock-A-Bye Baby on the tree-top." $85.00.

Ideal Catalog.

Magic Flesh Vinyl Head Doll (1953) 16" Vinyl head, arms and legs, molded hair, cotton-filled body, sleep eyes, open mouth with upper and lower teeth, cry voice organdy dress and bonnet, unies, shoes and socks. Catalog #2490. $100.00.

Courtesy Millie Caliri.

Magic Flesh Vinyl Head Doll with Saran Wig (1953) 16" (shown), 18", 20", 22", 24" Geon™ polyvinyl head, vinyl limbs, oil cloth cotton-stuffed body, saran wig, blue sleep eyes, painted lower lashes, open/closed mouth, cry voice, shoes and socks not original, came dressed in organdy dress, bonnet, slip, undies, shoes and socks, with flower barrettes in hair. Came with plastic curlers. Catalog numbers: #2497, #2407, #2417, #2427, #2437. Marks: 16", 16/IDEAL DOLL. $125.00.

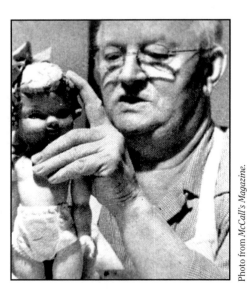

Photo from *McCall's Magazine*.

Bernard Lipfert (1953) Sculptor of many Ideal dolls for over 50 years including **Snoozie**, **Shirley Temple**, and **Betsy McCall**.

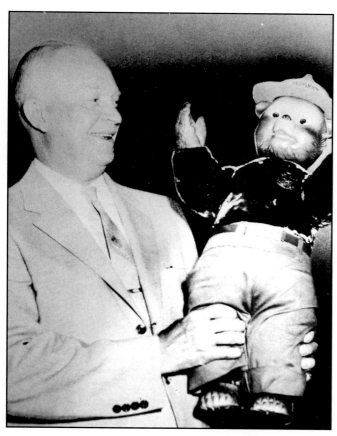

Ideal publication . Courtesy Mel Poretz.

President Dwight D. Eisenhower with **Smokey the Bear (1953)**.

Ideal Ad.

Smokey the Bear (**1953**) 18" and 25" (shown) Bakelite vinyl resins face and paws, rayon plush stuffed body, missing removable vinyl forest ranger hat, badge, and shovel. Symbol of U.S.A. National Forest Service. Wears Smokey belt, twill trousers. Came with Junior Forest Ranger kit including window stickers, certificate, letter from Smokey, stamps, blotter, bookmark, statement, membership card. Issued on the 50th anniversary of the "Teddy Bear" originated by Ideal. Original price: 18", $4.98, $6.98 (deluxe) and 25", $14.95 (deluxe). In 1957 a talking version recited fire prevention messages. 18", $100.00; 25", $135.00; Talking Version, $150.00.

Courtesy Marge Meisinger.

Butterick Sew-Easy Designing Set Mannequin (**1953**) 14" Solid vinyl mannequin of adult woman, molded blonde hair, came with Butterick patterns and sewing accessories. Catalog #8540. $65.00.

Ideal Catalog.

Peggy's Snap-On Magic Wardrobe (**1953 – 1955**) 5¼" Hard plastic doll with interchangeable wardrobe which snaps on and off. Wardrobe consists of two bathing suits, pajamas, two coats, hat, two school dresses, and party dress. Catalog number #3160. $45.00.

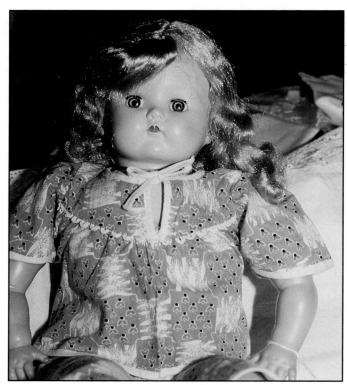

Courtesy Debra-lee Brule.

Plassie (**1950s**) Hard plastic head, vinyl arms, legs, cloth body, sleep eyes with lashes, mohair wig, crying voice. Reissue of 1942 doll. Marks: P-50/ IDEAL/MADE IN U.S.A. (on head) or IDEAL DOLL/MADE IN U.S.A. 3 2252077. $85.00.

Betsy Wetsy

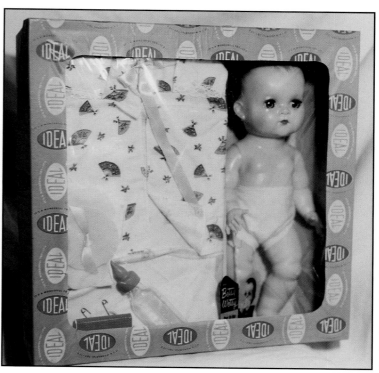

Betsy Wetsy® (**1954 – 1956**) 11½" Hard plastic (Celanese acetate) head, vinyl body and limbs, molded hair, sleep eyes. Drinks, wets, nose runs, water comes out of tear holes, cries when squeezed. Wearing diaper with layette consisting of bathrobe, bottle, soap, diaper pins, and diaper. Mint in box. Catalog #1001. Original price: $5.98. Marks: MADE IN U.S.A./ PAT.NO. 225207 (on head); IDEAL DOLL (on back). $100.00; MIB, $250.00.

Courtesy Eleanor Baker. Photo by Gary Faulkner.

Courtesy Eleanor Baker. Photo by Gary Faulkner.

Betsy Wetsy® (**1954 – 1956**) 13½" Hard plastic Celanese acetate head, soft vinyl body and limbs, wearing white dress and bonnet and curly caracul wig. Drinks, wets, cries, nose runs. In box with soap, bottle, tissues, clothespins, washcloth, diaper and pin, wearing booties. Marks: IDEAL DOLL/MADE IN U.S.A.(on head). $135.00; MIB, $285.00.

Betsy Wetsy® (**1954**) 13½" Hard plastic head, soft vinyl body. Marks: MADE IN U.S.A./Pat. No. 225207 (on head). Author's childhood doll.

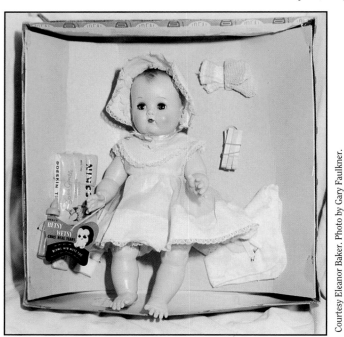

Courtesy Eleanor Baker. Photo by Gary Faulkner.

Betsy Wetsy® (**1954 – 1956**) 16" (shown) and 20" Hard plastic Celanese acetate head, soft vinyl body, drinks, wets, cries, nose runs. Molded or rooted curly wool hair. Wearing yellow dress and bonnet, in gift box with diapers, bottle, tissues, booties, and clothespins. Catalog #1011. Original price $9.98. Marks: 16/IDEAL DOLL/MADE IN USA(on head). 20" dressed in romper. 16", $150.00; MIB, $300.00; 20", $170.00; MIB, $325.00.

Courtesy Pam Keith. Photo by Gary Faulkner.

Betsy Wetsy® (**1954 – 1956**) 13½" Hard plastic head, vinyl body, drinks, wets, cries, nose runs, wearing diaper, t-shirt, with nine-piece layette in box including dress, bonnet, slip, diaper, baby powder, booties, bottle, soap, and clothespin. Catalog #1006. Original price: $7.98. Marks: 14/IDEAL DOLL/MADE IN USA. $135.00; MIB, $275.00.

Courtesy Dorothy Alford. Photo by Gary Faulkner.

Baby Big Eyes (**1954 – 1959**) 20" (shown), 23" soft vinyl head, vinyl arms and legs, curled separate fingers, vinyl coated soft body, blue sleep eyes with lashes, rooted curly blonde, red, or brunette saran wig, wearing pajamas and blanket, wears yellow, pink, blue, or green blanket and nightie. Also came in christening sacque. Catalog #0425. Original price $14.95. Marks: IDEAL DOLL/P6 (on head) or IDEAL DOLL/VS 18/20 (on head); IDEAL DOLL/P-19 (on back). 20", $65.00; 23", $85.00.

Ideal Catalog.

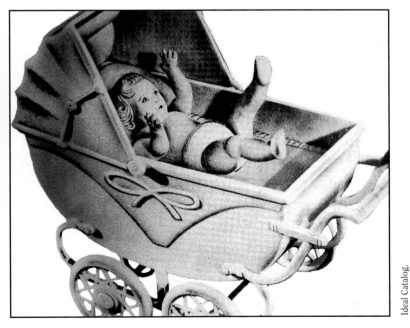

Ideal Catalog.

Pam's Pram (**1954**) 8" x 8¼" x 4¼" plastic baby carriage with plastic baby doll inside. When carriage is pushed, doll cries and moves its arms and legs. Doll has painted hair, features, and diaper. Catalog #4523. $35.00.

Large Gurlie Doll (**1954 – 1955**) 12" all plastic, jointed arms, sleep side glancing eyes, wig in assorted colors, can stand alone. Comes in cellophane bag. Catalog #3117. $25.00.

Courtesy Patty Massey.

Courtesy John Sonnier.

Posie (1954 – 1956) 17" and 23" (shown) Soft vinyl head, hard Celanese acetate plastic body, jointed bent knees, walker, rooted saran hair, flirty blue sleep eyes, walks, came with curlers, wears short dress. Pat. 1954. Catalog numbers #2650 and #2701. Original price $10.00 and $14.98. Marks: 17": IDEAL/ VP-17 (on head); IDEAL DOLL (on back); PAT.PENDING (on upper leg). 23": IDEAL DOLL/VP-23 (on head); IDEAL DOLL (on back); PAT. PENDING (on upper leg). 17", $125.00; 23", $150.00.

Posie (1954 – 1956) 17" and 23" all hard plastic. Flirty eyes and bending knees. Came with four pink curlers. Original price $15.98. Same face, body, and marks as Saucy Walker but with bending knees. Marks: IDEAL DOLL (on head); IDEAL DOLL (on back). 17", $150.00; 23", $200.00.

Courtesy Doris Blocker

Clarabelle (1954 – 1955) 16" (shown), 20" Mask face, soft stuffed cloth body, dressed in satin Clarabelle outfit. Missing noise box and attached horn. The clown from the Howdy Doody TV show, ©Kagran Corp. Catalog #7847. Original price $2.98. In 1955 also available with a vinyl face. $125.00.

Magic Lips (1955 – 1956) 23" Soft vinyl head and limbs, stuffed pink vinyl oilcloth body, rooted dark blonde or brown saran hair, blue sleep eyes, three lower teeth in open mouth, press her back she closes her lips, release she opens mouth with cooing sound, says "mama", wears flocked organdy dress, rayon slip, panties, plastic button shoes, comes with toothbrush, bottle, and curlers. Pat. 1955. Catalog #2350. Original price $14.98. Marks: None or IDEAL DOLL/T-25. 23", $130.00.

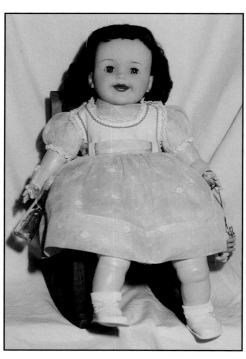

Courtesy Dorothy Alford. Photo by Gary Faulkner.

Ideal Catalog.

Davy Crockett and his horse (1955 – 1956) 4¾" x 5⅜" All plastic. Davy has painted features and sits astride his white stallion. Davy is dressed in simulated buckskin and wears a real coonskin cap. Can be removed from horse, holds bridle in hand. Catalog #3154. $50.00.

Campbell Kid Girl (1955) 8" Vinyl head, vinyl Magic Skin, one-piece body. Marks: CAMPBELL KID/MADE BY/IDEAL TOY CORP. $50.00.

Courtesy Judith Armitstead.

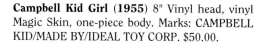

Ideal catalog.

Campbell Kids (1955 – 1957) 9½" Vinyl head, jointed arms, head swivels, one-piece Magic Skin vinyl soft stuffed body and legs. Boy and girl twins wearing chef's hats & aprons, painted eyes, molded painted hair. They coo when squeezed. Trademarks of Campbell Soup Company. Pat. 1955. Catalog #0100. Marks: CAMPBELL KID/MADE BY/IDEAL TOY CORP. $65.00.

Courtesy Carolyn Sharon.

Campbell Kid Girl (1950s) 8" All vinyl, molded hair, shoes and socks, jointed only at shoulder and neck. Marks: CAMPBELL KID/MADE BY/IDEAL TOY CORP.

Ideal Catalog.

Vinyl Doll with All Vinyl Body (**1955**) 16½" Vinyl head, molded hair, one-piece vinyl body, crying voice, sleep eyes, organdy dress and bonnet. Catalog #1290. $65.00.

Ideal Catalog.

Vinyl Doll with All Vinyl Body with Rooted Saran Hair (**1955**) 16½", 18½", 20½", 22½", 24½" Vinyl head, one-piece vinyl body, rooted saran hair, open mouth with teeth, crying voice, sleep eyes, organdy dress and bonnet. Came with card of curlers. Catalog numbers: #1295, #1305, #1315, #1325, #1335. $75.00.

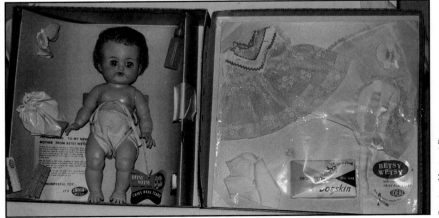

Courtesy Margaret Barron.

Betsy Wetsy® (**1956**) 11½", 13½" (shown), 16", 20" Soft vinyl head, vinyl body, rooted saran hair, drinks, wets, cries, sleep eyes. Came in layette or suitcase box (shown). Catalog numbers: #1025, #1026 (shown), #1027, #1020. Original price: $5.98, $7.98, $9.98. Marks of 13½", IDEAL DOLL/VW-2 (on head); and IDEAL/14 (on body). 11½", $50.00; 13½", $55.00; 16", $65.00; 20", $175.00; MIB; 16", $100.00.

Ideal Catalog.

Honeybunch (1956 – 1957) 15", 17", 19", 21", 23" (shown) Soft vinyl head, vinyl one-piece body and limbs stuffed with cotton. Rooted saran ponytail, sleep eyes, metal hole in back of neck for Ma-Ma voice. Dressed in pinafore dress or hat and coat. Catalog numbers: #1442, #1452, #1462, #1472, #1482. Marks on 15"": IDEAL DOLL/VP-15-2 (on head); IDEAL DOLL/VS 14 (on back). Also seen for 19", IDEAL DOLL/VP-19-2 (on head). $85.00.

Courtesy Kerry Israels.

Honeysuckle (1956 – 1957) 15", 17", 19", 21", 23" All soft vinyl with rooted brown saran wig, crying voice, sleep eyes with lashes, came in dress, christening gown or in wardrobe gift box. Catalog numbers: #1440, #1445, #1455, #1465, #1475, #1485. Marks: IDEAL DOLL (on head). $85.00.

Ideal brochure.

Twinkle Eyes (1957 – 1960) 17", 19", 21", 23", 25" Soft vinyl head and limbs, "rolling" flirty and sleep eyes, rooted saran ponytail, pinafore dress, and bonnet. Catalog numbers: #1459, #1469, #1479, #1489, #1499. Original price: $7.98, $9.98, $11.98, $13.98, $15.98. 17" and 19" also came in carrying case with accessories. 17", $65.00; 19", $75.00; 21", $85.00; 23", $95.00; 25", $105.00.

Courtesy Dave Koske.

Roy Rogers and Dave Koske (**circa 1957**) on a visit to the factory.
Ideal made plastic Roy Rogers horse, rider, and stagecoach.

Courtesy Anita Child.

David Rosenstein, Ben Michtom, Abe Katz at the 50th anniversary of Ideal Toy Co. (**1957**).

Courtesy Ruth Leif. Photo by Fred Leif.

Little Betsy Wetsy® (**1957**) 8" All vinyl, rooted saran hair, sleep eyes, drinks, and wets. Catalog #9600. Twelve outfits available separately. Marks: IDEAL DOLL/8 (on head and back), also seen IDEAL TOY CO./BW 9-4. $30.00; MIB, $55.00.

Courtesy Margaret Barron.

Little Betsy Wetsy® outfits (**1957**). Three of the 12 outfits available separately. $15.00.

9632 —
Corduroy overalls,
shirt, booties
. . . 2.00

9610 —
Romper,
bonnet, booties
. . . 1.00

9630 —-
Playsuit,
bonnet, booties
. . . 2.00

Little Betsy Wetsy® outfits (**1957**). As pictured in Ideal brochure.

Ideal Catalog.

Dolly Phone (**1957**) 15" soft vinyl head, felt or satin body, phone hand set serves as arms, bell on cord jingles, dial spins. Designed by puppeteer Bill Baird. $35.00.

J. Fred Muggs and Phoebe B. Beebe (**1957**) 15" vinyl face, hands, and shoes, pile plush body, dressed in assorted costumes. Comes in three different versions. $55.00.

Ideal Catalog.

Algy Doll and Algy Bear (**1957**) 10½" vinyl face and plush body with saran curls, painted features. Bear is 16" and has vinyl face with sleep eyes, plush body. Bear featured on TV's Ding Dong School. Non-allergenic materials, pat. 1951. Catalog #7152. Original price $4.98. $25.00.

Patti Prays (**1957**) 20" vinyl face and hands, stuffed cloth body and hat, plush hair, painted eyes, removable cotton nightie. Kneels, clasps hands, and recites bedtime prayer, "Now I lay me down to sleep" when wound. Catalog #7741. Original price $3.99. $55.00.

Ideal Catalog

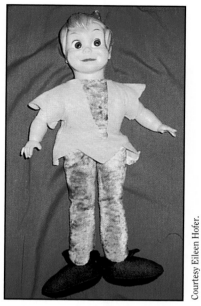

Courtesy Eileen Hofer.

Mighty Mouse (1957) 19" Vinyl head and hands and shoes. Plush body with satin cape and tights. Painted eyes. Has elastic string to make him fly. Doll also comes in either 11½" or 15" with a plush head, vinyl face, satin body and limbs, and cape. Terrytoon cartoon character, ©CBS Inc. $45.00.

Peter Pan (c. 1957) Vinyl head and arms, plush body, and felt feet. Marks: IDEAL TOY CORPORATION. $85.00.

15" Miss Revlon

Ideal Catalog.

Courtesy Chris's Collections, Chris & Joe Carrick.

Miss Revlon (1958 – 1959) 15" Vinyl with swivel waist, in Cherries A La Mode. $200.00.

Miss Revlon (1958 – 1959) 15" Vinyl with swivel waist, unusual flower print, no tag on dress.

Miss Revlon (1958 – 1959) 15" Vinyl, MIB. $350.00.

Miss Revlon (1958 – 1959) 15" Vinyl, blonde hair in blue and white striped dress.

Miss Revlon (1960) 15" Vinyl in black lingerie. 15", 18" and 20" were advertised in the Sears catalog in their black lingerie in 1960.

Courtesy Chris's Collections, Chris & Joe Carrick.

Miss Revlon (1958 – 1959) 15" Vinyl with "Ideal Doll" wrist tag.

Courtesy Susan Mobley.

Miss Revlon (1958 – 1959) 15" in outfit sold as a separate by Ideal. Hat has a bow in back.

18" Miss Revlon

Ideal Catalog.

Miss Revlon (1956 – 1959) 18" in brocade dress. Marks: VT-18/IDEAL DOLL. Dresses for the 18" and 20" dolls had ribbon tags on the outside front, none inside. 18", $175.00.

Courtesy Janice Aranoff.

Miss Revlon (1956 – 1959) 18" Vinyl, unusual cotton dress also came in yellow. Marks: VT-18/IDEAL DOLL.

Courtesy Jean Swanson.

Miss Revlon (1956 – 1959) 18" Vinyl, with lovely yellow outfit and hat. Doll in red dress is not Ideal.

Courtesy Jeanne Melanson.

Miss Revlon (1956 – 1959) 18" Most common size, narrow pinched-in face, left eye lower than right eye, long pink gown with pink pearl necklace and drop earrings. Some larger VT-18s have painted legs. Marks: IDEAL DOLL/VT-18 (on neck).

Courtesy Zelda Cushner.

Miss Revlon in box **(1957)** 18" Blonde hair, print dress, and matching reverse jacket #0940.

Courtesy Paula Manburg.

Miss Revlon (1956 – 1959) 18" in velvet top dress with red skirt, matches a Little Miss Revlon outfit.

Courtesy Jeanne Melanson.

Miss Revlon (1956 – 1959) 18" face comparison. Doll on left with longer face is from later production.

20" Miss Revlon

Ideal Catalog.

Miss Revlon (1956 – 1959) 20" in pink dress with white overlay lace.

Courtesy Dorothy Alford. Photo by Gary Faulkner.

Miss Revlon (1956 – 1959) 20" Vinyl Magic Touch skin head, vinyl teenage strung body, jointed at shoulders, waist, hips, and knees, high heel feet, rooted saran hair, sleep eyes with lashes, wearing navy "Cherries a la Mode" dress on left and dress from "Cherries a la Mode" series on right; comes with pierced ears with pearl earrings, pearl necklace, nylons, and hat. "Cherries a la Mode" dress also came in pink. Catalog numbers: #0945, #0965, #0985. Original price: $11.95, $15.95, $24.98. Marks: VT 20/IDEAL DOLL. 20", $200.00; MIB, $500.00.

Courtesy Sharon Jahraus.

Courtesy Margi Harris. Photo by Susan Mobley.

Miss Revlon (1956 – 1959) 20" vinyl with swivel waist, wearing nylon dress. Gloves, watch, and flowers at waist not original.

Miss Revlon (1956 – 1959) 20" vinyl in "Kissing Pink" striped pink and white dress with crinoline slip and pearl earrings and necklace.

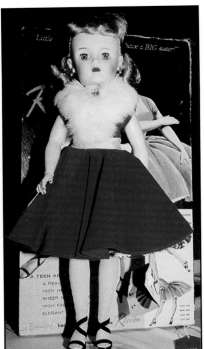

Courtesy Evelyn Roudybush.

Miss Revlon (**1956 – 1959**) 20" Wearing red velveteen dress with white fur stole, stockings, and high heel shoes.

Courtesy Mary Kangas.

Miss Revlon (1956 – 1959) 20" Hard plastic and vinyl. Doll on left wearing bridal outfit, doll on right wearing polka-dot dress.

Courtesy Anita Maxwell.

Miss Revlon (1957) 20" All vinyl, tosca hair, showing original slip that has matching panties.

23" Miss Revlon

Miss Revlon (1956 – 1958) 23" Vinyl, wearing "Queen of Diamonds" outfit #0990 with rabbit stole, rhinestone earrings, necklace, and ring. Also came in pink. The 23" dolls' dresses were untagged. Marks: VT-22/ IDEAL DOLL. 23", $275.00.

Courtesy Jeanne Melanson

Miss Revlon (1956 – 1958) 23"
Wearing lace dress with puffed
sleeves.

Courtesy Kathy Barna.

Miss Revlon (1956 – 1958)
23" Wearing strapless gown in
blue brocade with black velvet
top from the "Revlon Glamour
doll collection" of 10 different
glamorous dresses and gowns.

Courtesy Kathy Barna.

26" Miss Revlon

Courtesy Chris's Collections, Chris and Joe Carrick.

Miss Revlon (1957) 26" "Glamour doll," all vinyl
wearing navy with white lace-trimmed dress
#0933. These Glamour doll outfts only available in
1957 in 23" and 26" sizes with 10 separate fancier
fashions. Very rare size. Marks: VT-25/ IDEAL
DOLL. The 26" dolls' dresses were untagged.
$350.00.

Miss Revlon Walker

Courtesy Chris's Collections, Chris and Joe Carrick.

Courtesy Chris's Collections, Chris and Joe Carrick.

Miss Revlon (1959) 18" (shown on left) and 20" in Bridal Dress has a walker mechanism; push one leg forward it disengages, then re-engages when returned to normal position. Also has unusual arms. A rare doll. Marks: IDEAL DOLL/VT-18 (on head); none on the back. (On right) 18" doll in brown dress. Walker, $250.00.

Miss Revlon (1956 – 1957) 20" Straight leg walker wearing pink Cherries a la Mode.

Courtesy Zendelle Bouchard.

Miss Revlon (1957) 18" close-up of walker mechanism. Marks: IDEAL DOLL/VT-18 (on head), no marks on back. Marks: "18" near right armpit.

Courtesy Chris's Collections, Chris and Joe Carrick.

Courtesy Zendelle Bouchard.

Miss Revlon arm comparison. The Walking Doll on left has unusual thicker arms and hands. Perhaps they are the same as the arms on the Harriet Hubbard Ayer doll. Marks on arm: 18 (inside arm near armpit). Marks: IDEAL DOLL/VT-18 (on head); none on the back.

Miss Revlon (1957) 18" with walking mechanism. Has an unusual face, wide-set eyes and heavy eyebrows, pearl earrings, and unusual long gown of yellow taffeta and tulle that has Ideal tag instead of Miss Revlon tag on outside.

Miss Revlon – Other

Miss Revlon (1957) Ideal ad. A 26" size was available only in 1957.

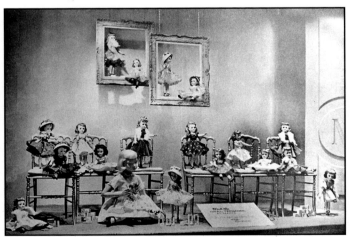

Ideal publicity photo. Courtesy Mel Poretz.

Miss Revlon window display **(1956)**.

Courtesy Jeanne Melanson.

Miss Revlon (**1959**) Body comparison of 15" and 23" dolls.

Miss Revlon with bent-knees. An unusual doll. One Revlon Doll offered by Sears in 1958 called the "5th Avenue" version was dressed in slacks and a cotton fleece jacket and had the bent-knee mechanism. $275.00.

Courtesy Chris's Collections, Chris and Joe Carrick.

Miss Revlon 17" Unusual size doll. Face slightly different, head marked VT-18 but shorter, unmarked arms and legs. Shown with 18" doll on left.

Crown Princess

Ideal Catalog.

Crown Princess (1957) 10½" All vinyl, swivel waist with rooted hair, came dressed in lingerie or in her royal cape and ballgown. All came with tiaras. Catalog #0800. Original price: $2.98. Marks: none. $100.00.

Crown Princess (1957) 10½" All vinyl with hard vinyl body and legs, soft flexible arms and head, high heel feet, non-pierced ears. Body is non-strung, limbs are flanged into body. Notice nylons and box. Came with a tiara. Catalog #0800-blonde. Swivel waist. Marks: 10½ R (inside right and left legs).

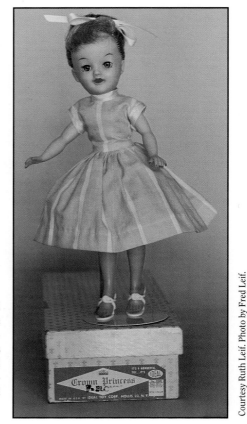

Courtesy Ruth Leif. Photo by Fred Leif.

Courtesy Ruth Leif. Photo by Fred Leif.

Crown Princess (1957) 10½" All vinyl with hard vinyl body and legs, soft flexible arms and head, high heel feet. Non-pierced ears. Body is non-strung, limbs are just inserted into body. Came with a tiara. Catalog #0800-blonde. Swivel waist. Marks: none.

Ideal Catalog.

Crown Princess (1957) 10½" All vinyl, swivel waist. This is the Crown Princess in Travel Case #0880 which comes with doll in royal cape, clothing, stockings, shoes, purse, hangers. Travel case also available separately #0889.

Comparison of **Crown Princess (1957)** and **Little Miss Revlon (1958).** Notice Crown Princess is taller and has different face.

Little Miss Revlon (1958)

Courtesy Jan Aranoff.

Courtesy Kathleen Tornikoski.

Little Miss Revlon (1958) 10½" in #9000 her "Formfit" bra and girdle, high heel shoes, and earrings. Marks: IDEAL VT-10½ (on head). $100.00.

Little Miss Revlon (1959) 10½" All vinyl with later Style Show box. Wearing #9023 Lounging outfit. Marks: IDEAL TOY CORP/VT-10½ (on head).

Ideal brochure.

Ideal brochure.

Little Miss Revlon (1958) 10½" in #9024 Knit Dress with stole, petticoat, shoes, purse. Original price, $2.00. Outfit MIB, $35.00.

Little Miss Revlon (1958) 10½" in #9030 Ice Skater outfit with skating shoes and hose, hat. Original price, $3.00.

Ideal brochure.

Little Miss Revlon (1958) 10½" in #9031 Prom Formal with crinoline, flowers, shoes. Original price, $3.00.

Ideal brochure

Little Miss Revlon (1958) 10½" in #9034 Taffeta Formal with crinoline, shoes. Original price, $3.00.

Little Miss Revlon (1958) 10½" in #9040 Bridal outfit with crinoline, flowers, shoes. Original price, $4.00.

Ideal brochure.

Little Miss Revlon (1958) 10½" in #9051 Scotch Dress with beret and plaid sash. Original price, $1.50.

Ideal brochure.

Little Miss Revlon (1958) 10½" in #9052 Cotton Plaid Dress with white lace around shoulders, with panty. Original price, $1.50.

Ideal brochure.

Little Miss Revlon (1958) 10½" in #9054 Halter Dress, black velvet halter, red bottom, with panty. Miss Revlon has same outfit.

Ideal brochure.

Little Miss Revlon (1958) 10½" in #9055 Raincoat with hood, boots, tote bag. Original price, $1.50.

Ideal brochure.

Little Miss Revlon (1958) 10½" in #9060 3-piece Playsuit with shoes, hat, toreador pants, sleeveless top, tie-on skirt. Original price, $2.50.

Ideal brochure.

Little Miss Revlon (1958) 10½" in #9061 Toreador outfit with blouse, shoes, and long waist sash. Original price, $2.50.

Ideal brochure.

Little Miss Revlon (1958) 10½" in #9070 Lassie Wool Coat with trimmed hat, purse. Original price, $3.50.

Little Miss Revlon (1959)

Little Miss Revlon (1959) 10½" in #9105 Torso Dress, daisy print dress with cowl collar from the School Series. Original price, $1.50. Outfit MIB $35.00.

Courtesy Jan Aranoff.

Little Miss Revlon (1959) 10½" in #9105 Torso Dress, showing print variation.

Courtesy Tricia Gullingsrud.

Courtesy Tricia Gullingsrud.

Little Miss Revlon (1959) 10½" in #9105 Torso Dress, showing print variation.

Little Miss Revlon (1959) 10½" in #9105 Torso Dress, showing print variation in pink.

Little Miss Revlon (1959) 10½" in #9114 School Dress, solid gold dress with design across chest from the School Series. Original price, $1.50.

Courtesy Tricia Gullingsrud.

Little Miss Revlon (1959) 10½" in three color versions of #9115 Polka Dot dress. Original price, $1.50.

Courtesy Jan Aranoff.

Courtesy Tricia Gullingsrud.

Little Miss Revlon (1959) 10½" in #9116 Calypso Blouse and skirt with crinoline, flowers. White blouse and a solid color skirt with rick-rack. Original price, $3.00. The skirt is tagged and came with the blouse which is not tagged.

Little Miss Revlon (1959) 10½" in #9116 Calypso blouse and skirt in variation of yellow blouse and print skirt. Variations seen are a solid color skirt and bodysuit for the blouse. Also the solid color skirt comes with variations of rick-rack colors.

Little Miss Revlon (1959) 10½" in #9117 Visiting Outfit with crinoline, hat, solid white ruffled blouse with striped skirt. Original price, $3.50.

Courtesy Tricia Gullingsrud.

Little Miss Revlon (1959) 10½" in #9118 Traveling Outfit with crinoline, hat, polka dot dress with rick-rack. Original price, $3.50.

Courtesy Tricia Gullingsrud.

Little Miss Revlon (1959) 10½" in #9119 Jumper with blouse underneath. Original price, $1.50

Ideal brochure.

Little Miss Revlon (1959) 10½" in #9120 Striped Dress with shoes, stockings, and purse. Original price, $2.00. Notice early diamond-shaped Little Miss Revlon box.

Courtesy Lee Collins.

Courtesy Jan Aranoff.

Little Miss Revlon (1959) 10½" in #9121 Striped School Dress with slip, shoes, and purse $2.00. Decorated belt. Missing purse.

Courtesy Jan Aranoff.

Little Miss Revlon (1959) 10½" in #9122 Party Dress with shoes, stockings, red purse. Short sleeve dress with ribbon around edge of shirt and bodice. Original price, $2.00.

Courtesy Jan Aranoff.

Little Miss Revlon (1959) 10½" in #9123 School Dress with shoes, stockings, purse. Original price, $2.50.

Courtesy Tricia Gullingsrud.

Little Miss Revlon (1959) 10½" in #9123 School dress in blue color variation with shoes, stockings, purse. Original price, $2.50. Notice Little Miss Revlon's hard-to-find original bob hairstyle.

Ideal brochure.

Little Miss Revlon (1959) 10½" in #9126 Pinafore with shoes, stockings, purse (clear net pinafore over dress with white pattern). #9127 Pinafore with shoes, stockings, purse (clear net pinafore over solid dress). Original price of each outfit, $3.00.

Ideal brochure.

Little Miss Revlon (1959) 10½" in #9130 Sailor Outfit with hat, solid color blue dress with snaps with middy collar. No tag, center hole starburst snap. Original price, $2.00.

Little Miss Revlon (1959) 10½" in #9131 Print Dress with rick-rack down front of bodice. Original price, $1.00.

Courtesy Jan Aranoff.

Little Miss Revlon (1959) 10½" in #9141 Sunday outfit with crinoline (striped skirt with solid top with tie and hat with netting), missing hat. Original price, $3.50

Courtesy Jan Aranoff.

Little Miss Revlon (1959) 10½" in #9142 Princess Style outfit with crinoline. Missing hat and purse. Original price, $4.00.

Ideal brochure.

Little Miss Revlon (1959) 10½" in #9143 velvet sheath with hat, purse. Original price, $3.50.

Ideal brochure.

Little Miss Revlon (1959) 10½" in #9157 lace formal (light color bodice with dark lace skirt) with shoes, stockings.

Courtesy Jan Aranoff.

Little Miss Revlon (1959) 10½" in #9158 nylon formal (print skirt). Original price, $4.00.

Courtesy Tricia Gullingsrud.

Little Miss Revlon (1959) 10½" in #9159 Debutante Gown (with black lace apron) with crinoline, flowers. Original price, $4.50. This is a variation on the skirt, which is tagged. Two other variations have been seen.

Courtesy Jan Aranoff.

Little Miss Revlon (1959) 10½" in #9160 Taffeta formal with shoes, stockings. Same as Miss Revlon's pink gown. Original price, $4.00

Courtesy Jeanne Melanson.

Little Miss Revlon (1959) 10½" in #9170 debutante bridal gown.

Ideal brochure.

Little Miss Revlon (1959) 10½" in #9171 Bridesmaid Outfit with hat, flowers, shoes, stockings. #9172 Bridal with shoes, stockings (with hair netting). Original price of each outfit, $4.50.

Ideal brochure.

Little Miss Revlon (1959) 10½" in #9176 Hostess Gown with matching robe. Original price, $3.00.

Ideal brochure.

Little Miss Revlon (1959) 10½" in #9177 Shorty Nightgown. Original price, $1.00.

Courtesy Lee Collins.

Little Miss Revlon (1959) 10½" #9174 Pajamas. Original price, $1.50.

Little Miss Revlon (1959) 10½" in #9179 Lounging Pajamas. Original price, $2.00.

Ideal brochure.

Little Miss Revlon (1959) 10½" in #9205 Coolie Beach Outfit, playsuit with sleeveless wrapper and cloth coolie hat with dark border, with sunglasses. Original price, $3.00.

Courtesy Lee Collins.

Little Miss Revlon (1959) 10½" in #9207 TV Lounging Outfit, diamond shape patterned top with solid ribbed pants, with sunglasses. Came in yellow or red. Original price, $2.50.

Ideal brochure.

Little Miss Revlon (1959) 10½" in #9208 Pedal Pusher Outfit with sunglasses. #9209 Jeans and shirt with hat. Original price for each outfit, $2.50.

Ideal brochure.

Little Miss Revlon (1959) 10½" in #9210 Skirt and Blouse with shoes, stockings, and purse (print skirt with white blouse). Original price, $2.50. #9212 Sweater and Skirt Outfit with shoes, stockings, purse (felt skirt). Original price, $3.00.

Courtesy Jan Aranoff.

Little Miss Revlon (1959) 10½" in #9211 Sunsuit, shorts with shirt and coolie hat. Original price, $2.50.

Ideal brochure.

Little Miss Revlon (1959) 10½" in #9215 Two-piece Playsuit (shorts with short sleeve skirt). Original price, $1.00.

Courtesy Jan Aranoff.

Little Miss Revlon (1959) 10½" in #9216 Sun Dress and Bonnet. Original price, $1.50.

Ideal brochure.

Little Miss Revlon (1959) 10½" in #9218
Two-Piece Pajama set, dark toreador length
pants, A-line dotted top. Original price, $1.00.

Ideal brochure.

Little Miss Revlon (1959) 10½" in #9240
Checked coat, hat, purse. Original price, $3.00.

Ideal brochure.

Little Miss Revlon (1959) 10½" in #9241 Flared
Woolen Coat. Original price, $2.00.

Ideal brochure.

Little Miss Revlon (1959) 10½" in #9249
Negligee Set with shoes, curlers. Original
price, $3.00.

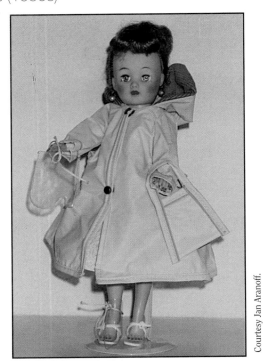

Courtesy Jan Aranoff.

Little Miss Revlon (1959) 10½" in #9252 Raincoat, clear plastic boots, tote bag. Raincoat was solid color or print. Original price, $2.00.

Courtesy Jan Aranoff.

Little Miss Revlon (1959) 10½" in #9254 Five-Piece Striped Suit with hat (striped car coat length coat, straight skirt). Original price, $4.00.

Courtesy Tricia Gullingsrud.

Little Miss Revlon (1959) 10½" in #9255 Five-Piece Redingote Outfit, polka-dot sheath with polka-dot coat lining, hat, purse, and belt. Original price, $3.50.

Ideal brochure.

Little Miss Revlon (1959) 10½" in #9256 Nurse Outfit with cap, shoes, stockings. Original price, $3.00.

Little Miss Revlon (1959) 10½" in #9257 Artist's Out-fit with beret, pedal pushers, smock, and shoes. Origi-nal price, $3.00. Showing two color variations.

Courtesy Tricia Gullingsrud.

Little Miss Revlon (1959) 10½" in #9258 Balle-rina Outfit with shoes, flowers. Original price, $2.00.

Ideal Brochure.

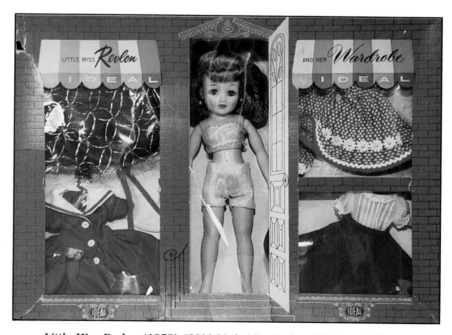

Little Miss Revlon (1959) #9010 Little Miss Revlon Gift Box (Doll & 4 outfits). Retail price $8.00. Miss Revlon Gift Set. Two of the dresses (the red knit and the navy felt skirt) are tagged: IDEAL (in an oval) Toy Corp./HOLLIS, N.Y. (inside outfit). However, two of the outfits (the black dress and the blue middy) are not tagged. MIB set, $250.00.

Courtesy Sharon Kriby.

Little Miss Revlon (1959) #9289 Little Miss Revlon Travel Case. Also available in 1958. $45.00.

9285	Eyeglasses (assorted colors)	.25
9286	Set of six hangers	.30
9299	Little Miss Revlon Doll stand	.60
9280	Crinolines (set of 2)	1.00
9284	Shoes and stockings (2 pair ea.)	1.00
9287	Hat in hat box	1.00

Little Miss Revlon (1959) #9280-9299 Accessories available for Little Miss Revlon.

Little Miss Revlon (1959) 10½" in unidentified untagged black strapless ballgown that came in Gift Box. Has black snap with four holes which can be sewn in back.

Little Miss Revlon (1959) 10½" Unidentified tagged red and white knit dress with scarf that came in Gift Box. Has circle dot starburst snap.

Little Miss Revlon (1959) 10½" unidentified tagged blue felt skirt and white blouse that came in Gift Box. Skirt has silver round circle snap that shows material in the middle.

Little Miss Revlon (1959) Store display of outfits from that year.

Ideal brochure . Courtesy Rita Dubas.

Courtesy Tricia Gullingsrud.

Ideal Catalog.

LITTLE MISS Revlon ACCESSORIES

9285-8	Eyeglasses	$ .10
9299-9	Doll Stands	.60
9380-9	Crinolines (2 in a box)	1.00
9284-1	Shoes and Stockings (2 pair each)	1.00

9354-2 Strapless Percale Print Dress, Net Overskirt, Panties outfit only retail $1.50.

9427-6 Felt Coat with Knit Collar and Hat Trim, Purse outfit only retail $2.00

Little Miss Revlon (1959 – 1960) 10½" in #9354-2 Strapless percale print dress, net overskirt, panties. Original price, $1.50.

Little Miss Revlon (1960) #9354 Strapless Percale print dress and #9427-6 Felt coat with knit collar and hat trim, purse. Also lists accessories that are available #9285 Eyeglasses, #9299 Doll Stands, #9380 Crinolines, #9284 Shoes and Stockings (2 pair each).

Courtesy Tricia Gullingsrud.

Ideal Catalog.

Little Miss Revlon (1959 – 1960) 10½" in #9357-5 Strapless Taffeta Party dress, panties. Original price, $1.50. Dress is tagged, dark purple variation showing lace variation around collar. Hat not original to outfit.

Little Miss Revlon (1959 – 1960) #9357-5 Strapless Taffeta Party Dress, #9350-0 Two-Piece Cotton Print Sleeping Outfit and #9422-7 Cotton Striped Dress and matching stole.

Courtesy Jan Aranoff.

Little Miss Revlon (1959 – 1960) 10½" in #9364 Bridal Outfit with flowers, pearls, and crinoline. The top is identical to the catalog but there is silver rick-rack instead of lace on skirt. Veil and flowers are original. Original price, $4.00.

Ideal Catalog.

Little Miss Revlon (1959 – 1960) #9420 Rick-Rack Cotton School dress, original price, $1.00 (also available in 1960); #9431 Velvet Cocktail Suit, original price, $3.00; and (1959 – 1960) #9360 Ice Skating Outfit, sweater, skates, leotard, leopard print skirt, and headband, original price, $3.00.

Courtesy Tricia Gullingsrud.

Little Miss Revlon (1958 – 1960) 10½" in #9420-1 Rick-Rack Cotton School Dress, original price, $1.00; and #9350-0 Two-Piece Cotton Print Sleeping Outfit, original price, $1.00. Outfit on right is tagged but unidentified and shown in the 1958 Sears Christmas catalog, green hat not original.

Ideal Catalog.

Little Miss Revlon (1960) #9421 Blue denim outfit, plaid short sleeve blouse, original price, $1.50; #9425 Cotton check bolero outfit, original price, $2.50; and **(1959 – 1960)** #9361 Velvet flared coat, white fur hat, and muff. Original price, $3.00.

Courtesy Chris's Collections, Chris and Joe Carrick.

Little Miss Revlon (1958 – 1960) 10½" in unidentified tagged pink gown.

Courtesy Tricia Gullingsrud.

Courtesy Tricia Gullingsrud.

Little Miss Revlon (1959) 10½" in two unidentified outfits. Coat and dress are tagged. Pants outfit is untagged but pictured in Wards 1959 catalog. Could be a variation of #9218 Two-Piece Pajama Set.

Little Miss Revlon (1958 – 1960) 10½" in unidentified tagged black top with check skirt dress.

Courtesy Valerie Myers.

Courtesy Valerie Myers.

Little Miss Revlon (1958 – 1960) 10½" in unidentified tagged full skirt in a taffeta material with navy blue iridescent checks with some gray. Navy blue bolero type jacket of shiny iridescent material as in the checks on the skirt. The blouse is a thin dotted swiss material. Red satin hat has a navy/white trim piece that matches the jacket and skirt.

Little Miss Revlon (1958 – 1960) 10½" in unidentified tagged outfit print pedal pushers and white blouse.

Courtesy Tricia Gullingsrud.

Courtesy Tricia Gullingsrud.

Little Miss Revlon (1958 – 1960) 10½" in unidentified dress with no tag. Similar to Torso Dress #9105. Hat goes to outfit #9240.

Little Miss Revlon (1958 – 1960) 10½" in two unidentified tagged dresses.

Courtesy Tricia Gullingsrud.

Little Miss Revlon (1958 – 1960) 10½" in unidentified tagged yellow ballgown.

Courtesy Tricia Gullingsrud.

Little Miss Revlon (1958 – 1960) 10½" in four unidentified outfits.
Three outfits on left are untagged. Red print outfit is shown in the 1959
Sears Christmas catalog. One on right is tagged and shown in the 1958
Sears Christmas catalog.

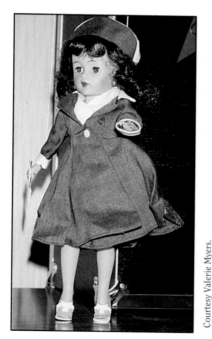

Courtesy Valerie Myers.

Little Miss Revlon (1958 – 1960) 10½" in
unidentified tagged brown coat and hat.

Courtesy Valerie Myers.

Little Miss Revlon (1958 – 1960) 10½" in unidentified tagged blue velvet coat and white fur hat and
muff.

Little Miss Revlon (1958 – 1960) 10½"
in unknown number tagged striped blue
and white dress.

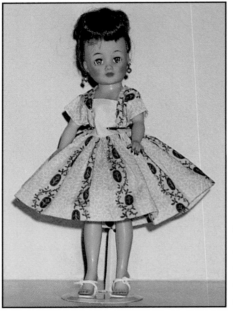

Little Miss Revlon (1958 – 1960) 10½" in unknown
number tagged blue print dress with white V-inset front.

Other 1958 Dolls

Photo by Anthony L. Colella.

Baby Jesus (1958) 8½" Vinyl infant with jointed head and arms, molded hair, molded swaddling cloth, inset brown glass eyes, painted teeth in smiling mouth. Came in maroon book-shaped box called "The Most Wonderful Story." Marks: none. $55.00.

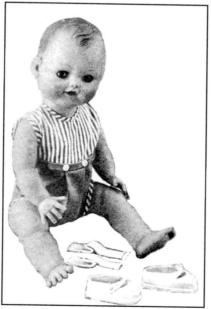

Sears catalog.

Baby Coos (1958) 19", 21", 24" All vinyl, sleep eyes, molded hair, fully jointed, makes cooing sound. Wears one-piece playsuit. Sears exclusive. Original price, $4.98 – 8.98. $65.00.

Shirley Temple

Courtesy Anita Child.

Shirley Temple Black, the actress, with Lionel Weintraub (c. 1957), combing Miss Revlon's hair.

Courtesy Anita Child.

Shirley Temple Black with Abraham M. Katz, Benjamin M. Michtom, and David Rosenthal (c. 1957).

THE FAMOUS
Shirley Temple
DOLL

with a fabulous wardrobe collection

Shirley Temple (1958) Ideal brochure showing Shirley Temple Black the actress with the new vinyl Shirley Temple doll.

Courtesy Mel Poretz.

Shirley Temple (1958) prototype in Ideal publicity photo.

12" Shirley Temple (1958)

Courtesy McMasters Doll Auctions.

Shirley Temple (1958) 12" Dressed in slip, mint in box. 12", $250.00.

Courtesy Donna Carr.

Shirley Temple (1958) #9501 Two-Piece Pajama Set, solid red top with striped cuffs, striped pants. Original price, $1.50. MIB outfits, $55.00.

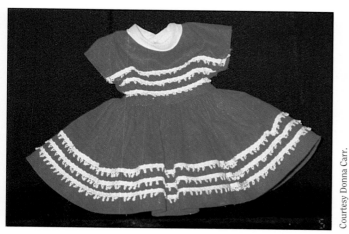

Courtesy Donna Carr.

Shirley Temple (1958) #9503 Cotton dress with loop detailing on bodice and around the bottom of skirt, came with petticoat and purse. Original price, $2.00.

Courtesy Donna Carr.

Shirley Temple (1958) #9504 Bolero Dress with petticoat and purse. Came in red or blue. Different prints seen in skirt. Original price, $2.00.

Ideal brochure.

Shirley Temple (1958) #9505 Quilted housecoat in pink or blue. Original price, $2.00.

Ideal brochure.

Shirley Temple (1958) #9506 Insignia Dress (navy blue) with petticoat and purse. Original price, $2.00.

Ideal brochure.

Shirley Temple (1958) #9507 Striped Percale Pinafore with white yoke trim and purse. Original price, $2.00.

Shirley Temple (1958) #9509 White or yellow dress with embroidery trim with petticoat and purse. Original price, $2.00.

Shirley Temple (1958) #9510 Multicolor Belted Raincoat with attached hood, tote bag. Original price, $1.50.

Shirley Temple (1958) #9525 Overall Outfit with shirt and hat. Original price, $2.50.

Ideal brochure.

Shirley Temple (1958) #9526 Pedal Pusher outfit with plaid cuffs and shirt, eyeglasses. Original price, $2.50.

Ideal brochure.

Shirley Temple (1958) #9527 Two-piece Playsuit Outfit with purse. Original price, $2.50.

Shirley Temple (1958) #9530 Bolero Dress with navy/red trim with petticoat, hat with veil, and purse. Original price, $2.00.

Shirley Temple (1958) #9532 Nylon Party Dress with hat, petticoat, and purse in assorted colors. Original price, $3.00.

Ideal brochure.

Shirley Temple (1958) #9535 Wool Flared Coat in assorted colors with velvet beret, muff, collar trim. Original price, $4.00.

Ideal brochure.

Shirley Temple (1958 – 1959) 12" Wearing unknown number fleece coat outfit shown in Spiegel's 1958 Christmas catalog.

Courtesy Iva Mae M. Jones.

Shirley Temple (1959) In TV Wardrobe package with handle on top. Showing outfit, right front, red print jumper dress which is shown in Sears 1958 Christmas catalog.

Courtesy Veronica Phillips.

12" Shirley Temple (1959)

Shirley Temple (1959) in outfits #9540 – #9564 shown on back of boxes from separate outfits. Prices for outfits ranged from $1.50 to $3.00. Dressed dolls ranged from $5.50 to $7.00.

Shirley Temple (1959) in #9541 cotton knit two-piece pajamas.

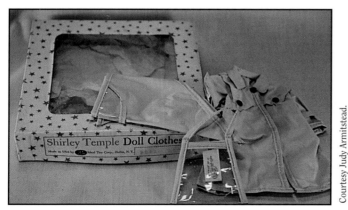

Shirley Temple (1959) #9540 Raincoat showing earlier "star" box.

Shirley Temple (1959) showing box for outfit #9541. Later box.

Ideal publicity photo courtesy Rita Dubas.

Shirley Temple (1959) #9542 School Dress with white apron.

Courtesy Donna Carr.

Shirley Temple (1959) #9543 Sailor Dress, short blue dress with red stars and middy, white sailor hat, red Shirley purse.

Courtesy Audrey Fletcher.

Shirley Temple (1959) #9545 Scotch Dress, plaid with sash and (1960) #9717 Nylon Visiting Dress.

Ideal publicity photo courtesy Rita Dubas.

Shirley Temple (1959) #9546 Embroidered Pinafore in assorted colors, panty, purse.

Ideal publicity photo courtesy Rita Dubas.

Shirley Temple (1959) #9547 Heidi outfit with checked skirt.

Courtesy Veronica Phillips.

Shirley Temple (1959) #9549 Nylon Visiting Dress in assorted colors, panty, purse, petticoat.

Courtesy Audrey Fletcher.

Shirley Temple (1959) #9550 Rebecca of Sunny-brook Farm overalls and #9564 Capt. January outfit.

Courtesy Donna Carr.

Shirley Temple (1959) #9551 Red velvet jumper with two flowers at waist, white nylon sleeves and collar, panty, purse.

Courtesy Audrey Fletcher.

Shirley Temple (1959) #9561 Ice Skater Outfit with matching hatband, replaced skates.

Courtesy Iva Mae M. Jones.

Shirley Temple (1959) #9562 Nylon Party Dress with hat, yellow, MIB.

Courtesy Iva Mae M. Jones.

Shirley Temple (1959) #9562 Nylon Party Dress, blue color variation, with hat, purse, shoes, pearl necklace in assorted colors.

Ideal publicity photo courtesy Rita Dubas.

Shirley Temple (1959) #9563 Corduroy Flared Coat, hat, purse, socks and shoes.

Courtesy Judith Armitstead.

Shirley Temple (1959) 12" in unidentified outfit similar to outfit #1410 on 17" doll.

Courtesy Barbara Patrick.

Shirley Temple (1959) unnumbered nylon dress with straw hat outfit shown in 1958 Sears Christmas catalog.

Courtesy Donna Carr.

Shirley Temple (1959 – 1960) In #9520 TV Wardrobe package with handle on top. Contains doll dressed in tagged pink slip and panties, shoes and socks. Wardrobe includes play outfit, school dress, party dress, purse, raincoat, hat, totebag, sparkly eyeglasses, Shirley script pin, and pearl necklace.

Courtesy Donna Carr.

Shirley Temple (1959) 12" in #9542 Blue School Dress (in box). Also shows 15" in pink School Dress, #1400.

12" Shirley Temple (1960)

Shirley Temple (1960) #9724 Sailor Girl Outfit, cap, leotards, panties, shoes $3.00; #9713 Cotton School Dress, embossed blouse, panties, purse $1.50; #9716 Flowered Pinafore on embossed dress, panties, purse $2.00.

Ideal Catalog

Courtesy Iva Mae M. Jones.

Shirley Temple (1960) #9724 Sailor Girl Outfit, cap, wearing replaced socks.

Shirley Temple (1960) #9718 Cowgirl outfit, boots, sombrero.

Ideal Catalog.

Courtesy Iva Mae M. Jones.

Shirley Temple (1960) #9718 Cowgirl outfit, replaced boots, missing sombrero.

Shirley Temple (1960) #9720 Nylon Party Dress, straw hat, petticoat, panties, shoes, socks, $3.00; #9712 Rick-Rack School Dress, panties, purse, $1.50; #9714 Felt Jumper Outfit, headband, blouse, panties, purse $2.00.

Shirley Temple (1960) #9715 Velvet Dropped Shoulder Dress, panties, and purse, $2.00, #9717 Nylon Visiting Dress, attached petticoat, panties, and purse, $2.00, #9721 Chromespun Taffeta Coat, straw hat, purse, shoes, socks, $3.00.

Shirley Temple (1960) #9717 Nylon Visiting Dress, attached petticoat, panties, and purse. $2.00.

Shirley Temple (1959 – 1960) #9711 Raincoat, matching scarf, totebag. $1.50.

9722-0
"Heidi" Outfit,
Headband
•
outfit only
retail
$3.00

9560-4
"Wee Willie Winkie"
Outfit
•
outfit only
retail
$3.00

9719-6
"Rebecca of
Sunnybrook Farm"
Outfit
•
outfit only
retail
$2.00

9564-6
"Captain January"
Outfit
•
outfit only
retail
$3.00

Ideal Catalog.

Shirley Temple (1960) Movie Classics Outfits: #9722 Heidi, #9560; Wee Willie Winkie; #9719 Rebecca of Sunnybrook Farm; #9564 Captain January.

Courtesy Veronica Phillips.

Shirley Temple (1960) Movie Classics Outfit #9722 Heidi, felt vest, print skirt, white blouse, white apron.

Courtesy McMasters Doll Auctions.

Shirley Temple (1960) Movie Classics Outfit #9560 Wee Willie Winkie, usual costume color. MIB, $600.00.

Courtesy Iva Mae M. Jones.

Shirley Temple (1960) Movie Classics Outfit #9560 Wee Willie Winkie, unusual color variation.

Courtesy Judy Armitstead.

Courtesy Judy Armitstead.

Shirley Temple (1959 – 1960) Movie Classics Outfit #9564 Captain January, navy color variation, also came in white. A dress with a middy collar was also called Captain January.

Shirley Temple (1960) Movie Classics Outfit #9719 Rebecca of Sunnybrook Farm, seersucker overalls and red blouse. Advertised in another Ideal catalog, a jumper and check shirt outfit was also called Rebecca.

12" Shirley Temple (1961)

Courtesy Donna Carr.

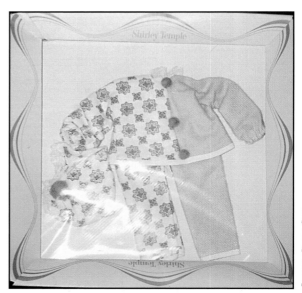

Courtesy Donna Carr.

Shirley Temple (1961) #9775 Leatherette car coat, felt slacks, scarf, matching felt cap, shoes, $4.00. MIB. Marks: Shirley Temple on top and bottom. $65.00.

Shirley Temple (1961) #9755 Two-piece flannelette turquoise and pink pajamas with stocking cap, $1.50. MIB. Marks: Shirley Temple on top and bottom. $65.00.

Shirley Temple (1961) 12" outfits available: **#9500** Two-piece play outfit, $1.00; **#9750** Two-piece play outfit (shorts); **#9755** Two-piece flannelette pajamas, stocking cap (like clown), $1.50; **#9756** Piqué School Dress, stripe trim, purse $1.50; **#9757** Cotton print school dress (V front), solid trim, purse, $1.50; **#9760** Two-piece pedal pusher, print shirt, pique trim, straw hat, $2.00; **#9765** Flocked nylon party dress (ties at shoulders), panty, petticoat, purse, $2.50; **#9766** Felt coat, matching beret with tassel, medallion, purse, $2.50; **#9767** Ballerina outfit, flower headband $2.50; **#9768** Cotton pinafore outfit, stripe and velvet trim, panty, purse, $2.50; **#9770** Nylon party dress, velveteen top, straw hat, purse, panty, shoes and socks, $3.50; **#9771** Three-piece cardigan suit, pleated skirt, panty, purse, shoes and stockings, $3.50; **#9775** Leatherette car coat, felt slacks, scarf, matching felt cap, shoes, $4.00.

Ideal Catalog.

12" Shirley Temple (1962)

Courtesy Donna Carr.

Courtesy Victoria Reinert.

Shirley Temple (1962) 12" in gift box with outfits and script pin shown in Spiegels 1962 catalog. Notice new type of raincoat.

Shirley Temple (1962) 12" in #9500-0 Basic Shirley Doll dressed in playsuit. Came with Shirley Temple name pin. Socks did not come with basic doll.

12" Shirley Temple (not dated)

Courtesy McMasters Doll Auctions.

Shirley Temple (1958 – 1963) 12" in 1960 Bedtime Outfit, tagged, shown in Spiegel 1960 Christmas catalog and 1961 Felt Coat with medallion and matching beret with tassel. Doll in the middle is not wearing Ideal outfit.

Shirley Temple (1958 – 1963) 12" in 1959 #9549 Nylon Visiting Dress. Other outfits from top right: 1959 #9563 Corduroy Flared Coat; unidentified red and white check dress; 1959 #9540 raincoat in green color variation; 1961 #9756 Pique School Dress; unidentified yellow dress with red rick-rack; 1961 #9757 Cotton print skirt with V-neck red front; unidentified brown pants with striped tie jacket. Doll with outfits, $550.00.

Courtesy Iva Mae M. Jones.

Courtesy Marcella Borzik.

Shirley Temple (1958 – 1963) 12" in black velvet dress with dotted white swiss blouse with puff sleeves. Tagged.

Shirley Temple (1958 – 1963) 12" in unidentified blue print dress, MIB.

Courtesy Donna Carr.

Shirley Temple (1958 – 1963) 12" in pink cotton and nylon dress. Original vinyl purse, shoes and socks.

Courtesy Donna Carr.

Shirley Temple (1958 – 1963) 12" in blue nylon dress with white lace trim, replaced shoes and socks. Marks: ST-12-N (on head and back).

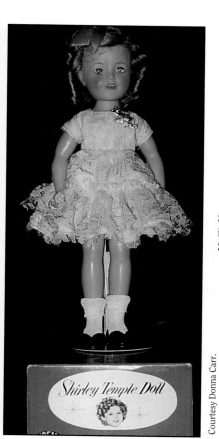

Courtesy Donna Carr.

Shirley Temple (1958 – 1963) 12" in pink party dress with lace overlay. Shown with box.

Courtesy Dona Carr.

Shirley Temple (1958 – 1963) accessories, shoes in socks in plastic case. Marks: "MADE IN U.S. A. BY IDEAL TOY CORPORATION, HOLLIS, NY."

15" *Shirley Temple*

The most famous doll in the world...Shirley Temple.. is as beautiful as Shirley herself was when she was America's favorite little girl. She has blond, curly rooted Saran hair and dimpled cheeks.

Shirley's lovely wardrobe consists of outfits she wore in her most popular movie classics: a colorful Tyrolean outfit from "Heidi," a blue denim suspender dress with matching headband from "Rebecca of Sunnybrook Farm," the attractive sailor dress she wore in "Captain January," and the Scotch kilt outfit from "Wee Willie Winkie." Shirley's wardrobe also features a red and white polka dot nylon dress.

NO.	SIZE	WEIGHT
1400-1	15"	22 lbs.
PACK: Window box, 1 doz. per ctn., packed assorted		
1410-0	17"	17 lbs.
PACK: Window box, ½ doz. per ctn., packed assorted		
1420-9	19"	15 lbs.
PACK: Window box, ½ doz. per ctn., packed assorted		

"CAPT. JANUARY"   "HEIDI"   "REBECCA"   "WEE WILLIE WINKIE"

Shirley Temple (1959) 15" in pink nylon dress trimmed with lace with blue velvet ribbon and flower at waist. Marks: "S.T./15/1958." Shown with her box. 15", $275.00.

Shirley Temple (1960) 15", 17", 19" outfits available this year: Capt. January, Heidi, Rebecca, and Wee Willie Winkie, also red and white polka dot nylon dress.

Courtesy Donna Carr.

Shirley Temple (1961) 15" in Little Bo Peep outfit from the "Fairytale Heroine" series of outfits. Also available that year in 15" dolls were: Little Red Riding Hood, Cinderella, and Alice in Wonderland, and #1408, a party dress to "pretend she's at a ball."

Shirley Temple (1961) 15" in Little Red Riding Hood outfit of red hooded cape, blue long-sleeve dress with printed flowers, and white apron from the "Fairytale Heroine" series.

Courtesy Veronica Phillips.

Shirley Temple (1961) 15" #1403 Cinderella.

Courtesy Susan Mobley.

Shirley Temple (1961) 15" #1403 Cinderella in skirt variation.

Courtesy Iva Mae M. Jones.

Shirley Temple (1961) 15" #1405 Alice In Wonderland from the "Fairytale Heroine" series in a short blue dress with collar and short sleeves and white frilly pinafore.

Montgomery Ward catalog.

Shirley Temple (1962) 15" outfits sold include party dress with matador type sleeves.

Ideal Catalog.

Shirley Temple (1962) 15" Outfits available: #1415 four dress styles: short sleeve party dress with open lattice work on bodice; jumper with rounded collar and white blouse; party dress with buttons on dark bodice and white skirt with large embroidered rick-rack trim; solid color party dress with matador type sleeves, three layers of ruffles.

Ideal Catalog.

Shirley Temple (1963) 15" only size sold in 1963. Looks like new head mold.

Courtesy Millie Caliri.

Shirley Temple (1959 – 1963) 15" in Heidi type outfit offered by Sears in 15" and 17" sizes.

Courtesy Iva Mae M. Jones.

Shirley Temple (1959 – 1963) 15" in unidentified tagged outfit of blue cotton with black rick-rack. Marks: IDEAL DOLL/ST-15-N (on head): IDEAL DOLL/ST-15 (on back).

Courtesy Miriam Gittleson

Shirley Temple (1959 – 1963) 15" in unidentified tagged outfit of yellow cotton.

Courtesy Anita Maxwell.

Shirley Temple (1959 – 1963) 15" in unidentified two-piece navy skirt outfit with white sheer blouse. $225.00.

Courtesy Susan Mobley.

Shirley Temple (1959 – 1963) 15" in unidentified tagged outfit of blue nylon with black velvet ribbon trim.

17" Shirley Temple

Courtesy Donna Carr.

Shirley Temple (1957) 17" in white nylon dress with red velvet vest and red flocked flowers. Notice Ideal tag, dress tag, and red purse with Shirley's name on it. 17", $300.00.

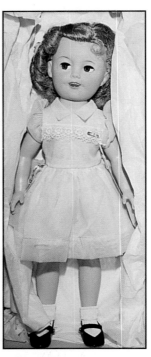

Shirley Temple (1959 – 1963) 17" in unidentified tagged white nylon dress with blue sleeves and collar and sash outfit, mint in box.

Courtesy Iva Mae M. Jones.

Shirley Temple (1959 – 1963) 17" in unidentified tagged pink nylon dress. Marks: IDEAL DOLL/ST-17 (on back).

Courtesy Iva Mae M. Jones.

Shirley Temple (1958 – 1963) 17" in yellow nylon dress, Shirley Temple tag. Original box and wrist tag. Marks: ST-17-1 (on head and back).

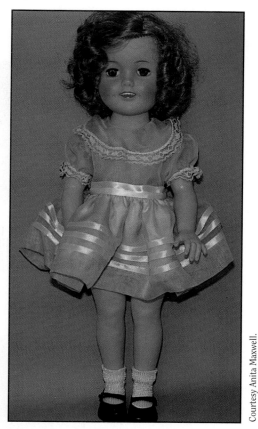

Courtesy Anita Maxwell.

Shirley Temple (1959 – 1963) 17" in unidentified tagged blue nylon dress with ribbon trim.

Courtesy Iva MaeM. Jones.

Shirley Temple (1959 – 1963) 17" in unidentified tagged white nylon dress with blue flowers. Shoes replaced.

Courtesy Iva MaeM. Jones.

Shirley Temple (1959 – 1963) 17" in unidentified tagged blue nylon dress with square collar. Shoes and socks replaced.

Ideal Catalog.

Shirley Temple (1959) 17" #1410 in yellow dress and 19" #1420 in plaid dress with bolero top. 17" (on left) Marks: IDEAL DOLL/ST-17-1 (on head) IDEAL DOLL/ST-17 (on back) and 19" (on right) Marks: ST-19-1(head); IDEAL DOLL/ST-19 (on body).

19" Shirley Temple

Shirley Temple (1959 – 1963)
19" in unidentified tagged blue
nylon dress. $325.00.

Courtesy Iva Mae M. Jones.

Shirley Temple (1959 – 1963)
19" in unidentified tagged blue
nylon dress with black ribbon
trim. Notice original star box and
tag promoting her "Twinkle Eyes."

Courtesy Iva Mae M. Jones.

Courtesy Pam Zampiello.

Shirley Temple (1959 – 1963) 19" in
unidentified tagged blue cotton play-
dress advertised in Sears catalog on a
15" doll. Button not original to dress.
Hair has been cut.

Shirley Temple (1959 – 1963)
19" in unidentified tagged white
nylon dress with blue sleeves
and collar. Notice original star
box and tag.

Courtesy Iva Mae M. Jones.

Courtesy Iva Mae M. Jones.

Shirley Temple (1959 – 1963) 19" in unidentified rare floral cotton print dress. Marks: IDEAL DOLL/ ST-19-1 (on head); IDEAL DOLL/ ST-19 (on body). Dress tagged: SHIRLEY TEMPLE Made By Ideal (in oval) Toy Corp.

Courtesy John Sonnier.

Courtesy Donna Carr.

Shirley Temple (1959 – 1963) 19" in white dress with red polka-dot dress with Shirley Temple Walker (1960).

Shirley Temple (1959 – 1963) 19" in blue cotton dress with nylon pinafore, wearing Shirley Temple script pin. Marks: IDEAL DOLL/ST-19-1 (on head); IDEAL DOLL/ST-19 (on back).

Courtesy Donna Carr.

Shirley Temple (1959 – 1963) 19" tagged dresses, pink and blue nylon with flocked flowers.

Courtesy John Sonnier.

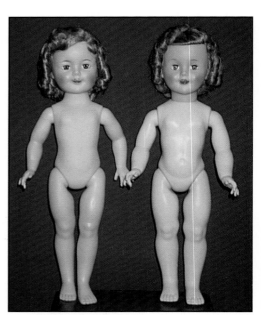

Courtesy John Sonnier.

Shirley Temple (1960) 19" Walker body (right) comparison to regular 19" doll (left). Notice walker body jointed at bottom of neck and appears lighter in color.

Shirley Temple Walker (1960) 19" Walker, all vinyl, sleep eyes, curly blonde hair, open mouth with teeth, dimpled cheeks. Marks: IDEAL TOY CORP/ST-19-R (on head): IDEAL TOY CORP/G-18 (on body).

Shirley Temple – Other Items

Courtesy Georgia Naylor.

Shirley Temple (1959 – 1963) 26" rare size with flirty eyes. Marked: IDEAL DOLL/ST-26 (on head). Clothes not original. $500.00.

Courtesy Anita Child.

Shirley Temple Black and Abe Katz (1963) on the occasion of the 50th anniversary of the Shirley Temple doll at the Plaza Hotel, New York.

Courtesy Donna Carr.

Shirley Temple (1959) Comparison of 19", 15", and 12" dolls all wearing Heidi outfit.

Courtesy Donna Carr.

Shirley Temple (1958) Carry-all for her hair curlers. Marks: "Shirley Temple" across the front side of box. Measures 2⅞" by 4".

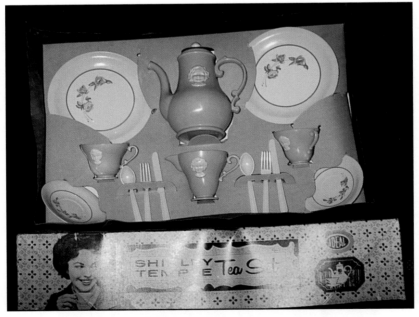

Courtesy Donna Carr.

Shirley Temple (1959) pink plastic tea set. Set is unusual because plates and saucers have flower design instead of usual Shirley Temple monogram.

Shirley Temple Playpal Doll

Courtesy McMasters Doll Auctions.

Courtesy John Sonnier.

Shirley Temple Playpal Doll (1960) 36" Vinyl head and hands and plastic body, rooted saran hair, sleep eyes, open/closed mouth with painted teeth, dimples. Some have jointed wrists. Marks: IDEAL DOLL/ST-35-38-2 (on head); IDEAL (in circle)/35-5 (on body). $1,200.00.

Shirley Temple Playpal Doll (1960) 36" Vinyl and plastic, rooted saran hair, sleep eyes, open/closed mouth with painted teeth, dimples. Wearing rare Heidi outfit. Some came with white pantaloons. Marks: IDEAL DOLL/ST-35-38-2 (on head); IDEAL TOY CORP. (in circle)/35-7 (on body). $1,400.00.

Courtesy John Sonnier.

Shirley Temple Playpal Doll (1960) 36" showing the dress color variations: yellow, blue and pink. Notice original tag on doll on right. Pin in center not original.

Ideal Catalog.

Courtesy Iva Mae M. Jones.

Cream Puff (1959 – 1962) 19", 21" (shown), 24" Lightweight, all vinyl with rooted hair, watermelon mouth, sleep eyes with lashes, dimpled cheeks, coo voice, rooted saran hair, yellow nylon dress and bonnet. Catalog numbers: #1351, #1352, #1353. Original price: $7.99, $10.97. In 1960 redesigned mouth and no coo voice. $150.00.

Cream Puff (1959 – 1962) 23" all vinyl, watermelon mouth, dimples on cheeks. Marks: IDEAL DOLL/B-23-L (on head); none on back.

Ideal Catalog.

Playtex Dryper Baby (1959) 21" and 23" All vinyl (blow molded body), ball-jointed arms, jointed legs, rooted curly brown saran hair, sleep eyes, drinks, wets, coos, actual size of a three-month-old baby, comes with a layette of Playtex disposable drypers, undershirt, gown, playclothes, washcloth, soap, and bottle. Catalog #1510 and #1515. Original price, $14.00. Marks: IDEAL DOLL/OB23-3 (on head); IDEAL (in oval)/23 (on body). 21", $200.00; 23", $225.00.

Courtesy Carol Fetherman.

Playtex Dryper Baby (1959) 21" and 23" Rooted brown hair, wearing red dresses.

Ideal Catalog.

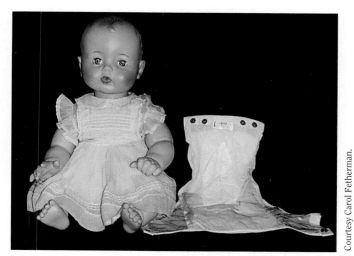

Courtesy Carol Fetherman.

Playtex Dryper Baby (1959) 21" and 23" All vinyl (blow-molded body), molded hair, sleep eyes, drinks, wets, coos, actual size of a three-month-old baby, comes with a layette of Playtex disposable drypers, undershirt, gown, playclothes, washcloth, soap, and bottle. Catalog #1510 and 1515. Original price $14.00.

Playtex Dryper Baby (1959) 23" Molded hair. Shown with her diaper. Dress not original.

Ideal Catalog.

Ideal Catalog.

Baby Coos (**1959**) 21" All vinyl (blow-molded), sleep eyes, molded hair, wears dress, bonnet, panties, shoes, and socks. Catalog #1375. Marks: SP-1/IDEAL DOLL/MADE IN U.S.A. (on head). $85.00.

Baby Coos (**1959**) 19", 21" All vinyl (blow-molded), sleep eyes, rooted hair, wears dress, bonnet, panties, shoes, and socks. Catalog #1370, #1371. Marks: SP-1/IDEAL DOLL/ MADE IN U.S.A. (on head).

Ideal Catalog.

Ideal Catalog.

Betsy Wetsy (**1959 – 1962**) 11½", 13½", 16" With molded hair. Shown with items she comes with in window gift box. Also shows rooted saran hair doll.

Betsy Wetsy® (**1959 – 1962**) 11½", 13½" (shown), 16" All vinyl with rooted saran hair, redesigned face, sleep eyes, separate fingers and toes, sleep eyes, molded or rooted saran hair, drinks, wets, and cries. 11½" came with 13-piece layette. All sizes also came in suitcase with 13-piece layette or trunk with 14-piece layette. Marks: 16": IDEAL TOY CORP./PW-20. 11½", $40.00; 13½", $45.00; 16", $50.00.

Ideal Catalog.

Courtesy Genevieve Bethyon.

Betsy Wetsy (1959 – 1962) 11½" and 13½" with rooted saran hair Deluxe Betsy Wetsy In Trunk.

Big Baby Betsy Wetsy®️ (1959 – 1960) 21" (shown), 23" All vinyl with rooted saran (shown) or molded hair, drinks, wets, cries, sleep eyes, hole in upper back, widespread, well-defined fingers and toes, wears dress, bonnet, petticoat, shoes, and socks, and came with bottle. Size of a one-year-old. Came with wind-up swing in 1960. Catalog #1151, #1152, #1231-0 for $17.00. Marks: IDEAL DOLL/VC-22 OR IDEAL DOLL/B-23 (on head) Also available 1965 through 1973. 21", $75.00; 23", $85.00.

Patti Play Pal & Family

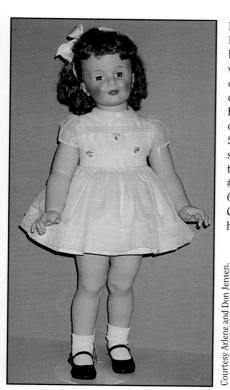

Courtesy Arlene and Don Jensen.

Patti Play Pal (spelled Playpal in 1960 catalog) **(1959)** 35" Rotational molded vinyl head, blow-molded vinyl body, jointed wrists with vinyl hands, blue sleep eyes, rooted curly or straight saran hair with bangs, closed mouth, individual fingers, strung. Blonde hair most common. Wears blue dress or red and white check dress with pinafore. Size of a three-year-old. Nonwalker had strung arms and legs, jointed wrists. Harder to find since only made one year. Catalog #1550 (curly hair) and 1551(straight hair). Original price $30.00. Marks: IDEAL TOY CORP./G 35 OR B-19-1 (on head). Straight hair, $300.00; curly hair, $350.00.

Courtesy Betty Hopkins.

Patti Play Pal (1959) 35" with most common hairstyle, long straight hair with bangs. Shown with the box she came in. MIB, $500.00.

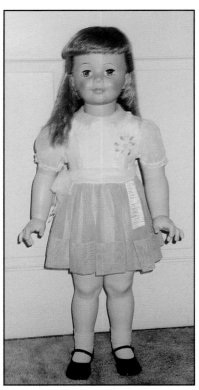

Courtesy Terrie Richardson.

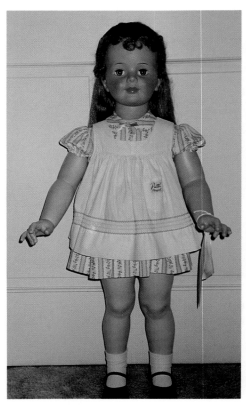

Courtesy Terrie Richardson.

Patti Play Pal (1959). 35" vinyl, blue sleep eyes, rooted blonde saran hair with bangs, individual fingers, wears blue and white dress. Size of a three-year-old child. Marks: IDEAL DOLL/G 35 (on head).

Patti Play Pal (1959) 35" Vinyl, blue sleep eyes, less common hairstyle, rooted auburn hair with spitcurls, individual fingers, original print dress with pinafore. Marks: IDEAL DOLL/G 35 (on head); IDEAL TOY CORP./G-35-4/PAT.PEND. (on body).

Courtesy Cris Johnson.

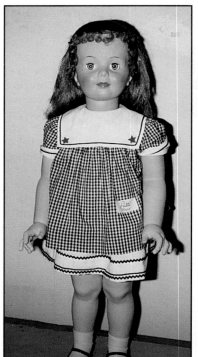

Courtesy Patti Anderson.

Patti Play Pal (1961) 35" with hardest to find platinum color hair, wearing a green velvet jumper and white blouse, a walker. Locket is not original.

Walking Patti Play Pal (1960 – 1961) 35" with long hair and spitcurls, wearing navy and white check sailor type outfit. Walkers had flanged arms and legs. $250.00.

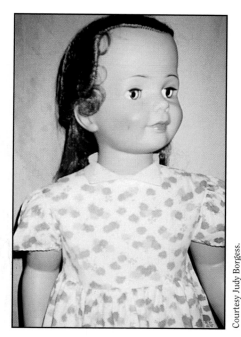

Courtesy Judy Borgess.

Patti Play Pal (1959) 35" with original unusual hairdo with side curls and hard-to-find original print dress, missing pinafore.

Courtesy Kathy Reed.

Patti Play Pal (1959) 35" Reddish brown hair with bangs, in unusual plaid dress. Shown with Patti (1964).

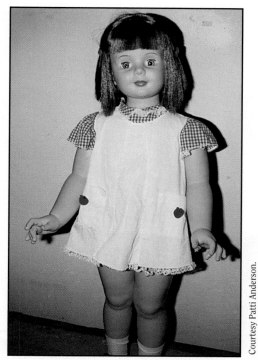

Courtesy Patti Anderson.

Patti Play Pal (1959) 35" with auburn hair with unusual part. Doll also has green eyes and auburn eyelashes. Wearing common white pinafore with apple appliques.

Patti Play Pal (1959) 35" Dark brunette. Close-up of her lovely realistic face sculpted by Neil Estern. Wearing blue variation of white pinafore outfit.

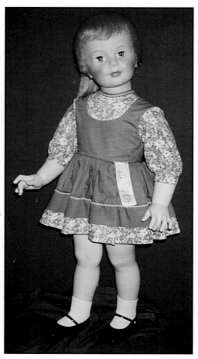

Courtesy John Sonnier.

Courtesy Chris's Collections, Chris and Joe Carrick.

Patti Play Pal (**1960 – 1961**) 35" Hard-to-find "Carrot-top," vinyl, blue sleep eyes, rare orange rooted saran hair with bangs, is a walker. There were two types of walkers, early, and later with metal rods attached to end of legs so doll walks better. Marks: IDEAL DOLL/G 35 (on head). $500.00.

Patti Play Pal (**1959**) 35" with unusual hairstyle, thick hair pulled back. Bow probably not original.

Ideal Catalog.

Ideal Catalog.

Patti Play Pal (**1959**) 35" Showing her entire family in 1959. Missing Peter Playpal who was introduced in 1960.

Patti Play Pal (**1959**) and **Penny Play Pal** (**1959**) 32" Plastic head, vinyl blow-molded jointed body, strung head and arms, rooted curly blonde or brown saran hair, blue sleep eyes, individual fingers, wears blue organdy dress, vinyl shoes, and socks. Patti's 2-year-old sister, made only one year. Marks: IDEAL DOLL/ 32-E-L or B-32-B PAT.PEND. (on head); IDEAL in oval (on back). $300.00.

Play Pal Family

Courtesy Terrie Richardson.

Courtesy Carolyn S. Cutrer. Photo by Todd Cutrer.

Penny Play Pal (**1959**) 32" Brunette, mint with box.

Penny Play Pal (**1959**) 32" All vinyl, blue sleep eyes, rooted curly blonde saran hair, individual fingers, wears original pink dress, and black vinyl shoes. Socks not original. Size of a two-year-old child. Marks: IDEAL DOLL/32-E-L (on head); IDEAL (in oval) (on body).

Ideal Catalog.

Suzy Play Pal (**1959 – 1960**) (spelled Suzie Playpal in 1960) 28" Plastic head, blow-molded vinyl jointed body, rooted curly short blonde saran hair, blue sleep eyes, wears purple dotted dress, white shoes. Patti's one-year-old sister. Catalog #1530. Marks: IDEAL DOLL/O.E.B -28-5 or 24-3 (on head); IDEAL in oval (on back). $400.00.

Courtesy Serena Henderson.

Suzy Play Pal (1959 – 1960) 28" Curly brown hair, wearing dotted swiss dress. Notice molding of hands with third and fourth fingers down. Marks: IDEAL DOLL/OB 28-5 (on head).

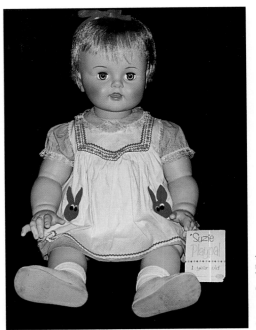

Courtesy Carol Fetherman.

Suzy Play Pal (1959 – 1960) 28" Straight dark blonde hair, wearing adorable dress with bunnies on pinafore. Notice molding of hands with third and fourth fingers down.

Ideal Catalog.

Johnny Play Pal (1959) (on left) 24" Vinyl, blue sleep eyes, molded hair, wears purple and white check outfit with booties. Patti's three-month-old brother. Size of a three-month-old boy. Catalog #1522. Johnny's marks: IDEAL DOLL/BB-24-3 (on head); IDEAL (in oval)/23 (on body). **Bonnie Play Pal (1959)** (on right) 24" Plastic head, blow-molded vinyl body, rooted blonde hair, blue sleep eyes, Patti's three-month-old sister, wears blue and white check outfit with white shoes and socks. Size of a three-month-old girl. Catalog #1523. Original price $12.00. Made only one year. Bonnie's marks: IDEAL DOLLl/O.E.B.-24-3 (on head); IDEAL (in oval on body). Johnny, $350.00; Bonnie, $350.00.

Courtesy Lana Norlin.

Bonnie Playpal (1959) 24" Wearing original dress. Notice all fingers of left hand bent down. Marks: IDEAL DOLL/OEB 24-23 (on head).

Courtesy Mary Bono.

Peter Playpal (**1960**) 38" Vinyl, gold sleep eyes, freckles, pug nose, rooted blonde hair, original clothes, black plastic shoes. Marks: ©/IDEAL TOY CORP./BE-35-38 (on head); ©/IDEAL TOY CORP./W-38/PAT.PEND. (on body). $600.00; MIB, $950.00.

Courtesy Iva Mae M. Jones.

Peter Play Pal (1960) 38" Vinyl. Wearing shorts variation of pants outfit.

Courtesy Terrie Richardson.

Peter Play Pal™ (**1960 – 1961**) 38" Vinyl, close-up of face, gold sleep eyes, freckles, pug nose, rooted brunette hair, rare navy blue outfit, black plastic shoes. Catalog #1570-1. Original price $35.00. Marks: ©/IDEAL TOY CORP./BE-35-38 (on head); ©/IDEAL TOY CORP./W-38/PAT.PEND. (on body).

Ideal Catalog.

Walking Patti and **Peter PlayPal**™ (**1960 – 1961**) 36" All vinyl walker, blow-molded hands jointed at wrist, comes in three different dresses and vinyl strap shoes and socks. Catalog #1552-9. Walking Patti still available in 1962.

Courtesy Neil Estern.

Neil Estern (**1959**) Sculptor of the Patti Play Pal line of dolls.

Pattite (**1960**) 18" All vinyl, rooted golden, auburn, or brown saran hair, sleep eyes, wears red and white check dress with white pinafore with her name on it. Looks like a small Patti Play Pal so collectors have called her Little Patti Playpal. Doll is strung. Catalog #1535-4. Marks: IDEAL TOY CORP/G-18. Walker in 1961. $500.00.

Courtesy Marge Meisinger. Photo by Ned McCormack.

Saucy Walker (1960 – 1961) 28" (shown) and 32" All vinyl, rooted blonde saran hair, blue sleep eyes, closed grin, short straight rooted "pixie" hairdo, walker, original red print dress and pinafore, white tights, with box. Catalog #1545-3. Marks: ©IDEAL TOY CORP./T28X-60 or IDEAL TOY CO/BYE S285(on head); IDEAL TOY CORP./T-28/Pat. Pend. (on body). Made in 1961 wearing dress with socks. 28", $200.00.

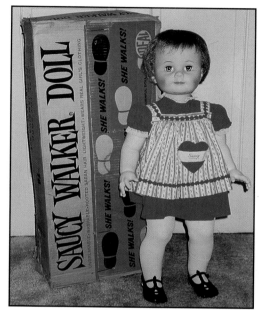

Courtesy Terrie Richardson.

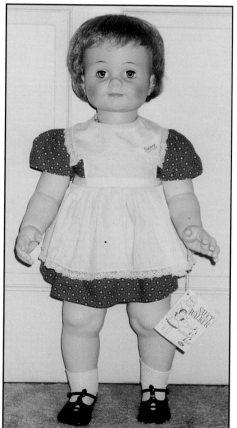

Courtesy Terrie Richardson.

Ideal Catalog.

Saucy Walker (1960) 28" and 32" (shown) All vinyl, rooted blonde saran hair, original blue print dress and white pinafore, wrist tag. Catalog #1546-1. Original price $25.00. Marks: ©IDEAL TOY CORP./BYE-32-35 (on head); IDEAL TOY CORP./B-32-W/Pat. Pend. (on body). 32", $250.00.

Betsy Wetsy® (1960 – 1962) 16" and 23" All vinyl, redesigned face, rooted saran hair, sleep eyes, drinks, wets, and cries. Wears romper with her name on bib. Came with bathtub or swing. Catalog #1230-2, #1240-1. Original price $17.00 – $23.00 Marks: 23" IDEAL DOLL/B-23 (on head). Wind-up swing, $100.00; 16", $60.00; 23", $70.00.

Bonnie Baby (**1960**) 12" All vinyl with sleep eyes and molded hair, open mouth, drinks, and wets. Came with dress with bonnet, booties, diaper, and bottle. Catalog #0119-8. $100.00.

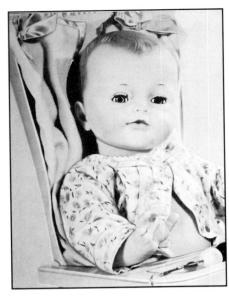

Bye-Bye Baby™ (**1960 – 1961**) 25" All vinyl, sized to look like a six-month-old with realistically sculpted fingers and toes, all vinyl, fully jointed, molded painted brown hair, blue or yellowish-brown sleep eyes, drinks and wets, came with snowsuit or kimono and blanket, comes in car seat with tray, has a seven-piece layette set of nightgown, blanket, diaper, washcloth, booties, soap and regulation size infant's bottle. Catalog #0470-5. Retail price $24.95. Marks: IDEAL TOY CORP./L25NB (on head); IDEAL TOY CORP./NB 25 (on back). 25", $300.00.

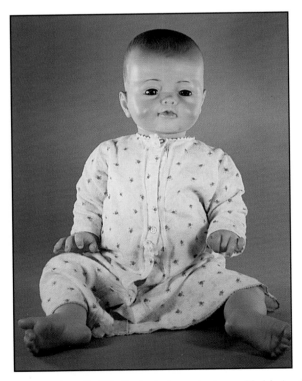

Bye-Bye Baby (**1960**) 25" all vinyl strung body, molded hair, sleep eyes, wearing original flannel bathrobe. Beautifully detailed hands and feet designed by Neil Estern. Hole in mouth, metal hole in back. Marks: ©IDEAL TOY CORP./L25NB (on head); ©IDEAL TOY CORP./NB-25 (on body).

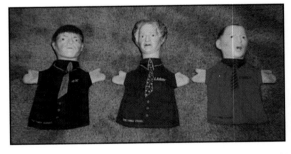

Three Stooges® hand puppets (**1960**) 9" Vinyl head and fabric bodies. Larry, Curly, and Moe, molded features. Retail $1.00. Catalog #7015-1. $300.00.

Miss Ideal

Courtesy Cris Johnson.

Courtesy Todd Cutrer.

Miss Ideal (**1961**) 25", and 30" (shown) All vinyl, brunette rooted nylon hair, jointed ankles, wrists, waist, arms, and legs. Closed watermelon shaped mouth, sleep eyes, came with beauty kit with comb, curlers, wave lotion. Wearing original Capri outfit. Catalog #1620-4. Original price: $15.99, $19.99. Marks: ©IDEAL TOY CORP. SP-25-S (on head); ©IDEAL TOY CORP. P-25 (on body). 25", $250.00; 30", $300.00.

Miss Ideal (**1961**) 25" and 30" (shown) All vinyl, rare platinum rooted nylon hair, also came in blonde; jointed ankles, wrists, waist, arms and legs. Sleep eyes, came with beauty kit with comb, curlers, wave lotion. Wearing original blue "Town and Country" sundress. Marks: ©IDEAL TOY CORP./SP-30-S (on neck); ©IDEAL TOY CORP./G-30-S (on back). 30", $325.00.

Miss Ideal (**1961**) 30" Blonde wearing campus outfit (jacket, check shirt, and straw hat) with strap shoes. Shown with her box and all her accessories including Playwave kit, hatbox, and instructions.

Courtesy Terrie Richardson.

Lori Martin from National Velvet (1961) 30" and 38" (shown) All vinyl, fully jointed body with swivel waist and ankles, some have swivel wrists, blue sleep eyes with lashes, individual fingers, long rooted dark hair, dressed in check shirt, dungarees, and black vinyl boots. From TV show "National Velvet." Catalog #1631-1, 1632-7. Marks: Metro Goldwyn Mayer Inc./Mfg. by/IDEAL TOY CORP./38 (on head); ©IDEAL TOY CORP./G-38 (on back). 30", $750.00; 38", $800.00.

Lori Martin

Lori Martin from National Velvet (1961) 30" and 38" (shown) All vinyl, swivel waist, notice graceful individual fingers, sleep eyes, long rooted black hair, dressed in check shirt, dungarees, felt hat (not original), and vinyl boots.

Courtesy Terrie Richardson.

Courtesy Carolyn S. Cutrer. Photo by Todd Cutrer.

Courtesy Juley Teuscher.

Courtesy Patty Massey.

Lori Martin from National Velvet (1961) 30" (shown) and 38" All vinyl with swivel waist and jointed ankles. Doll is strung. Clothing not original. Marks: Metro Goldwyn Mayer Inc./Mfg. by/IDEAL TOY CORP/30 (on head); IDEAL TOY CORP./G-30 (on body).

Lori Martin from National Velvet (1961) 42" all vinyl. Very rare size. Apparently only 50 were made as store displays. Original clothing. Marks: Metro Goldwyn Mayer Inc./Mfg. by/IDEAL TOY CORP(on head); IDEAL TOY CORP./G-42 (on body). $2,000.00.

Daddy's Girl

Courtesy Terrie Richardson.

Courtesy Terrie Richardson.

Daddy's Girl (1961) 38" and 42" (shown) Vinyl head and arms, plastic body with swivel waist and jointed ankles, rooted blonde saran hair, blue sleep eyes with lashes, closed grin, represents pre-teen girl of age 12-13. Wears red plaid dress and straw hat. Catalog #1630-3, #1640-2. IDEAL TOY CORP./G-42-1 (on head); IDEAL TOY CORP./G-42 (on body). 38", $1,200.00; 42", $1,400.00.

Daddy's Girl (1961) 42" Plastic body with swivel waist and jointed ankles, rooted brunette saran hair, blue sleep eyes with lashes, closed grin, represents pre-teen girl of age 12-13. Marks: IDEAL TOY CORP./G-42-1 (on head); IDEAL TOY CORP./G-42 (on body).

Daddy's Girl (1961) 42" Blonde.

Courtesy Carolyn S. Cutrer. Photo by Todd Cutrer.

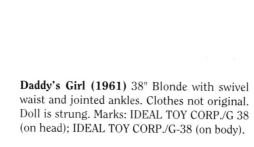

Courtesy Juley Teuscher.

Daddy's Girl (1961) 38" Blonde with swivel waist and jointed ankles. Clothes not original. Doll is strung. Marks: IDEAL TOY CORP./G 38 (on head); IDEAL TOY CORP./G-38 (on body).

Ideal Catalog.

Thumbelina (1961) 16" Vinyl head and limbs, soft cloth body, painted eyes with three outer lashes, rooted saran hair, open/closed mouth, wind the knob in her back, and she moves her body and wriggles. Marks: IDEAL TOY CORP. /OTT-16 (on head). IDEAL TOY CORP/ US PAT NO 3,029,552 (on plastic knob in back).

Thumbelina (1961 – 1962) 16" (shown) and 20" Vinyl head and limbs, soft cloth body, painted eyes with three outer lashes, rooted saran hair, open/closed mouth; wind the knob in her back and she moves her body and wriggles. Shown in box. Catalog #0515-7. Cries in 1962. 16", $200.00; 20", $250.00.

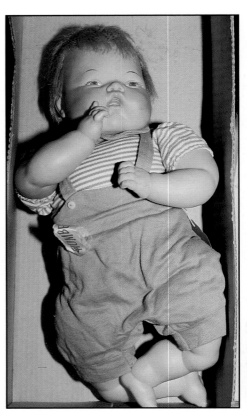

Courtesy Robin Randall.

Ideal Catalog.

Kissy (1962) Outfits available in 1962 for Kissy: #1310 Sun Suit, #1311 Romper Suit, #1312 Pajama Set, #1313 Creeper Set, #1314 Hat and Coat. Also there was a Deluxe Kissy line of fancy organdy dresses, #1305.

Kissy (1961 – 1964) 22½". Soft vinyl head and hands, hard vinyl body, rooted saran hair, sleep eyes, lashes, jointed wrists, wears t-strap shoes; press her hands together her mouth puckers up and makes a kiss with a kissing sound. Came in eight different outfits. Catalog #1300-3. Original price $8.00. Marks: ©IDEAL CORP./K-21-L (on head); IDEAL TOY CORP./K22/PAT.PEND. (on body). 22", $100.00; black, $150.00.

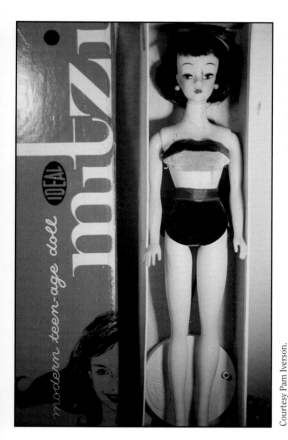

Courtesy Pam Iverson.

Mitzi™ (**1961**) 11¾" Barbie look-alike, plastic and vinyl jointed at neck and shoulders with rooted red-brown saran hair, painted blue eyes, molded lashes, wears two-piece swimsuit, pearl earrings. Box says "Modern Teenage doll with pedestal stand." Marks: MITZI/© IDEAL TOY CORP./MCM LX/Z or/1 seen (on back). Box says #9820-1, also #9820-2. $100.00.

Courtesy Barbara Mitchell.

Mitzi (1961) 11¾" with platinum hair, wearing original dress with bodice same fabric as the Samantha Bewitched gown.

Ideal Catalog.

Jackie (1962) 15" All vinyl, blue sleep eyes, rooted saran hair, individually molded fingers. Rare since named for the First Lady but taken off market quickly. Marks: IDEAL TOY CORP./G-15-L (head), IDEAL TOY CORP/M-15 (on body). $900.00.

Courtesy Lora Lawler.

Jackie (1962) 15" All vinyl, blue sleep eyes, rooted saran hair, individually molded sleep eye. Notice sleep eyes as differentiated from Carol Brent/Liz.

Montgomery Ward catalog.

Liz or Carol Brent (**1961**) Ad for 15" made as a special for Montgomery Ward called Carol Brent.

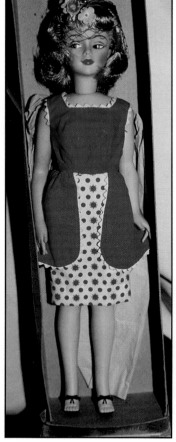

Courtesy Kathy Tornikoski.

Liz or Carol Brent (**1961**) 15" Soft vinyl head and arms, hard vinyl jointed body, swivel waist, rooted blonde, brunette, or red saran hair, painted side glancing eyes, closed mouth, high heel feet. Dressed in a variety of suits or dresses. Box says "Jackie." Catalog #0850-8. 15" was made as a special for Montgomery Ward, called Carol Brent. Marks: IDEAL DOLL/VT 10½ (on head); 15": IDEAL TOY CORP./M-15-L (on head): IDEAL TOY CORP./M-15 (on body). $85.00.

Liz (**1962**) 15" Vinyl head jointed at bottom of neck, in bathing suit that came in her gift set. Marks: ©IDEAL TOY CORP./M-15-L (on head); ®IDEAL TOY CORP./M-15 (on body).

Liz (1962) 15" Vinyl in leopard print pants, black jersey top, and straw hat that came in her gift set. Gift Set $250.00.

Liz (1962) 15" Vinyl in negligee that came in her gift set.

Liz (1962) 15" underwear set, MIB, $45.00.

Ideal Catalog.

Liz (1962) Fashions. Eight haute couture outfits available. $45.00 each.

Dick Tracy Puppet (1961) Rubber heads, cloth bodies. Came with record of TV voices of characters. Also was a Hemlock Holmes and Joe Jitsu Puppet. $50.00.

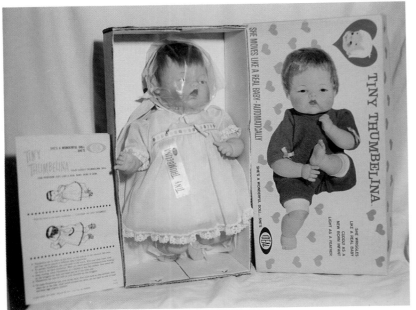

Courtesy Pam Keith. Photo by Gary Faulkner.

Tiny Thumbelina (1962 – 1968) 14" Vinyl head and limbs, soft cloth body, painted eyes, rooted saran hair, six outfits sold separately; wind key in back and she wriggles and turns head. Items that could be bought for her in 1964 included dressing table with utility pockets, rocking crib with see-through slats and heart design with her picture inside it, vinyl carrying cases, feeding kits, changing kits, and bath kits. Also outfits for playing, sleeping and traveling. Catalog #0401-0. Original price $10.00. Marks: IDEAL TOY CORP./OTT-14 (on head) or U.S. PAT.#3029552 (on body). $125.00.

Montgomery Ward catalog.

Bouncing Baby Coos (1962 – 63) 20", 25" Vinyl head, soft body, rooted ash blonde saran hair, redesigned face with blue sleep eyes, open yawning mouth with molded tongue; pat her she coos, squeeze her she cries. 20" wears striped pajamas and cap with pom-pon and booties. 25" wears pink nylon dress. Catalog #0601-5, #0611-4. Original price $12.98. Marks: IDEAL TOY CORP./YTT-19-L-5 (on head). $75.00.

Ideal Catalog.

Terry Twist (1962) 25" Soft vinyl head, vinyl body, rooted long saran hair in various colors, watermelon closed mouth, sleep eyes, came in slack outfit, artist's outfit, or cheerleader's outfit with name on ribbon; can turn at waist, ankles, shoulders and neck. Catalog #1603-0. $150.00.

Courtesy Evelyn Roudybush.

Terry Twist (1962) 25" Soft vinyl head, vinyl body, rooted long saran hair in various colors, watermelon closed mouth, sleep eyes; can turn at waist, ankles, shoulders, and neck. Replaced megaphone. Same doll as Miss Ideal. Marks: IDEAL TOY CORP/SP-25-S.

Ideal catalog.

Baby Toddler (1962) 16" and 19" All vinyl, rooted saran hair, sleep eyes, open/closed mouth, hands bent upwards, dressed in toddler styled dresses with matching bonnet. Catalog #1000-9, #1010-8. $50.00

Tammy

Photo by Joe Guerriero.

Tammy (**1962**) 12" Vinyl head and arms, plastic body and legs, teen doll, rooted hair, painted side glancing eyes; has 20 different outfits that could be purchased separately. Photo shows variations of hair color. Catalog #9000-1. Original price, $3.00. Marks: © IDEAL TOY CORP./BS-12/1 (on head); © IDEAL TOY CORP./BS-12/2 (on back) for the platinum hair doll; BS-12/3 for dirty blonde hair; and BS-12/4 for brown hair doll. $55.00; black, $75.00.

Tammy (**1962 – 1964**) Outfit #9091 Underwear Set. MIB outfit, $35.00.

Tammy (1962 – 1964) in blue playsuit she came in and outfit #9092 Sleepy-time; #9115 Pizza Party; #9153 Dream Boat (different jacket than shown in Ideal brochure); #9172 Travel Along.

Montgomery Ward catalog.

Tammy (1962 – 1964) Outfit #9117 Beau and Arrow. MIB outfits, $55.00.

Tammy (1962 – 1964) in outfit #9113 Tennis the Menace, #9115 Pizza Party, #9118 Tee Time, #9119 Purl One, #9120 Nurse's Aide (hard-to-find outfit). $75.00.

Tennis The Menace retail $2.50   9115-7 Pizza Party retail $2.50   9118-1 Tee Time retail $2.50   9119-9 Purl One retail $2.50   9120-7 Nurse's retail $2.5

Ideal Catalog.

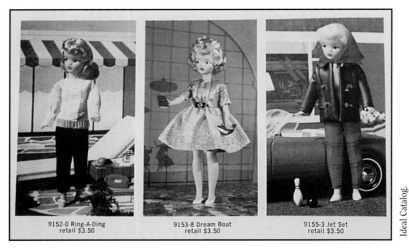

Ideal Catalog.

9152-0 Ring-A-Ding
retail $3.50

9153-8 Dream Boat
retail $3.50

9155-3 Jet Set
retail $3.50

Tammy (1962 – 1964) Outfit #9152 Ring-A-Ding, #9153 Dream Boat, #9155 Jet Set.

9169-4 Beauty Queen
retail $4.00

Tammy (1964) Outfit #9169 Beauty Queen, retailed for $4.00. Hard-to-find outfit. $75.00.

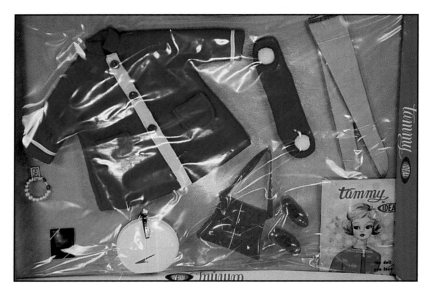

Tammy (1962) Outfit #9173 Model Miss. Hard-to-find outfit. MIB, $75.00.

Tammy (1962 – 1964) Outfit #9174 Sorority Sweetheart. MIB, $55.00.

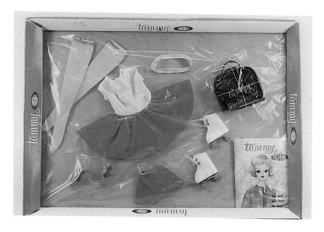

Tammy (1963) Outfit #9177 Skate Date, roller skates. MIB, $65.00.

Tammy (1962) Outfit #9211 Snow Bunny. MIB, $65.00.

Tammy (1963) Outfit #9212 Figure Eight. MIB, $65.00.

Tammy (1964) Outfit #9213 Wedding Belle, $60.00.

Ideal Catalog.

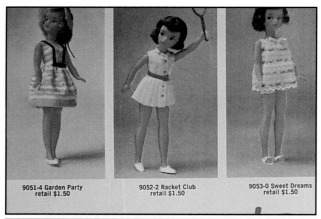

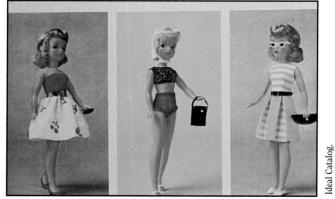

Ideal Catalog.

Tammy (1964) Outfit #9051 Garden Party, #9052 Racket Club, #9053 Sweet Dreams, #9055 Dance Date, #9056 Beach Party, #9054 Sunny Stroller. Only available after Spring, 1964.

Tammy (1963) #9570 Carrying case. $40.00.

Tammy's 1963 Car (1963 – 1964) #9700 Mediterranean blue 1963 M.G.V. sportscar, 18" long. Wheels roll, red upholstery. MIB, $150.00.

Tammy's Bed, Vanity, and Chair Set (1963)
#9701 Red velvet headboard, red velvet
spread with red and white peppermint stripe
skirt, and bolster pillow. Plastic vanity table
and chair. MIB, $55.00.

Tammy's House (1963) #9702 has
metal lock on top. Marks: MADE IN
USA/IDEAL TOY COMPANY/HOLLIS,
NY. $100.00.

Courtesy Dorothy Hesner. Photo by Carol Stover.

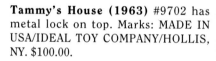

Ideal Catalog.

Tammy's Boat (1963) #9705 Plastic
with plastic sail. $250.00.

Courtesy Dawn Thomas.

Grown-Up Pos'n Tammy (1965) 12" Vinyl head with soft flexible vinyl arms and legs, plastic body, new smaller head with pageboy hairdo, poseable limbs. Catalog #9105-8. Wearing "Formal Feathers" outfit from Sears catalog, missing feather boa. Marks: IDEAL TOY CORP/T-12-E (on head); ©1965/IDEAL (in an oval)/T-12 (on back hip). $50.00, MIB $100.00.

Playthings Magazine.

Grown-Up Pos'n Tammy (1965) in striped crop top and skirt. Also showing Misty, Tammy's friend. MIB, $100.00.

Courtesy Anita Child.

Robert F. Kennedy, Attorney General of the United States, during his campaign for the United States Senate seat from New York with (from left): Lionel Weintraub, Abraham Katz, and Benjamin F. Michtom at the Ideal factory (**circa 1964**). Notice Tammys in foreground.

Courtesy Juley Teuscher.

Black Tammy (1964) 12" Black vinyl, long black rooted hair, brown side glancing painted eyes. Marks: IDEAL TOY CORP/BS-12 (on head), BS-12 (on right hip). $525.00.

Ideal Catalog.

Tammy Family (1964) Store display of Tammy's family: Mom, Dad, Tammy, Ted, and Pepper. $300.00.

Tammy (1962) and **Pepper (1963)** with their boxes. Rare red hair. MIB, $75.00.

Courtesy Audrey Fletcher.

Pepper (1963) 8" in variation of standard playsuit. $35.00; MIB, $50.00.

Pepper (1963) #9306 Budding Ballerina includes tutu, head piece, ballet slippers, and satin bag. MIB outfits, $45.00.

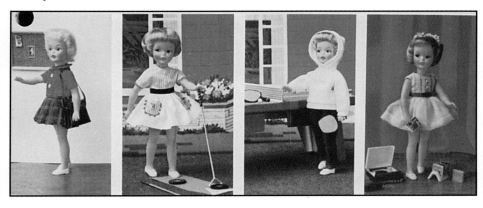

Ideal Catalog.

Pepper (1963) #9308 Teacher's Pet, #9317 Happy Holiday, #9318 After School, #9326 Birthday Party. MIB, $45.00.

Pepper (1963) #9326 Birthday Party includes nylon dress shoes, flower hair decoration, record player, albums, records, and record rack. MIB, $45.00.

9331-0 Miss Gadabout
retail $3.00

9339-3 Snow Flake
retail $3.50

Ideal Catalog.

Pepper (1963) #9311 Miss Gadabout and #9339 Snow Flake, complete with sled. MIB, $45.00.

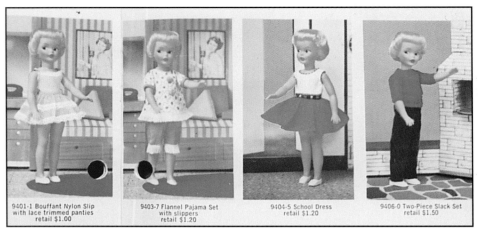

9401-1 Bouffant Nylon Slip
with lace trimmed panties
retail $1.00

9403-7 Flannel Pajama Set
with slippers
retail $1.20

9404-5 School Dress
retail $1.20

9406-0 Two-Piece Slack Set
retail $1.50

Pepper (1963) Clothing which came on cards, #9401 Bouffant Nylon Slip, #9403 Flannel Pajamas, #9404 School Dress, #9406 Two-piece Slack Set. MOC, $25.00.

Pepper and Dodi (1964) Raincoat outfit and **Tammy (1964)** #9052 Racket Club.

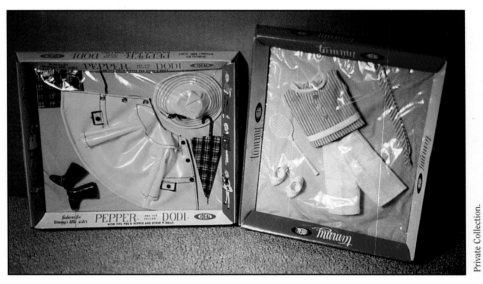

Private Collection.

Pepper (1963) carrying case and **Pepper and Dodi (1964)** carrying case. $35.00.

Private Collection.

Courtesy Juley Teuscher.

Ideal Catalog.

Pepper's Pony (1964) 10" long x 8" tall plastic shown with box. Marks on box: Tammy's sister Pepper's Pony "34-9720-4/980V086F." Pony is unmarked, box is dated 1964. Extremely rare. $300.00.

Pos'n Pepper (1964) 9¼" Vinyl head, arms, and legs, plastic body, flexible limbs, freckles; wears blue and white dress. Catalog #9405-2. Original price $2.00. Marks: ©IDEAL TOY CORP./G9-E (on head); IDEAL TOY CORP./G-9-W/1 (on body). $40.00, MIB, $75.00.

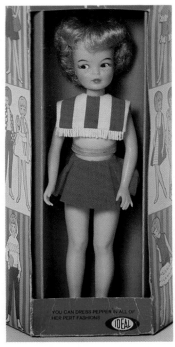

Photo by Anthony L. Colella.

Photo by Joe Guerriero.

New Pepper (1965) 9¼" Soft vinyl head and arms, soft plastic legs and body, new smaller face, rooted blonde hair, painted side glancing eyes with three painted lashes, freckles; wears red and white fringed playsuit. Catalog #9350-0. Marks: ©1965/IDEAL TOY CORP./P9-3 (on head); 1964©/IDEAL (in oval)/2DO-9 (on body). $35.00; MIB, $75.00.

Tammy's Mom and Dad (1963) 12½" Vinyl and plastic. Mom has rooted blonde hair, painted side glancing blue eyes, painted long black eyeliner to side of eye, high heel feet. Six outfits sold separately. Catalog #9395-5. Original price $4.00. Mom marked: ©IDEAL TOY CORP./W-13-L (on head) and ©IDEAL TOY CORP./W-13 (on body). Dad has painted molded hair, painted features, brown eyes, gray on temples. Ten outfits sold separately. Catalog #9396-3. Original price $4.00. Dad marked ©IDEAL TOY CORP./M-13 2 (on head) and ©IDEAL TOY CORP.//B-12½/2 (on body). Mom, $45.00; MIB, $75.00. Dad, $45.00; MIB, $75.00.

Courtesy Cheri Miller.

Dad (1963) 12½" Vinyl, different head mold, perhaps earlier dolls or prototype doll. Used in Ideal advertising. Marks: IDEAL TOY CORP/M 12-L (on head); B 12 1/2 (on body). $65.00; MIB, $110.00.

Dad and Ted (1963) Outfit #9461 red blazer. MOC Outfits, $25.00.

Dad and Ted (1963) Outfit #9462 blue cardigan and knee socks. MOC, $25.00.

Ideal Catalog.

Mom (1963) and Ted 12½" in outfit they came in, shown in Tammy's House.

Ideal Catalog.

Mom (1963) Outfit #9415 Nighty Nite, #9422 Lounging Luxury, #9418 Lazy Days fleece brunch coat, #9412 Evening in Paris brocade sheath with stole, MIB Outfits $40.00.

Dodi (1964) 9" Vinyl head and arms, plastic legs and body, long rooted ash blonde or red hair, painted blue eyes, wears navy blue felt dress with tassel and red sweater. Pepper's friend. Catalog #9300-5. Original price $2.60. Marks: ©1964/IDEAL TOY CORP./DO-9-E (on head); 1964©/ IDEAL (in oval)/1 DO-9 (on body). $40.00; MIB, $75.00.

Ted (1963) 12½" Vinyl head and arms, plastic legs and body, molded painted light brown hair, painted brown eyes, Tammy's big brother. Catalog #9450-8. Original price $3.50. Marks: ©IDEAL TOY CORP./B-12½-H 2 (on head), W-2 also seen; ©IDEAL TOY CORP./B12½ (on back), /2 also seen as additional line. $45.00; MIB, $65.00.

Private Collection.

Courtesy Marlene Tartaglia.

Pos'n Salty or Pos'n Pete (1964) 7¾" Vinyl Pepper's friend or Tammy's little brother. Catalog #9449-0. Salty had striped shirt. Pete had solid color shirt. Both wore dungarees. Marks: ©1964/IDEAL TOY CORP (on head); ©1964/IDEAL TOY CORP/P8 (on back). Hard to find. $75.00; MIB, $125.00. Also showing New Pepper and Grown-Up Pos'n Tammy.

Patti (1964) 9" Vinyl rooted dark brown hair, painted side glancing blue eyes. Pepper's friend, a Montgomery Ward Exclusive. Marks: ©IDEAL TOY CORP./G9-L (on head); ©IDEAL TOY CORP/G-9-W/2 (on back). $125.00; MIB, $200.00.

Tearie Dearie

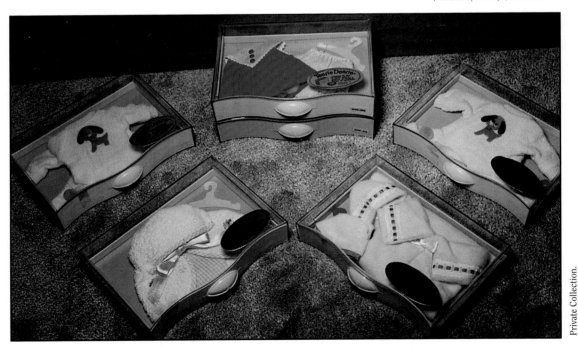

Private Collection.

Tearie Dearie (1963 – 1967) Outfits available for 8" Tearie Dearie. The cases stacked like a chest of drawers. #8011 Scotch Lass, short sleeveless playsuit with plaid trim and plaid and white sun bonnet; #8012 Sleepyhead, cuddly one-piece sleeper with pom-pon; #8016 Lotsa Dots, polka-dot piqué dress; #8017 Sandbox Sweetheart, one-piece playsuit with matching front buttoning vest; #8021 Bath Bunny, hooded plaid trimmed bathrobe and diaper; #8022 Really Ruffled, short sleeve blouse and coordinated pants with daisies; #8026 Party Perfect, velveteen party dress, matching panties; #8027 Snuggle Bunting, soft flannel with satin ribbon trim. All outfits not pictured. MIB, $15.00.

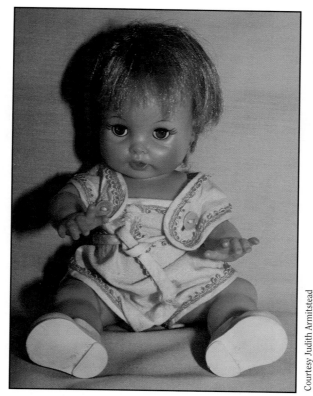

Courtesy Judith Armitstead

Tearie Dearie (**1963 – 1967**) 9" All vinyl, fully jointed, sleep eyes roll whenever she's picked up, lower painted lashes, rooted saran hair; drinks, wets, and cries real tears, blows bubbles with her bubble pipe, comes with a bottle in plastic package that converts to rocking cradle. Dressed in assortment of baby outfits, each with matching diaper. Eight outfits sold separately. Catalog #1100-7. Original price $2.00. Uses Little Betsy Wetsy® Body from 1957. Advertised on TV. Marks: IDEAL TOY CO/BW 9-4. $35.00.

Courtesy Jessie Williams.

Tearie Dearie Twins (**1963**) 9" Vinyl, fully jointed, rooted hair, sleep eyes; drinks, wets, comes in package that converts to cradle with bottle. Eight outfits sold separately. Marks: IDEAL TOY CO/BW 9-4. $80.00/set.

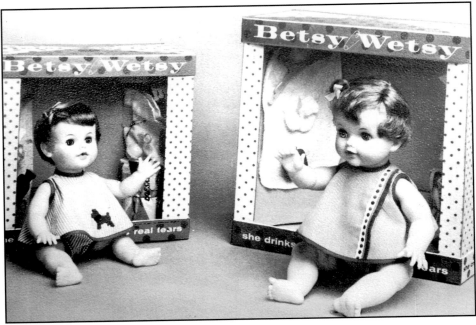

Ideal Catalog.

Betsy Wetsy® **(1961 – 1963)** 11½" and 13½" All vinyl, redesigned faces, straight saran hair, sleep eyes; drinks, wets, cries real tears. Comes with seven-piece layette set. 11½", $40.00, 13½", $45.00.

Lolly (**1963**) 19", 21", 23" Vinyl head and limbs, soft body, rooted saran hair, sleep eyes, open mouth, party dress, bonnet, and baby doll. Catalog #1361-5, #1362-3, #1363-1. $45.00.

Ideal Catalog.

Twins In A Blanket (**1963 – 64**) 14" Vinyl head and limbs, cloth body, rooted saran hair, sleep eyes, boy has happy open mouth, girl has sad pouty mouth. Both dressed in rompers. Also came in frilly tote basket, boy dressed in rompers with organdy shirt, girl in silk dress. Catalog #0531-4. Original price $11.00. $60.00/set.

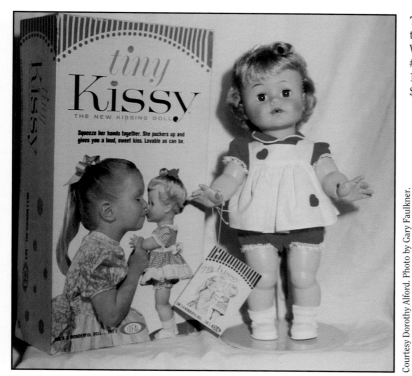

Courtesy Dorothy Alford. Photo by Gary Faulkner.

Tiny Kissy (1963 – 1968) 16" Vinyl head and body, pull hands together and she puckers her lips. Smaller version of Kissy. Wears red outfit with white pinafore with hearts. Catalog #1304-7. Original price $9.98. Marks: IDEAL TOY CORP./K-16-1 (on head); IDEAL TOY CORP./K-16-2 (on body). 16", $80.00; black, $90.00.

Ideal Catalog.

Kissy Baby (1963 – 1964) 22" Vinyl head, body, arms, and bent baby legs, rooted saran hair, sleep eyes; bring hands together and she puckers and makes a kissing sound. Catalog #1303-7. Original price $8.00. Marks: IDEAL TOY CORP./K-21-L-1 (on head); IDEAL TOY CORP. K-22/US Pat.No. 3,054,215 (on body). $50.00.

Ideal Catalog.

Tiny Kissy (1965) 16" Vinyl; press her arms together and she kisses. Wears red dotted dress with sailor collar or blue and white romper suit with pleated skirt. Catalog #1304. $80.00. **Cuddly Kissy** (1965) 16" Vinyl head and limbs, cloth body. Rooted blonde saran hair. Squeeze her tummy and she kisses. Dressed in corduroy or dotted Swiss dress trimmed with bows and lace and white booties. Catalog #1330-0. Original price $7.00. $85.00.

Courtesy Cris Johnson.

Tiny Kissy (1966) 16" auburn hair in new package. Marks: ©IDEAL TOY CORP-K-16-1 (on head); K-16-2 (on body).

Pebbles

Ideal Catalog.

Courtesy Laura Meisner.

Baby Pebbles (**1963 – 1964**) 14" Vinyl head, arms, and legs, soft body, blue side glancing painted eyes, rooted hair with topknot and bone, leopard print nightie, flannel blanket. Catalog #0710-4. Original price $5.00. $90.00; MIB, $160.00.

Tiny Pebbles (**1964 – 1966**) 12" vinyl. Mint in box complete with bone in hair. $80.00; MIB, $140.00.

Courtesy Laura Meisner.

Baby Pebbles (**1963 – 1964**) cradle. Inner lining is animal print cardboard. Also available was a Cave House and a Dino rider. MIB, $60.00.

Ideal Catalog.

Pebbles (1963 – 1964) and **Tiny Pebbles (1964 – 1966)** 16" and 12" All vinyl, jointed body, rooted saran hair with top knot, painted blue eyes, dressed in leopard print outfit, characters from the Flintstones cartoon, Hanna-Barbera Productions. Pebbles: Catalog #0700-5. Original price $6.00. Tiny Pebbles: Catalog #0720-3. Original price $3.00. Small version of Pebbles came with a plastic "log" cradle in 1965. Pebbles 16", $90.00; MIB, $160.00. Tiny Pebbles 12", $80.00.

Baby Pebbles in Cave House (1966) 8¼" Vinyl head and arms, light brittle vinyl body and legs. Came in simulated rock cave house package. Different from 14" Baby Pebbles in that she is all vinyl. Marks: ©HANNA BARBERA PRODUCTIONS INC./IDEAL TOY CORP./FS-8 1/4/1965 (on head); ©HANNA BARBERA PRODUCTIONS INC./IDEAL TOY CORP./FS-8 (on right rear end). Also was 8¼" Baby Bamm-Bamm in 1966. $60.00; MIB, $100.00.

Tiny Bamm-Bamm (1964) 12" All vinyl, painted brown side glancing eyes. Jointed right elbow as well as neck, shoulders, and legs. Wears felt loincloth with bone and cap. Complete with club and extra outfit with Barney printed on shirt. Marks: ©HANNA-BARBERA PRODS., INC./IDEAL TOY CORP./BB-12 (on head and body). Clothes untagged. $80.00; MIB, $140.00.

Ideal Catalog.

Bamm-Bamm (1964) 16" All vinyl head and jointed body, rooted blonde saran hair, painted blue side glancing eyes, leopard skin suit and cap, club. Catalog #0705-4. Original price $6.00. $90.00; MIB, $160.00. **Tiny Bamm-Bamm (1964 – 1966)** 12" Smaller version of Bamm-Bamm. Catalog #0721-1. Original price $3.00. $80.00; MIB, $140.00.

Petite Princess

Private Collection.

Fantasy Family Dolls (1964 – 1965) 3⅞" to 5½" Vinyl miniature doll family shown with mint in box Petite Princess Fantasy Furniture – piano, telephone, chairs, cabinet. Bendable arms and legs. Father has gray felt jacket and pants with painted yellow hair. Mother has brown upswept wig and dress. Little girl has yellow braids and red dress. Boy has molded brown hair, felt pants. Catalog #4466-9, #9710-5 (1964). Original price $3.00. Family, $80.00. For furniture prices, see page 343.

Courtesy Miriam Gittleson.

Fantasy Family boy doll (1964) in Princess Patti Music Room setting. $100.00.

Ideal Catalog.

Petite Princess (1964 – 1965) Royal Boudoir bedroom set. This elaborate line of furniture was called Petite Princess in 1964 and Princess Patti in 1965. Shown: #4416-4 Little Princess 5" satin bed, $45.00; #4417-2 Royal Dressing Table/stool, $45.00; #4420-6 Palace Chest, $25.00; #4408-1 Boudoir Chair Lounge, $35.00. Fits the Petite Princess Fantasy Rooms which came in three colors. Was advertised on television's "Magilla Gorilla Show."

Courtesy Iva Mae Jones.

Petite Princess (1964 – 1965) Living Room pieces: #4439-6 real brass Royal Candelabra, $15.00; #4424-8 Rolling Tea Cart, $25.00; #4425-5 4" long Royal Grand Piano, $75.00; #4437-0 Occasional Table Set (missing cigarette lighter, ashtray, picture frame, and Buddha statue), $25.00; #4407-3 Salon Curved Sofa, $35.00; #4410-7 Brocade Salon Wing Chair, $35.00.

Courtesy Juley Teuscher.

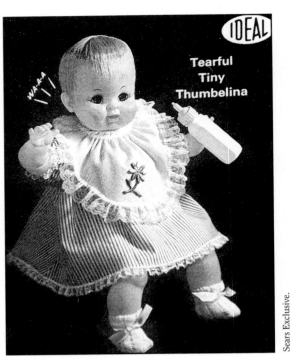

Sears Exclusive.

Snoozie (1964 – 1965) 20" Vinyl head and limbs, cloth body. Rooted curly or straight saran hair, blue sleep eyes, cries. Turn knob on back and she opens and closes eyes, head moves from side to side and cries. Wears pajamas. Catalog #0800-3. Original price $9.50. Marks: IDEAL TOY CORP./YTT-19-E (on head); IDEAL TOY CORP./U.S. PAT. No. 3,029,552 (on knob in back). $80.00.

Tearful Tiny Thumbelina (1964) 14" vinyl head and limbs, cloth body, rooted hair. Drinks from a bottle, dressed in blue stripe dress with pink bib. When stomach is pressed her eyes tear. Wind her up she moves and stretches like a real baby. $8.88 retail. $50.00.

Ideal ad.

Ideal's **1964** doll line: (J) **Cuddly Kissy** 16", (K) **Tearie Dearie**, (L) **Tiny Thumbelina**, $80.00, (M) **Snoozie** 20", (O) **Pebbles** and **Bamm-Bamm**, (P) **Pos'n Tammy** 12" Vinyl head, flexible vinyl arms, legs, plastic body. Wears red ballet outfit, comes with curlers. Catalog #9005-0. Original price $2.40. $45.00. (Q) **Pos'n Pepper**, (R) **Betsy Wetsy**®.

Courtesy Rosalie Whyel Museum of Doll Art. Photo by Charles Backus.

Courtesy Richard J. Armitstead.

Mr. Magoo (1964) 15" Vinyl face, cloth body and limbs, molded hat, closed eyes. Cartoon character. Marks: ©1962 UPA PICTURES, INC/All Rights Reserved. Catalog #7853-5. $65.00.

The Addams Family: Fester, Gomez, Morticia (1964) Vinyl head with painted features, hand puppets with cloth bodies from TV show "The Addams Family." Marks: ©FILMWAYS PROD.INC./ 1964/IDEAL TOY CORP. $80.00 each.

Courtesy Richard J. Armitstead.

Superman (1965) (on right) Vinyl head, cloth hand puppet body. Represents George Reeves as Superman. Trademarks: ©1965/NAT.PER.PUB.INC./SM-P-HL3/IDEAL TOY CORP. **Batman (1966)**(on left) Vinyl head, cloth hand puppet body, molded features. Marks: ©1966/NAT'L PERIODICALS PUBS. INC., IDEAL TOY CORP./BM-P-H17. $150.00 each.

Ideal Catalog.

Baby Snoozie (1965) 14" vinyl head and arms, cloth body. Wind knob and doll squirms, stretches, and closes her eyes slowly. Cries until she is picked up and cuddled. Pink, blue, or yellow flannel pajamas with bunny trim. $60.00.

Courtesy Dorothy Alford. Photo by Gary Faulkner.

Goody Two Shoes (1965) 19" All vinyl walking doll, rooted long blonde hair, blue sleep eyes, wears blue dress, has two pairs of shoes. Battery operated on-off switch on back. Catalog #0570-2. Original price $10.00. Marks: 1965/IDEAL TOY CORP./TW18-4-LH4 (on head); 1965/IDEAL TOY CORP./WT 18/PAT.PEND. (on body). $100.00.

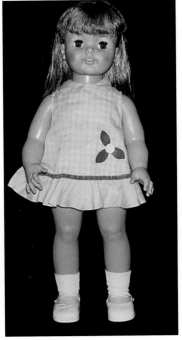

Courtesy Carol Fetherman.

Talking Goody Two Shoes (1966) 27" Vinyl, jointed body, rooted saran hair, walks and talks, says "I'm Goody Two Shoes", etc. Two D-cell batteries. Catalog #0535-5, original price $12.00. $110.00.

Glamour Misty, The Miss Clairol® Doll (1965 – 1966) 12" Vinyl head and arms, plastic legs and body, rooted platinum blonde saran hair, side glancing eyes. Original underwear outfit. Comes with three markers to color hair blonde, red, or brunette. Doll has straight legs. Catalog #9809-5. Original price, $3.25. Marks: ©1965/IDEAL TOY CORP/ W-12-3 (on neck); 2 on derriere, or ©1965 IDEAL (in oval) 12M-12 (on hip). $55.00, MIB, $125.00.

Pos'n Misty (1965 – 1966) 11½" Vinyl poseable arms and legs. Marks: ©1965/IDEAL TOY CORP./W12-3 (on head); body unmarked. Comes in phone booth case. MIB, $100.00.

Courtesy Dawn Thomas.

Playthings Magazine

Honey Moon (1965) 14" Soft vinyl head and limbs, stuffed cotton body, white string hair, painted eyes, blue and silver original costume with removable clear plastic space helmet. Doll had blue and white or brown and white painted eyebrows. Cries when you press stomach. Baby character from Dick Tracy Comic strip by Chester Gould, daughter of Junior Tracy and Moon Maid. Original price $9.98. Marks: ©1965-C.T.-N.Y.N.S./IDEAL TOY CORP./HM/4-2-2H. $65.00.

Honey Moon (1965) Abe Kent, Ideal's vice president with Honey Moon doll.

Betsy Baby (1965) 11½" (shown), 13½", and 17" Vinyl, fully jointed, saran hair. Drinks, wets, and cries. Eyes slowly close during feeding, don't automatically close when laid down. Wearing blue flowered bib type outfit. Comes with bottle, nipple, diaper. 11", $30.00; 13½", $35.00; 17", $40.00.

Courtesy Sharon Criscione.

Courtesy Sharon Criscione.

Prototype 21" Ideal doll never produced. Doll designed by Neil Estern and clothing designed by Judy Albert. Marks: IDEAL TOY CORP./G-21. Not produced due to expense of costume.

Prototype 21" Ideal doll never produced. Doll designed by Neil Estern and clothing designed by Judy Albert. Marks: IDEAL TOY CORP./G-21.

Samantha

Courtesy Arnold Gargiulo II.

Courtesy Danny and Christy Young.

Samantha The Bewitched Posing Doll (1965 – 1966) 12" all vinyl, brown painted side glancing eyes. Marks: IDEAL DOLL/M-12-E-2 (on head); IDEAL in oval/1965 (on body). Mint in box. Box reads: "SAMANTHA is portrayed by Elizabeth Montgomery." $600.00; MIB, $1,000.00.

Samantha The Bewitched Posing Doll (1965 – 1966) 12" Vinyl, side glancing brown eyes. Legs can be posed. Marks: IDEAL DOLL/M-12-E-2 (on head and body).

Courtesy Arnold Gargiulo II.

Samantha The Bewitched Posing Doll (1965) Notice variety of costumes, color, and style. Note doll second from left is Center-Eyed Misty. She has same marks as Samantha doll but has blue center facing eyes, and is redressed.

**Samantha The Bewitched Posing Doll
(1965)** Close-up, doll has been redressed.

Samantha and Tabatha (1966) showing
Tabatha's costume. Marks: ©1966/IDEAL
TOY CORP./TAT-14-H-62. $600.00.

Those "Devil-may-care" Dolls...

SAMANTHA
and her new baby **TABATHA**
stars of ABC-TV's "Bewitched" show

9829-3 SAMANTHA—This exclusive "down-to-earth"
doll version of TV star, Samantha, finds her dressed
in sparkling wine red witch's costume with her golden
blonde Saran hair swooping out from beneath a
matching peaked hat. 12" high, Samantha has poseable arms and legs and comes "bewitchingly" seated
on a sky-riding broom stick in a clear, window box.
Pack per doz: 1   Wgt: 16 lbs.

1150-2 TABATHA—Introducing Tabatha, TV's newest
off-spring and the latest addition to the top-rated "Bewitched" show. Our 14" version has a soft, squeeze-
able body and pert, pixie face that's topped with short,
shiny silver hair. Dressed for a trip to Dreamland,
Tabatha wears a two-piece pajama set and seems to
"float" over the house tops in her all-new window box.
Pack per doz: 1   Wgt: 15 lbs.

Samantha ©1966 Screen Gems
Tabatha ©1966 Screen Gems

They're wonderful
dolls ...they're **IDEAL**

Ideal Catalog.

Comparison of Samantha and Center-Eyed Misty (1966) 12"
Vinyl Samantha with brown/green side glancing eyes on left
and Center-Eyed Misty with blue eyes on right. Center-Eyed
Misty was first Misty doll made, only made for a short time.
Notice differences in hair line; Samantha's hair is swept back
and Misty has side bangs.

Ideal Catalog.

Ideal Catalog.

Go Go Gogi The Disco-Doll (1966) 30" Vinyl head and hands, vinyl foam bendable body, long straight rooted hair, sleep eyes, dressed in "mod" fashions. Catalog #1065-2. Original price, $9.00. $50.00.

Katie Kachoo (1966) 17" Vinyl head, vinyl jointed body, rooted hair; tilts head back and sneezes when arms are raised. Comes with ice bag, thermometer, and water pan. Marks: ©1966/IDEALTOY CORP/SN-17-EH-37. Catalog #1005-8. Original price, $7.00. $60.00.

Private Collection.

Mini Monsters: Franky, Vampy, Dracky, Wolfie (1966) 8½" Vinyl head and jointed squeezable body, painted hair and eyes, rubber removable shoes. Catalog #0740-1, #0743-5, #0741-9, #0742-7. Original price, $1.50. Vampy Girl, white streak in hair, plastic with vinyl arms and head, molded eyelids, open/close mouth. Marks: Wolfie (© 1966 IDEAL TOY CORP/8¼ MW-H-8); Vampy (/8¼ MV-H-8); Dracky (/8¼ MD-H-8); Franky (/8¼ MF-H-8). $65.00.

Captain Action

Captain Action (1966 – 1968) Marks: ©1965/IDEAL(in an oval)/H-93 (on head); ©1966/IDEAL TOY CORP./2 (on back). There were 13 outfits available for Captain Action. They are marked: Ideal Captain Action. $250.00.

Captain Action (**1966 – 1970**) 12" Vinyl head, poseable arms and legs, wears uniform with CA in triangle on chest with tights and cap, lightning sword, scabbard, gun, gun belt, removable boots. Catalog #3400-9. Original price, $2.50. Can become any one of 12 favorite comic strip super heroes with extra outfits such as: **Superman** (**#3401-7**), **Batman** (**#3402-5**), **Flash Gordon** (**#3403-3**), **Sgt. Fury** (**#3404-1**), **Steve Canyon** (**#3405-8**), **Lone Ranger** (**#3406-6**), **Phantom** (**#3407-4**), **Aquaman** (**#3408-2**), **Captain America** (**#3409-0**). **Green Hornet** (**#3413-2**) Outfits, $125.00+. **Action Boy** (**1967**) 9" Vinyl head, poseable body, young friend of Captain Action, wears tights outfit with AB in triangle on chest with beret, utility belt, boots, boomerang, knife, and black panther with leash. Catalog #3420-7. Marks: ©1966/IDEAL (in an oval) (on head); ©1967/IDEAL TOY CORP. (on body). $350.00.

Captain Action in Spiderman Set (1967) #3414-0 and **Action Boy in Robin Set (1967)** 9" vinyl. Other sets available for Action Boy were Superboy and Aqualad. MIB outfits, $150.00+.

Captain Action in Tonto Set (1967) and Buck Rogers Set #3416-5 (1967). Outfits MIB, $150.00.

Courtesy Danny Young.

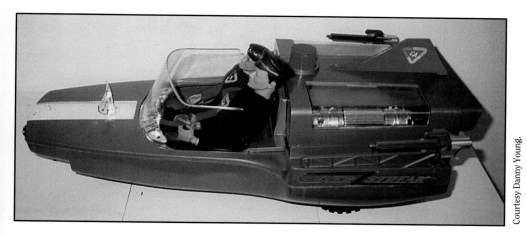

Captain Action in Silver Streak Amphibian Vehicle (1967) missing two spring operated turbo red rockets. #3449-6 vehicle is 21½" long. Marks: ©1967/IDEAL TOY CORP. $300.00.

Courtesy Danny Young.

Dr. Evil (1967) (on right) #3465-2 12" Blue vinyl with jointed wrists, arms, and legs. Dressed in dark pajama type outfit, comes with various face masks. Marks: IDEAL/1968/H-112 (on head); ©1966/IDEAL TOY CORP. (on body). Dr. Evil Lab Set (1968) #3466-0 Dr. Evil Gift Set figure, lab coat, disguise mask pieces on left, reducer wand, hypo gun, hypnotic eye, very rare. Dr. Evil, $250.00; Dr. Evil Lab Set, $2,000.00.

Courtesy Danny Young.

Courtesy Dorothy Alford. Photo by Gary Faulkner.

Courtesy Debbie Garrett.

Giggles (**1967 – 1969**) 18" Vinyl head, vinyl body with jointed wrists, rooted blonde hair, side glancing eyes; pull hands together and she giggles. Catalog #1012-4. Marks: 1966/IDEAL TOY CORP./GG 18 H 77 (on head); 1967/IDEAL TOY CORP./ GG 18 (on body). 18", $65.00.

Giggles (**1967 – 1969**) 18" Black Giggles, notice different box. Black, $120.00

Ideal Catalog.

Tubsy (**1967 – 1968**) 18" Vinyl head and jointed plastic body, rooted hair, sleep eyes, uses two D-cell batteries, dressed in terry robe and diaper; splashes when placed in water up to her tummy. Six outfits sold separately. Catalog #0840-9. $50.00.

Comic Heroines

Ideal Catalog.

Ideal Catalog.

Jet Set Dolls: Stefanie, Chelsea, and Petula (1967) 24" Vinyl head, poseable polyurethane body, rooted long straight hair, young teen dolls, dressed in mod fashions, earrings, strap shoes. It is questionable whether these dolls were ever produced. Catalog #1085-0. $45.00.

Comic Heroines: Mera, Queen of Atlantis; Bat Girl; Super Girl; and Wonder Woman (1967 – 1968) 11½" All vinyl, poseable bodies, rooted hair, painted side glancing eyes, dressed as comic strip characters from National Periodical Publishers. Catalog #9855-8. Marks: 1965/Ideal Toy Corp./W-12-3 (on head); 1965/Ideal (in oval)/2 M-12 (on hip).

Courtesy John Medeiros.

Comic Heroines: Batgirl (1967 – 1968) 11½" All vinyl poseable body. Green eyes, eyeshadow. Same body as Poseable Tammy. All Comic Heroines came with comic art decorated box. MIB, $900.00.

Courtesy John Medeiros.

Comic Heroines: Mera Queen of Atlantis (1967 – 1968) 11½" All vinyl poseable body. Flippers not original. MIB, $900.00.

Comic Heroines: Wonder Woman (1967 – 1968) 11½" All vinyl poseable body. Should have red shoes. Lasso not original. MIB, $900.00.

Courtesy John Medeiros.

Courtesy John Medeiros.

Comic Heroines: Super Girl (1967 – 1968) 11½" All vinyl poseable body. MIB, $900.00.

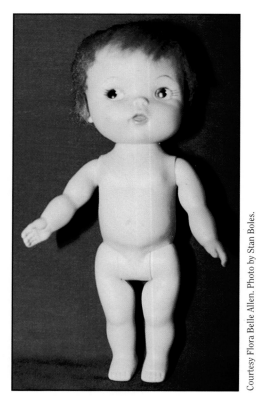

Courtesy Flora Belle Allen. Photo by Stan Boles.

Ideal Catalog.

Honeyball (1967) 9½" Vinyl head, vinyl foam body, saran rooted hair, painted side glancing eyes, six outfits sold separately. Catalog #1066-0. $35.00.

Posie Dolls: Lily, Daisy, Petal, and Rosie (1967) 18" Vinyl head, poseable soft foam bodies, painted eyes, rooted saran hair, non-sleep eyes with lashes, baby dolls. Catalog #1075-1. Lily has platinum hair and a different face from others, with an open mouth; Daisy has red braided hair, open mouth with teeth, polka dot outfit; Petal has blonde hair, felt petal trimmed jumper, open mouth with teeth; and Rosie has brunette hair, striped jumper, open mouth with teeth. $55.00.

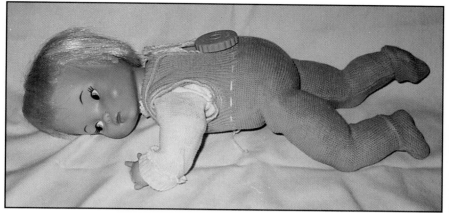

Courtesy Dawn Thomas.

Thumbelina (1968) 14" vinyl head, soft vinyl body, painted side glancing blue eyes, rooted platinum hair. Has knob in back of body. Wearing knit set. Marks: ©1966/IDEAL TOY CORP./TAT-14-H-62. This doll has the same head as Tabatha (1966). $85.00.

Courtesy Lori Grabel.

Newborn Thumbelina (1968 – 1972) 9" Vinyl head and arms, foam stuffed body, rooted blonde hair, painted eyes; squirms when string is pulled. Catalog #0411-9. "Negro" version also available. Doll also came with accessories such as carriage and cradle. Layette also available. $60.00.

Courtesy Aida Tejaratchi.

Newborn Thumbelina (1968 – 1972) 9" in box that came with cradle, pull string and she rocks cradle. #49-30757. $60.00.

Courtesy Lori Gabel.

Newborn Thumbelina (1968 – 1972) Adorable 9" with red pigtails, shown with box.

Courtesy Aida Tejaratchi.

Toddler Thumbelina (1969 – 1971) 9" On rocking horse, dressed as an Indian Princess (#0431-7). Vinyl head and limbs, soft body, rooted hair, painted eyes. Also wears pink middy dress, painted white shoes and socks; pull string and her head and legs move, and she toddles away in her walker. Advertised as sister to Newborn Thumbelina. Seven-piece layette available separately. Marks: 1968/Ideal Toy Corp/BTT9-H-124 (on head). MIB, $85.00.

Courtesy Aida Tejaratchi.

Toddler Thumbelina (1969 – 1971) Pull string in back and her head and legs move and she toddles away in walker. Catalog #0430-9.

Courtesy Aida Tejaratchi.

Toddler Thumbelina (1969 – 1971) 9" Vinyl head and limbs, soft body. Pull string in back and her head and legs move. Wearing yellow outfit. MIB.

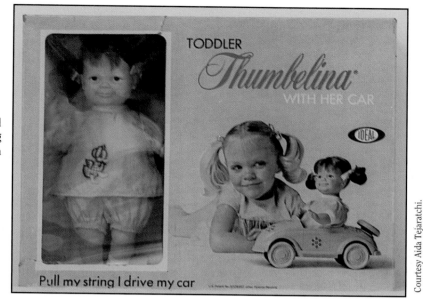

Toddler Thumbelina (1971) 9" Vinyl head and limbs, soft body. Pull string in back and her head and legs move. In car #0432-5. MIB.

Courtesy Aida Tejaratchi.

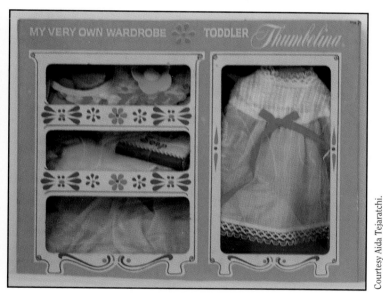

Courtesy Aida Tejaratchi.

Toddler Thumbelina (1969 – 1971) 9" MIB outfit, $40.00.

In-A-Minute Thumbelina (1971) 9" Vinyl, rooted hair, painted eyes; pull string and she bangs cup on her high-chair tray. Also includes spoon and feeding dish. Catalog #0460-6. $70.00.

Courtesy Aida Tejaratchi.

Little Lost Baby (**1968**) 22" Vinyl head with three faces, soft body, cries, coos, laughs, sleeps. Head changes mechanically, voice operates on battery. Body is soft foam. Sculpted by Neil Estern. Catalog #0555-3. Marks: 1967/IDEAL TOY/3F-18-H-111 (on neck). $65.00.

Tearie Betsy Wetsy® (**1968**) 9", 11½", and 17" All vinyl dolls, redesigned face with rooted blonde hair, drink, wet, and cry. Catalog #1130-4, #1158-5, #1165-0. $35.00, $45.00, $55.00.

Baby Giggles (**1968**) 15" All vinyl, rooted hair. When you move her hand up and down, her head and eyes move side to side, and she giggles. Catalog #1019-9. Head sculpted by Neil Estern. Marks: ©1968/IDEAL TOY CORP./BG.-16-H-18 (on head). $60.00.

April Shower (**1969**) 14" Vinyl, painted eyes, rooted platinum hair. Open mouth with two painted teeth. Automatically turns head and arms when placed in water. Marks: ©1968/IDEAL TOY CORP./BT-11-H128 (on head); A-8283©IDEAL 1969 PAT. 3,436,859/MADE IN JAPAN. $45.00.

Posie Doll – Daisy (shown), **Petal, Lily** (1969) 18" Vinyl head and hands, poseable foam body, sleep eyes. Daisy has open mouth with two teeth, long blonde straight hair, wears suede-like fringed vest and bell-bottoms, headband, print shirt, and moccasins. Petal has platinum curly poodle cut and wears knit shirt with paisley scarf and slacks. Lily has brunette banana curls and wears polka dot percale pantsuit, lace jabot, and felt boots. Catalog #1072-8, #1073-6, #1071-0. $60.00.

Ideal catalog.

Diana Ross (1969) 17½" All vinyl, rooted black bouffant hairdo, came in two versions. "On-stage" (Catalog #0920-9) was a gold fabric sheath with feathers and gold shoes. "Off stage" (Catalog #0921-7) was a chartreuse knit mini dress with print scarf and black shoes. From the "Supremes" singing group. $300.00.

Ideal Catalog.

Betty Big Girl (1969 – 1970) 32" All vinyl, rooted hair, sleep eyes, says phrases such as: "My name is Betty Big Girl." Works on one D-cell battery, wears culotte and vest outfit, blouse, and paisley scarf, tights, and vinyl loafers. Catalog #0540-5. Marks: 1968/IDEAL TOY CORP./HD-31-H-127 (on head); 1969/IDEAL TOY CORP./HB-32 (on back). $100.00.

Ideal Dolls
(1970s)

Courtesy Aida Tejaratchi.

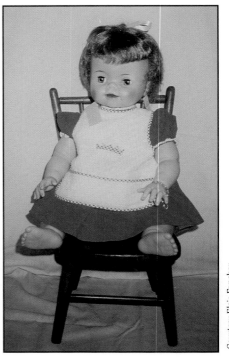

Courtesy Elsie Fancher.

Kissin Thumbelina (1970) Vinyl head and limbs, rooted brown hair, blue sleep eyes. Pull-string in back makes head and body move, right arm swings out to simulate throwing a kiss. Plastic carriage. Catalog #0408-5. MIB, $70.00.

        Bibsy (circa 1970) 23" Vinyl, rooted blonde hair, blue sleep eyes, open mouth with molded tongue; mouth puckers and mades baby sounds when squeezed. Original outfit, bib marked Bibsy in script. Marks: IDEAL TOY CORP./D-20-2 (on head); IDEAL TOY CORP./D-23 (on back). $45.00.

Flatsy

Courtesy Miriam Gittleson.

Flatsy (1970 – 1971) Individual Flatsy in pink raincoat and hat in plastic oval. $45.00.

Flatsyville™: Grandma Baker in a Victorian House (shown), **Sleepy in a Victorian House, Keely in a California Ranch, Munchie in a California Ranch, Kookie in a California Ranch, Nana in a Cape Cod House, Carrie in a Cape Cod House, Shaina in a Cape Cod House (1971)** 4½" Vinyl Flatsy wears dress with apron, rooted platinum hair, eyeglasses, black vinyl shoes. Catalog #0159-4. New additions to the Flatsy line. $55.00.

Courtesy Joedi Johnson.

Fashion Flatsy – Ali the City Girl (1970)
8" vinyl poseable doll with orange hair and green eyes. Outfits were Orange Mini Dress & Vest (#0363-2), Tie Dyed Jeans (#0364-0), and Crochet Gown (#0365-7). Her box is a town house setting. $45.00.

Courtesy Joedi Johnson.

Fashion Flatsy – Cory the Model (1970) 8" vinyl poseable doll with pink hair and blue eyes. Outfits were Bridal Outfit (#0366-5), Cocktail Mini Dress (#0367-3), and Silver Evening Pants Suit (#0368-1). Her box is a photo studio setting. $45.00.

Fashion Flatsy – Dale the Actress (1970) 8" vinyl poseable doll with aqua hair and blue eyes. Outfits were Wet Look Suit (#0369-9), Checked Suit (#0370-7), and Maxi Coat (#0371-5). Her box is a the-atre setting. $45.00.

Courtesy Joedi Johnson.

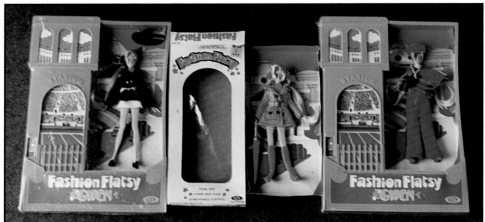

Courtesy Joedi Johnson

Fashion Flatsy – Gwen the Student (1970) 8" Vinyl poseable doll with green hair and green eyes. Outfits were Raincoat and Boots (#0360-8), Suit Outfit (#0361-6), and Poncho and Slacks (#0362-4). Her box is a sports stadium setting. Notice box in middle also found.

Patti Partridge™(**1971**) Vinyl head and limbs, soft body, open mouth with one tooth, rooted hair wig; mechanism in back makes her yawn, suck her thumb open and close mouth, clap hands, and wave. "Tracy's (Partridge) very own performing doll" from TV show "Partridge Family." Catalog #0543-9. $85.00.

Ideal Catalog.

Ideal Catalog.

Bizzie Lizzie (1971 – 1972) 18" Vinyl head and jointed body, rooted blonde hair, sleep eyes; she irons, vacuums, and uses feather duster. Power back uses two D-cell batteries. Also came in black version. Catalog #0867-2. $60.00.

Play 'n Jane (1971) 15" Vinyl head and jointed body, rooted hair, came with sports equipment; launches ball into playing base, uses battery. Catalog #0851-6. Marks: ©1971/IDEAL TOY CORP./TIC-18P-H-181/HONG KONG (on head); ©1971/IDEAL TOY CORP/TIC-16 (on body). $45.00.

Ideal Catalog.

Belly Button Babies: Me So Glad, Me So Silly, Me So Happy (1971) 9½" Vinyl head and body, rooted hair, painted eyes, curved legs; press button in belly makes arms, legs, and head move. "Me So Glad" black version wears white dress, white version wears blue swiss. "Me So Happy" boy in yellow shorts romper, girl with bangs and long straight blonde hair in yellow dress. "Me So Silly" girl with tongue sticking out wearing blue and white plaid set has pigtails, girl wearing red and white plaid has poodle cut, tongue sticking out of mouth, open mouth. Girl and boy version. Catalog #1016-5. White, $35.00; black, $45.00; MIB, $55.00.

Belly Button Baby: Me So Happy (1971 – 1972) 9½"
Boy with brown eyes in yellow romper. MIB.

Belly Button Baby: Me So Glad (1971 – 1972) 9½" Girl in blue romper. MIB.

Belly Button Baby: Me So Glad (1971 – 1972) 9½" Girl with green eyes in white outfit, no shoes, came with rattle and hair bow. Black version. Mint in later box. Marks: ©1970/IDEAL TOY CORP/ E9-2-H165 also seen E9-5-H169/ HONG KONG (on head); IDEAL TOY CORP/ HONG KONG/ 2A-0156 (on back). Dress tagged: IDEAL IN OVAL/ BELLY® BUTTON BABY/ DRESS MADE IN HONG KONG.

Crissy

Beautiful Crissy (1969) 17½" Showing both white and black versions. First Crissy had hair down to floor, later ones had shorter hair. Marks: ©1969/IDEAL TOY CORP./GH-17-H 129 (on head); 1969/IDEAL TOY CORP./GH-18/U.S.PAT.3162976 (on back). Hair to floor version, $100.00. White $45.00, black $65.00.

Courtesy Carol Fetherman.

Courtesy Susan Mobley.

Beautiful Crissy (1969) Five of the six original Fashion Boutique outfits available for Crissy the first year: Walking Jump Suit also known as Groovy Jump Suit, Sporty Blazer and Miniskirt, Cape Coat, Pom Pon Hat, Bell Bottoms, Blouse, and Tie; "Party Outfit" a metallic gold eyelash minidress. Also includes a Boudoir Ensemble. MIB $45.00.

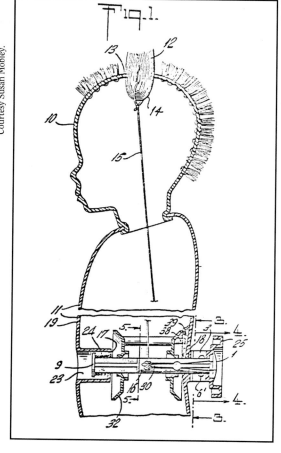

Patent for Doll Having Adjustable Lock of Hair (Patent filed 1971). The mechanism for Crissy®'s family growing hair. Inventors Francis Amici, Robert David, and Richard Levine.

Private Collection.

Beautiful Crissy box (1969) and Crissy's Fashions Tote. $35.00.

Courtesy Susan Mobley.

Beautiful Crissy (1969 – 1970) in brown and white polka dot dress from Crissy's Fashion Boutique.

Courtesy Susan Mobley.

Beautiful Crissy (1969 – 1970) Looking groovy in Peace Poncho and White Dress. Also 1971 outfits: The Drenched Trench, Gypsy, and Funky Feathers.

Talky Crissy (1971) 17½" All vinyl, wearing original long pink satin robe and pink shoes. Growing hair, comes with hair care accessories; pull string and she says 12 sentences. Catalog #1084-3. Original price $9.97. There was also a Spanish-speaking Talky Crissy. Body heavier vinyl than other Crissy bodies, put together with screws. 1972 version said only six phrases and did not come with hair accessories. Marks: ©1969/ITC/GH-17-H120 (on neck); ©1970/ITC/U.S.Pat 3162976/OTHER PATENTS PEND (on back). $55.00; Spanish Talky, $65.00.

Courtesy Susan Mobley.

Ideal Catalog.

Beautiful Crissy (1972) Dress-Up Collection.

Beautiful Crissy (1972) Dress-Down Collection.

Ideal Catalog.

Velvet
Crissy's Cousin

Talky Velvet (1971 – 1973) 15" Vinyl head and body, growing hair, comes with hair accessories, butterfly pull tab; says six sentences when string pulled, such as "Hi, I'm Velvet," and "I want to be your friend." Catalog #1095-9. Original price $9.97. 12 different outfits available this year. Marks: ©1969/IDEAL TOY CORP./GH-15-H-157 (on head); ©1971/IDEAL TOY CORP./TV 15/US PAT 3162973/OTHER PATENTS PEND. (on back). $45.00.

Movin' Groovin' Velvet (1971) 15½" All vinyl, in pink dress. Has a swivel waist and growing hair. Also came in a black version. Catalog #0127-2. $35.00, black $55.00.

Courtesy Janet Thiel.

Ideal Catalog

Velvet (1972) Dress-Up Collection.

| 8121-6 Superstars | 81... Ch... Mov... | 8123-2 Kinky Kolors | 8124-0 Loverly | 8127-3 Short Cuts | 8125-7 Dandy Denims | 8122-4 Frontier Gear | 8120-8 Lemon Hang-up |

Ideal Catalog.

Velvet (1972) Dress-Down Collection.

Courtesy Susan Mobley.

Velvet's Beauty Braider (1973). 15" Black Velvet in white dress with lilac flowers. Also came in a white version. Has plastic hair accessory to help braid hair. $35.00.

Courtesy Marian Schmuhl.

Velvet with Swirly Daisies (1974) 15" Vinyl head and body, platinum blonde growing hair, comes with purple daisy hair accessory, comes with extra dress. Daisy shape gro-hair knob in back. Marks: ©1969/IDEAL TOY CORP./GH-15-H-157 (on head); ©1970/IDEAL TOY CORP./GH 15/2M 5169-01 (on right side of buttocks); MADE IN HONG KONG (on left side of buttocks). $35.00

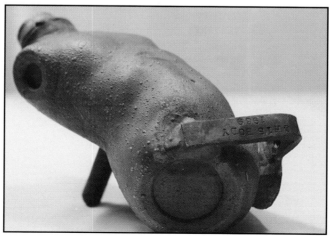

Courtesy Matthew Hollwedel.

Velvet body mold (dated **1969**) Marks: GH-15.

Tressy (**1970**) 17½" All vinyl. Black growing hair, blue sleep eyes, closed smiling mouth, Sears exclusive. Marks: 1970/IDEAL TOY CORP./SGH-17-161/HONG KONG (on head); 1969/IDEAL TOY CORP./GH-18/U.S.PAT. 3,162,976 (on right hip). Also was a black version. White, $65.00; black, $80.00.

Courtesy Susan Mobley.

Mia (**1971**) 15" Vinyl head and body, dark rooted hair, blue eyes, growing hair, open mouth with upper painted teeth, violet sleep eyes with lashes, shown with original blue romper she came in. Velvet's friend, six outfits sold separately to fit Velvet in Glad Plaid (on left) and Mia in Play Dots in middle. Catalog #1059-5. Marks: 13EYE (on head); ©1970/IDEAL TOY CORP./NGH-16-H 178 (on neck); ©1970/IDEAL TOY CORP./GH-15/2M 5169-01 (on back). $50.00.

Courtesy Carol Fetherman.

Kerry (**1971**) 17½" Vinyl head and body, blonde rooted hair, green eyes, growing hair. Crissy®'s friend, in elephant print dress, eight outfits sold separately to fit Kerry and Crissy®. Catalog #1056-1. Marks: ©1970/IDEAL TOY CORP./HGH-18-H-172/HONG KONG/18EYE (on head); 1969/IDEAL TOY CORP./GH-18/U.S.PAT.-#3,162,976 (on back). $55.00.

Posin' Cricket (1971) 15½" Vinyl head and body, auburn rooted hair, brown sleep eyes, growing hair, painted teeth, swivel waist; wearing original orange check dress. Shown with box. Marks: ©1970/IDEAL TOY CORP./CR-H-177/HONG KONG P (on shoulder); ©1970/IDEAL TOY CORP./MO15/HONG KONG (on shoulder). $65.00.

Courtesy Rosalie Whyel Museum of Doll Art. Photo by Charles Backus.

Courtesy Mary-Ellen Smiley.

Dina (1972 – 1973) 15" All vinyl, growing hair doll, member of the Crissy® family. Vinyl head and body, platinum blonde hair, painted blue eyes, open/close mouth with painted teeth, swivel waist, "glowing" tan, growing hair, butterfly tattoo on leg, dressed in purple romper, Velvet's friend. Catalog #1037-1. Original price: $4.70. Marks: ©1971/IDEAL TOY CORP./GHD-16-H-186/HONG KONG/IDEAL 1037-1 (on head); ©1971/IDEAL TOY CORP./MG-15/U.S. PAT.-3,162,976/ OTHER PAT. PEND. /HONG KONG P (on back). Also available in 1973. $50.00.

Brandi (1972 – 1973) 17½" Vinyl head and body, golden rooted hair, painted blue eyes, open/closed mouth with painted teeth, swivel waist, "glowing" tan, growing hair. Crissy®'s friend, shown with box. Catalog #1068-6. Original price $4.70. Marks: ©1971/GHB-18 H186/HONG KONG (on head);©1971/IDEAL TOY CORP./ MG-16/US-PAT-3-162-976/OTHER PAT.PEND./HONG KONG P (on back). $55.00.

Courtesy Marie Ceil Eastman.

Courtesy Carol Fetherman.

Courtesy Cathie Clark.

Cinnamon (originally called just **"Velvet's Little Sister"**) (**1972 – 1974**) 13½" Vinyl head and hair, painted eyes, rooted auburn growing hair, orange polka-dot outfit. Four outfits sold separately. Also came in black version. Shown with box. Catalog #1069-4. Original price, $2.99. ©1971/IDEAL TOY CORP./G-H-12-H18/HONG KONG/IDEAL 1069-4 (on head); ©1972/IDEAL TOY CORP./U.S. PAT-3-162-976/OTHER PAT.PEND./HONG KONG (on back). White, $60.00; black, $70.00.

Cinnamon (Velvet's Little Sister) (1972 – 1974) 13½" Vinyl. Shown with later box and her name and later playsuit.

Ideal Catalog.

Ideal Catalog.

Baby Crissy® (**1973 – 1976**) 24" Vinyl, jointed arms, legs, head, soft vinyl arms and legs filled with foam, rooted auburn grow hair, two painted teeth, brown sleep eyes. Catalog #1115-5. Original price $9.99. Marks: ©1972/IDEAL TOY CORP./2M-5511/B OR GHB-H-225 (on back). Also came in black version. Reissued in 1981. $75.00; black, $85.00.

Baby Velvet (1974) 20" foam body, lavender sleep eyes, blonde grow hair.

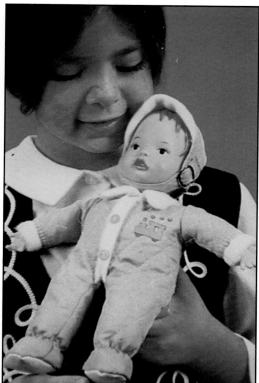

Lazy Dazy (1972 – 1973) Vinyl head and hands, soft body, sleep eyes close softly when she lies down. No batteries. Catalog #0866-4, original price, $4.59. $35.00.

Thumbelina Boy (1972) 9" Molded hair and painted eyes, dressed in aqua snowsuit with removable hat. Catalog #0465-5. Marks: 1970/IDEAL TOY CORP/STT-9-H-180/HONG KONG (on head). Tag reads "Newborn Thumbelina." $70.00.

Ideal Catalog.

Courtesy Cathie Clark.

Courtesy Hank Schuster.

Patti Playful (1973 – 1976) also called **Little Love**® in **1970**. 15" Vinyl head and limbs, soft body, rooted platinum hair, sleep eyes, two teeth. A puppet doll that can be moved by inserting hand in back of doll to made head and limbs move. Marks: ©1973/IDEAL TOY CORP./LL16-N-162. Original clothes, dress says her name in script. Came with white slippers with pom-pon. $55.00.

Harmony (1973 – 1976) 21" Vinyl head and body, long rooted hair, her arms strum guitar and head moves. One D-cell battery. Sound comes from changeable record in her amplifier. Catalog #1096-7. Original price $12.00. Marks: H-2000/1971 (Ideal in oval on head); 1972/Ideal Toy Corp. (on back).

Ideal Catalog.

Upsy Dazy™ (1973) 15" Vinyl head, soft foam body, hard arms and flat spindle hands, hard plastic red cap, painted eyes, blonde rooted hair. Doll somersaults with a unique mechanism. Catalog #0871-4. Original price, $9.50. Also came in black version. $30.00.

Shirley Temple

Courtesy Marge Meisinger.

Shirley Temple: "Wards Yesterday's Darling" (1972) 15" Vinyl offered exclusively by Montgomery Ward. Re-issue of 1958 – 1963 mold. Fully jointed body, wears flocked flower print ninon dance dress with velvet bodice, slip, panties, white vinyl shoes, socks. Original price, $7.99. Marks: IDEAL DOLL/ST-19-1 (on head); IDEAL ST-15/HONG KONG (on back). $150.00.

Courtesy Iva Mae Jones.

Shirley Temple (1973 – 1975) 16½" Vinyl head and plastic body, rooted blonde hair with curls, brown painted eyes, open mouth with teeth, polka dot dress from "Stand Up and Cheer." Four outfits sold separately in 1974, 1975. Marks: 1972/IDEAL TOY CORP./ST-14-H-213/Hong Kong (on head); Logo 1972/2M-5534-2 (on back). Catalog #1125-4. Original price $6.97. $135.00; MIB, $225.00.

Ideal Catalog.

Shirley Temple (1973 – 1975) Four outfits included Rebecca of Sunnybrook Farm, Heidi, Little Colonel, and Captain January. Could be bought separately. MIB outfits, $35.00.

Courtesy Dave Koske.

Shirley Temple and Dave Koske (**1973**) at a visit to the factory during the production of the 1973 line of **Shirley Temple** dolls.

Courtesy Pamela Martinec

Shirley Temple (1974) 12" Shirley Temple. Hard vinyl head, painted brown eyes, uses Cinnamon's body with grow hair feature. Patriotic outfit. Marks: ©1974 IDEAL TOY CORP/ST-12-H-237 (on head). Prototype made to coincide with 1976 Bicentennial. Apparently made only in very limited production.

Courtesy Pamela Martinec .

Shirley Temple (1974) 12" Shirley Temple, comparison with 1972 16" doll produced for Montgomery Ward. 1972 doll has soft vinyl head with same painted brown eyes with white highlights.

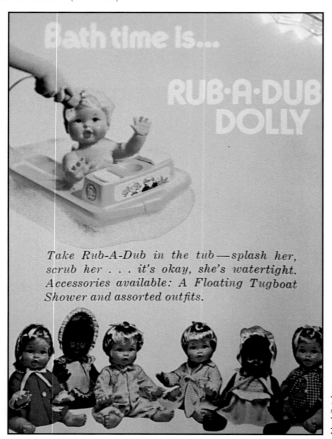

Take Rub-A-Dub in the tub—splash her, scrub her . . . it's okay, she's watertight. Accessories available: A Floating Tugboat Shower and assorted outfits.

Ideal Catalog.

Rub-A-Dub Dolly in Tugboat Shower (1974 – 1978) 17" All vinyl, moveable arms and legs, rooted hair, painted eyes, completely watertight, even floats. Four outfits sold separately. Catalog #1208-8. Original price, $7.99. Also came in black version. Marks: ©1973/IDEAL TOY CORP/RAD-16-H233 (on head); ©1973/IDEAL TOY CORP/HOLLIS NY 11423/RAD 17/2M-5852-01/2 (on body). Six outfits available in 1975: romper, dress and bonnet, robe, pajamas, dress, coat and hat. New face and hairstyle in 1979. $30.00.

Vincent DeFilippo (circa 1965), sculptor of many dolls for Ideal in the 1960s and 1970s, at work. **Rub-A-Dub Dolly** was his first complete commission.

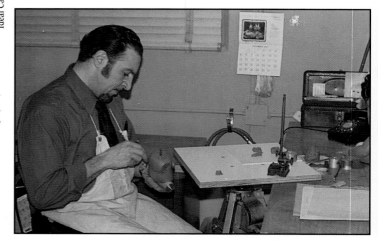

Ideal Catalog.

Evel Knievel (1974 – 1977) 7" All plastic stunt figure with stunt cycle, comes with helmet. Doll was so popular that Ideal even had an Evel Knievel line of play clothes for children, women, and men including pocketbooks, shirts, jackets, T-shirts, and long shirts. Catalog #3403-3. Marks: ©1972 IDEAL/HONG KONG (on back). $25.00.

Tiffany Taylor

Tiffany Taylor (1974 – 1976) 19" All vinyl, rooted hair, top of head turns so rooted blonde hair on one side changes to brown hair, painted eyes, long individual eyelashes, jointed arms and legs and head. Missing her light green sandals. Teenage body with high heel feet shown with one of the four outfits sold separately. Twelve outfits available in 1975, including a "mink" coat. Catalog #1202-1. Original price, $7.95. Also came in black version. Marks: IDEAL (in oval), Hollis NY 11429/2M-5854-01/1 (on back); 6 on rear or ©1974/IDEAL (in an oval), HOLLIS, NY 11423/2M 5854-01/2 (on head); ©1974/CG-19-H-230 HONG KONG (on back). White, $65.00.

Courtesy Dorothy Hesner. Photo Carol Stover.

Tiffany Taylor (1974 – 1976)
Black version. $75.00.

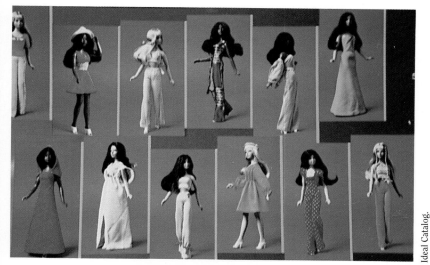

Ideal Catalog.

Tiffany Taylor (1974 – 1976) Separate fashions available in 1974.

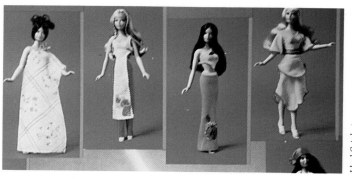

Ideal Catalog.

Tiffany Taylor (1974 – 1976) Separate fashions available in 1974.

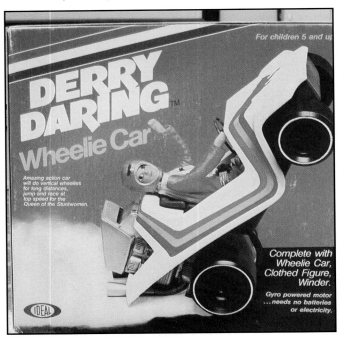

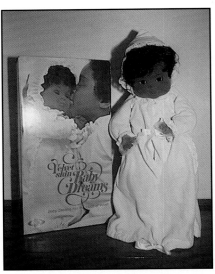

Courtesy Cathie Clark.

Black Baby Dreams™ — The Doll with the Velvet Skin (1975 – 1976) 17" Vinyl head, soft cloth body, floppy arms and legs of soft "velvet skin" (trademark), sleep eyes that close only when she lies on her side, rooted hair. Also came in white version. Catalog #1351-6. $45.00.

Derry Daring (1975) 7" Vinyl action figure, poseable body, rooted blonde hair to waist. Female counterpart to Evel Knievel. Marks: IDEAL DOLL/H-236D.d. (on head). Catalog #3354-8. $35.00.

Jody

Courtesy Debbie Garrett.

Jody: An Old Fashioned Girl (1975 – 1976) 9" All vinyl, rooted hair to her feet, dressed in turn of the century clothes, came with separate room settings such as Victorian Parlor, General Store. Came in three outfits: Gibson Girl, Calico Dress with Apron, and White Eyelet Dress. Came in red and white gingham outfit in 1976. Also came in black version. Catalog #1300-3. $35.00.

Jody: An Old Fashioned Girl (1975 – 1976) in velvet skirt and white blouse with cameo, Gibson Girl dress.

Jody (**1975 – 76**) 9" All vinyl. Called The Country Girl Doll in 1976. In her sideboard led by her horse, Duffy, from Horse and Farm Set (Catalog #1311-0). Includes barn, ducks, chickens, rabbits, and cat. $60.00

Ideal Catalog.

Jody (**1975 – 1976**) Black version. $45.00.

Courtesy Debbie Garrett.

Jody (**1975 – 1976**) in her Country Kitchen complete with over 30 accessories including stove, play utensils, and play food. Comes complete with Jody dressed in calico Apron Dress. $65.00.

Ideal Catalog.

Jody (**1975 – 1976**) in her Victorian Parlor complete with old fashioned gramophone, player piano, flocked velvet sofa. Comes complete with Jody dressed in White Eyelet Dress. $65.00.

Ideal Catalog.

Jody (1975 – 1976) in her General Store includes goodies to buy and Post Office window. Comes complete with Jody dressed in Gibson Girl outfit. $65.00.

Ideal Catalog.

Tuesday Taylor

Tuesday Taylor (1976 – 1977) 11½" All vinyl, poseable body, rooted hair, painted eyes, eyelashes, change color of hair with turn of head, wears aqua lace-front dress. Six outfits sold separately that convert into another: tennis dress to dress, bathing suit to gown, two-piece to lounge outfit, jeans to dress, jumpsuit to gown, undies to robe; 30 outfits sold separately in 1977. Suntan version available in 1977. Super-model version in 1978. Marks: ©1975 IDEAL H-248 Hong Kong (on neck); ©1975 IDEAL US Pat No 3903640 Hollis NY 11423 HONG KONG P (on rear). Clothing tagged "IDEAL Tuesday Taylor." Catalog #1250-0. $40.00.

Taylor Jones (1976 – 1977) 11" Black version, all vinyl, poseable body, rooted hair, painted eyes, eyelashes, change color of hair with turn of head, six outfits sold separately. Catalog #1251-8. $45.00.

Ideal Catalog.

Ideal Catalog.

Ideal Catalog.

Ideal Catalog.

Tuesday Taylor (1977) Outfits for Tuesday Taylor. There were 36 separate outfits sold in 1977 and 1978.

Tuesday Taylor (1977) Outfits for Tuesday Taylor. Clothing tagged "IDEAL Tuesday Taylor." Outfits MIB, $25.00.

Tuesday Taylor (1977) Outfits for Tuesday Taylor.

Tuesday Taylor (1977) Outfits for Tuesday Taylor.

Tuesday Taylor's Summer/Winter Vacation House (1977) Plastic house that changes from two-story ski chalet to A-frame beach house. $65.00.

Ideal Catalog.

Tuesday's Boyfriend Eric™ (1976) 12" Vinyl poseable body painted molded yellow hair, painted blue eyes. Dressed in turtleneck sweater, flared slacks, and Gucci-type loafers. #1254-2. Designed by Bera. $35.00.

Suntan™ Tuesday Taylor®, Suntan™ Eric®, and Suntan™ Dodi® (**1977 – 1978**) Plastic and vinyl poseable dolls that tan when exposed to the sun due to a photochronic substance in plastic. Painted eyes. Tuesday and Dodi have rooted blonde hair; Eric is Tuesday's boyfriend and has painted hair. Dodi is Tuesday Taylor's kid sister. Tuesday® is 11½", Eric is 12", and Dodi is 9". Catalog #1261-7, #1265-8, #1259-1. Marks: Tuesday, HONG KONG (on head); ©1975/Pat. No. HOLLIS NY 11423; Eric, ©1976 IDEAL (in oval)/Hollis N.Y. 11423/HONG KONG P (on back); Dodi, ©1964/IDEAL TOY CORP/DO-9-E (on head); HONG KONG/ ©1977 IDEAL HOLLIS N.Y. 11423 (on back). Tuesday, $40.00; Eric, $35.00; Dodi, $30.00.

Ideal Catalog.

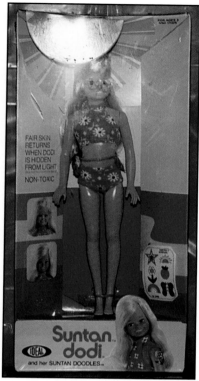

Courtesy Marcia Fanta.

Ideal Catalog.

Suntan Dodi (1977 – 1978) 9" All vinyl, painted eyes, rooted blonde hair. Tuesday Taylor's kid sister. Head is from same mold as 1964 Dodi from Tammy family. Has photochronic substance in skin that turns doll darker when exposed to sun.

Tuesday Taylor® Beauty Queen™ (1978) 11½" Vinyl head, plastic body, rooted sun-streaked blonde hair, magnetic shoes that go on platform stage. Marks: ©1964/ Ideal Toy Corp. D0-9-E (on head); Hong Kong/ ©1977 IDEAL(unreadable name) N.Y.11423 (on back). Catalog #1264-1. $30.00.

Courtesy Marcia Fanta.

Tuesday Taylor® Super Model™ (1978) 11½" vinyl poseable arms and legs. Super model version has "fashion stepper" accessory that allows her legs to be moved. Also comes in black version. Catalog #1240. Marks: ©1977 IDEAL (in an oval)/H-293/HONG KONG P (on head); ©1975/IDEAL (in an oval)/HOL-LIS/N.Y. 11423 Hong Kong P (on back). $30.00.

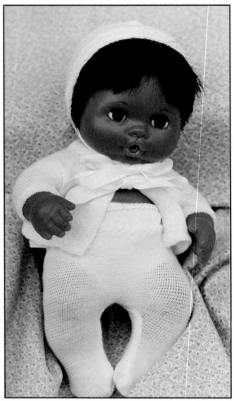

Courtesy Wenham Museum. Photo by Diane Buck.

Baby Baby a Handful of Love (1976 – 1977) 7" Black version, black vinyl head, one-piece vinyl body, black rooted hair, dressed in diaper and pink blanket; when given bottle the bottle moves in and out, turn bottle her eyes close. Also came in white version with blonde hair. Catalog #1340-9. Marks: 115/IDEAL (in oval); ©1974/B-6-B-52/HONG KONG. $25.00.

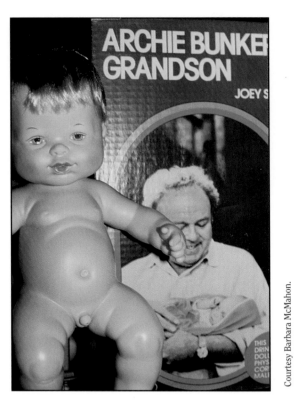

Courtesy Barbara McMahon.

Joey Stivic, Archie Bunker's Grandson (1976 – 1977) 14" Vinyl head, one-piece vinyl body, rooted blond hair, painted eyes, open mouth; drinks and wets, anatomically correct boy from TV show "All in the Family." Catalog #1380-5. Marks: IDEAL TOY CORP/J-14-H-253 (on head); ©1976/TANDEM PRODS.INC/ ALL RIGHTS RESERVED/IDEAL (in oval)/B-58 (on back). $45.00.

Ideal Catalog.

Baby Baby a Handful of Love (1976 – 1977). Six outfits sold separately: bunting, smock, white lace-trimmed dress, pajamas, overalls, kimono. MIB outfits, $15.00 each.

Wake-up Thumbelina (**1976**) 17" Vinyl head of "soft skin," vinyl head and arms, plastic body, cloth stuffed legs are part of outfit, rooted hair, painted eyes; raises head, turns from side to side, raises body, turns over, and holds up arms, two D-cell batteries. Catalog #1360-7. Marks: ©1976/IDEAL TOY CORP./WB-18-H-251 (on head); ©1976/IDEAL (in oval)/HOLLIS NY 11423 (on back). $30.00.

Ideal Catalog.

Courtesy Rosalie Whyel Museum of Doll Art. Photo by Charles Backus.

Tara (**1976**) 15½" All vinyl black doll with "authentic" black features, long black rooted hair that "grows" with turn of a knob, sleep eyes. Catalog #1239-3. Marks: ©1975/IDEAL TY CORP./H-250/HONG KONG (on head); ©1970/IDEAL TOY CORP/GH-15/M5169-01/MADE IN HONG KONG (on buttock). $75.00.

EVEL KNIEVEL™ PRECISION MINIATURES TV

Now there are 12 neat little Evel Knievel die cast stunt vehicles that look just as great at play . . . as they do on display! Any child who's thrilled by Evel's daring exploits — and what child isn't — will want a complete set. There's terrific appeal in the accurately scaled, highly detailed look of these miniatures. They look so real, you'd expect them to roar away at any moment! And that's just the point — because they do look so real, a child's imagination can easily create endless thrilling adventures with them. It's the whole world of Evel Knievel in miniature . . . big entertainment that's small enough to be carried anywhere.

EVEL KNIEVEL™ PRECISION MINIATURES
4323-2
STUNT CYCLE®
4301-8
CHOPPER
4302-6
FORMULA 1 DRAGSTER
4303-4
CANYON SKY CYCLE™
4304-2
FUNNY CAR
4306-7
FORMULA 5000
4305-9
(2 each of 6 styles.)
Pack: 1 doz. Wgt: 3 lbs.
Also available in open stock.

EVEL KNIEVEL™ PRECISION MINIATURES
4322-4
FORMULA "J" CAR
4316-6
RAT TRAP™ CAR
4317-4
SUPER STOCK CAR
4318-2
DRAG BIKE
4319-0
STRATOCYCLE™
4320-8
SUPER CYCLE
4321-6
(2 each of 6 styles.)
Pack: 1 doz. Wgt: 3 lbs.
Also available in open stock.

EVEL KNIEVEL™ PRECISION MINIATURES ASSORTMENT
4300-0
Assortment of all 12 styles, packed in a colorful display shipper.
Pack: 3 doz. Wgt: 8 lbs.

JAY J. ARMES™ FIGURE TV
4400-8
Jay J. Armes is more than a real-life character . . . he's bigger than life! J.J. overcame incredible odds to become the world's greatest investigator.

Today he lives in luxury . . . employs 240 agents . . . and earns up to $50,000 per case! We've reproduced J.J. as a 9½"-tall, fully poseable figure dressed in turtleneck, vest, and slacks. J.J. has no hands, but his spring-loaded hooks can be opened and closed to grasp objects. Or add one of his interchangeable action accessories . . . like a pair of suction cups for climbing walls . . . a magnet for hanging onto steel structure . . . a machete to cut his way out of tough situations . . . even a pair of false hands for undercover roles. And cleverest of all . . . the hook that flips over to become a pistol! J.J. actually has one, and it's saved his life more than once. Incredible but true . . . that's Jay J. Armes!
Pack: 2 doz. Wgt: 6 lbs.

J.J. ARMES
THE WORLD'S GREATEST INVESTIGATOR
J.J. ARMES
BIO-KINETIC HANDS

17
TOYS
PRE-SCHOOL
BICYCLE ACCESSORY
DOLLS
3-D GAMES
BOARD GAMES

Ideal Catalog.

Jay J. Armes (**1976 – 1977**) 9½" All vinyl poseable action figure. Molded hair, painted eyes, comes with interchangeable hooks for hands, resembles real life detective. Catalog #4400-8. $45.00.

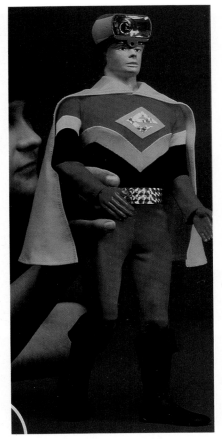

Ideal Catalog.

ElectroMan™ (1977) 16" All vinyl poseable action figure has miniature electronic circuit, power beam that senses motion or light change and issues warning sound when detects change. Also talks in computer-like noise. Battery operated. $45.00.

Ideal Catalog.

Magic Hair™ Crissy® (1977) 19" Vinyl head, poseable plastic body, rooted brown hair, velcro on head. Comes with five hair pieces that attach with velcro, painted eyes, teenage character, also came in black version. Catalog #1280-7. Marks: ©1977/IDEAL TOY CORP./M.H.C. -19-H-28I/HONG KONG (on head); ©1974/IDEAL (in an oval)/HOLLIS, N.Y. 11423/2M-5854-01/1 with a 6 and 7 (on derriere). $35.00.

Courtesy Edna Zeiler. Photo by Betty K. Jones

Tippy Tumbles (1977) 16½" Vinyl head and arms, plastic body, painted eyes, rooted hair; stands on her head and flops over, attached by wire to "pocketbook" battery pack; girl doll, also came in white version. Catalog #1194-0. Marks: ©1976/IDEAL TOY CORP./T-18G-H-276 (on head); U.S. PAT.NO. 3500577/IDEAL TOY CORP./HOLLIS NY 11423 (on back). White, $35.00; black, $40.00.

Timmy Tumbles (1977) 16½" Vinyl head and arms, plastic body, painted features, brown rooted hair; tumbles over, boy doll, has battery box in shape of tool kit which attaches on side of leg. Catalog #1196. Black version also available. Marks: ©1976/IDEAL TOY CORP./T-18G-H-276 (on head); U.S. PAT.NO. 3500577/IDEAL TOY CORP./HOLLIS NY 11423 /1977 (on back). White, $35.00; black, $50.00.

Dorothy Hamill™ (1978) 11½" Vinyl head, plastic poseable body, rooted short brown hair, comes on ice rink with ice skates, Olympic skating star, six separate outfits. Catalog #1290-6. Marks: 1977 DH/IDEAL (in oval); HONG KONG 1975 (on head); 1975 IDEAL (in oval)/US PAT. NO. 3903640/HOLLIS, NY 11423/HONG KONG P (on body). $35.00.

Snuggles™ (1978 – 1981) 12½" Vinyl head, cloth body and limbs, rooted blonde hair, painted eyes; holds a blanket, pillow, or Teddy bear. Pull string and she moves head and snuggles; also came with red hair or in a black version. Sculpted by Erin Libby. Marks: IDEAL TOY CORP. 1978/ MADE IN HONG KONG; also seen, ASSEMBLED IN HAITI. Catalog #1185-8. $30.00.

Ideal's Original Teddy Bear (1978 – 1981) All plush, button eyes, velvety yarn nose. Same as used for 75th Anniversary. $30.00.

Whoopsie™ (1978 – 1981) 13" Vinyl head and limbs, soft foam-filled body, blonde rooted hair, watermelon mouth, painted eyes, one-piece body. Push tummy and braids go up and she makes "whoopsie" sound. Came barefoot. Black version also available. Catalog #1190-8. Marks: 22/©IDEAL TOY CORP/ HONG KONG/ 1978/H298. Reissued in 1981. $35.00.

Ideal Catalog.

Snuggles and her Rocking Horse (1979) 12½" Vinyl head, cloth body and limbs, rooted blonde hair, painted eyes; holds a blanket, pillow, or Teddy bear. Rocking horse is polka dot with orange yarn mane, tail, and forelock. Pull string and she moves head and makes rocking horse move. Catalog #1154-4. $30.00.

Ideal Catalog.

My Bottle Baby (1979 – 1980) 14" Vinyl head, stuffed cloth body and limbs, rooted blonde hair with pigtails, painted eyes, open mouth; pull string and her head moves up and down and makes nursing sounds, stops drinking when you remove her bottle. Catalog #1104-9. $25.00.

New Rub-A-Dub® Dolly (1979) 17" Vinyl, rooted hair, painted eyes, new outfit and hairdo. Black version also available. Tugboat Shower could be bought separately. $35.00.

Brandi and Andy Gibb – Disco Dancin' with the Stars (1979) 7½" Vinyl with rooted blonde hair, painted eyes. Andy Gibb, star of "Shadow Dancin'," arms swing and bodies sway when put on dancing stands, comes with two dancing stands and light show with strobe light. Catalog #1470-4. Marks: S.G.L. IDEAL (in oval)/H-317/HONG KONG (on head); ANDY GIBB/IDEAL TOY CORP./HONG KONG (on back). $45.00.

Kissy (1979) 3" Vinyl with rooted hair, "rubber stamp-like" lips treated to leave kiss imprint, three hair colors: blonde, brunette, redhead. Catalog #1148-6. Marks: ©1978/IDEAL TOY CORP. $20.00.

Ideal Dolls
(1980s)

Ideal Catalog.

Ideal Catalog.

Karen and Her Magic Carriage (**1980 – 1981**) 14½" Vinyl head, cloth body, rooted blonde hair, painted eyes, open mouth. Came in blue and white carriage. Squeeze handle and she lifts both arms, waves, plays peek-a-boo, also does this when press tummy. Catalog #1362-3. $35.00.

Chew, Chew, Chew Suzy Chew Doll (**1980**) 14" Vinyl head and limbs, soft vinyl body, rooted blonde hair, painted eyes; opens mouth, chews solid food when press button on back, also came in black version. Catalog #1228-6. $35.00.

Photo by Anthony L. Colella.

Little Miss Marker™ – Sara Stimson (**1980**) 11½" Vinyl head and body, rooted brown hair, painted eyes, wearing beret, jacket and dress, brown high top shoes and white socks. Star of Universal Studio's 1980 remake of "Little Miss Marker™," Catalog #1382-1. Supposedly, only 6,000 were made. Marks: ©1979/UNIV. STUDIOS/IDEAL (in oval)/ H390/HONG KONG (on head); IDEAL (in a double oval)/HONG KONG P (on back). $25.00.

Sara Stimson (1980) Shown with prototype of 11½" Shirley Temple which was never produced.

Joseph C. Winkler, Executive Vice President and Chief Operating Officer and Lionel A. Weintraub, Chairman of the Board, President and Chief Executive Officer (**1980**). Ideal stockholders report.

Pretty Curls™ Dolls (1981 – 1982) 12½" All soft vinyl, rooted nylon hair, painted eyes, came with hair styling kit, three versions of hair color: blonde, brunette, redhead. Catalog #1161-9. Marks: ©1980/IDEAL TOY CORP./H-541. Black version also available. $25.00.

Ideal Catalog.

Ideal Catalog.

Perfume Dollys: Rosalie Rose, Joyful Jasmine, Nina Gardenia, Lola Lilac (**1981**) 3" Perfume bottles whose heads come off and have roll-on ball appplicator of perfume. Catalog #1512-3. $5.00. Shown with prototype of **Loni Anderson,** star of TV show "WKRP in Cincinnati" doll that was not produced.

Baby Kiss-a-Boo™ (**1981**) 12½" Soft vinyl head and one-piece body, rooted blonde hair, painted eyes, comes with boo-boo and kiss applicator, boo-boo coloring, and six bandaids. Catalog #1375-5. Black version also available. $25.00.

Ideal Catalog.

Laura™ and Robin™ (**1981**) 11½" Vinyl fashion doll, foam-filled soft body, rooted blonde hair, painted eyes, dressed in sweater and slacks, Robin is the black doll. Twelve outfits sold separately. Catalog #1074-4 and #1075-1. There is question of whether these dolls were ever produced on a large scale.

Courtesy Christian Bassick.

Ideal Catalog.

Patti Play Pal® (**1981 – 82**) 36" Vinyl doll reissued from 1959 mold. Blonde straight hair with bangs. Eyes do not close. Catalog #8535-7. Original cost $39.50. Black version available only in 1981 – 1982. White, $150.00; black, $175.00.

Baby Crissy® (**1981**) 24" Reissued from original 1973 molds. All vinyl, rooted auburn hair grows, brown glassene eyes with lashes, open/closed mouth with two painted teeth, dressed in white romper. Can wear real baby clothes. Reissue from original mold. Catalog #8526-6. Original cost $27.50. Also came in black version. $60.00, black $70.00.

Ideal Catalog.

Tiny Tears® (**1982 – 1985**) 14" One-piece vinyl body, inset blue eyes, bisque skin color, rooted (left) or molded hair (right), long lashes, two middle fingers of left hand curled under to palm, first two fingers of right hand molded to thumb, dressed in short dress, comes with bottle; drinks, wets, and cries. Marks: 1971 Ideal (in an oval on head); ©1971 IDEAL TOY CORP./TNT-14-8-34 (on body). Catalog #1367-2, #1364-9. Black version also available. $30.00.

Ideal Catalog.

Thumbelina (**1982 – 1983**) 7" All vinyl body is one piece, rooted hair, blue glassene eyes, comes in quilted carry-all, black and white version. Catalog #1320-1 and #1321-9 (left). Marks: 1974/IDEAL (in oval)/B-6-H361 (on head); IDEAL (in oval), 1974/B.B.-8-52 (on back). 16" **Thumbelina Soft Infant Doll** (**1982 – 1985**) rooted hair, open laughing mouth, vinyl head and limbs, sleep eyes, wears pink shirt and white blouse. Catalog #1393-8; 18" **Thumbelina Doll with molded hair** (**1982 – 1985**). 7", $20.00; 16", $30.00.

Photo courtesy Elsie Fancher.

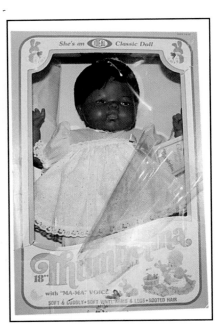

Courtesy Mary Kangas.

Tiny Tears® (**1982 – 1985**) 14" all vinyl, blue glassene eyes, bisque skin color, rooted hair; drinks, wets, cries. Shown wearing christening dress in her box.

Thumbelina (**1981**) 18" Vinyl head, arms, and legs, painted eyes, cloth body, "mama" voice, molded or rooted hair, open mouth. Reissued from the original 1960s mold. Black version also available. Catalog #1355-7, #1371-4. $40.00.

Ideal Catalog.

Country Fashion Crissy® Doll (1982 – 1983) (On left) 15" All vinyl, reissued from original Velvet body mold, glassene sleep eyes with lashes, wearing long plaid skirt, white blouse, and straw hat, growing auburn nylon hair. Catalog #1031-4. Doll is on Velvet body with brown eyes and red hair. $45.00. (Right) **Beautiful Crissy® Doll (1982 – 1983)** wearing short white dress. Catalog #1030-6. Also came in black version. White, $25.00; MIB, $45.00; black, $30.00; MIB, $50.00.

Jelly Belly™: Lemon Drop, Purple Punch, Bubble Gum (1982) 12" Vinyl faces, soft terrycloth bodies and cloth limbs, rooted hair, has non-toxic substance in belly that is soft and squishy. Dolls are scented according to color of costume: yellow (lemon drop), blue (purple punch), pink (bubble gum). Catalog #1010-8, #1011-6, #1012-4, #1013-2. Original price $7.25. $20.00.

Courtesy S. Swertman.

Courtesy Veronica Phillips.

Shirley Temple (1982) 8" (shown), 12" Vinyl in the six versions she came in: "Stand Up and Cheer," "Heidi," "Littlest Rebel," "Little Colonel," "Stowaway," "Captain January." Catalog #1330-0 (8") and #1340-9 (12"). Original price $11.00 and $17.00. Also produced in 1983 with different costumes. 8", $40.00; 12", $50.00.

Shirley Temple (1982) 8" in Captain January outfit, MIB.

Courtesy Dorothy Hesner. Photo by Carol Stover.

Shirley Temple (1982) 8" in Stowaway costume, MIB.

Ideal Catalog.

Angel Babies (1982) 3½" All vinyl jointed neck, arms, waist, mylar wings, each come with a wand that attaches by string to doll to make it fly, six versions, story book and cloud to stand on included; turn waist and wings pop up. Catalog #1517-2. Original price $3.95. $15.00.

Courtesy William Furnish.

Raggedy Ann and Andy (1983 – 1985) 16" Porcelain swivel head, shoulders, hands and feet, stuffed cloth body and limbs. Limited production collector's doll set, 6,000 sets produced worldwide. Red yarn wig, painted eyes. Ann wears a calico dress with white eyelet apron; Andy wears plaid shirt, navy shorts, blue hat. Has a signed numbered certificate of authenticity. Catalog #10003. Original price $500.00 for set. $150.00 each.

Ideal Catalog.

Baby's Thumbelina® Doll (1983 – 8194) (On left) 4" Vinyl face and hands, cloth fluffy fiber body forms outfit and hood, comes in pink, yellow and blue, rooted yarn hair, painted eyes. Also came in black version. Catalog #13003. (Middle) **Thumbelina (1983 – 1985)** 16" Vinyl head and limbs, soft cloth body, new face, rooted nylon hair with top-knot, glassene eyes with lashes, "mama" voice, dressed in pink dress. Black version also available. Catalog #13938. (Right) **Newborn Thumbelina (1983 – 1985)** 18" Vinyl head and limbs, soft body, light color vinyl, painted eyes, open mouth, "mama" voice, pink striped dress with eyelet apron. Black version also available. Catalog #13557.14", $20.00; 16", $30.00; 18", $40.00.

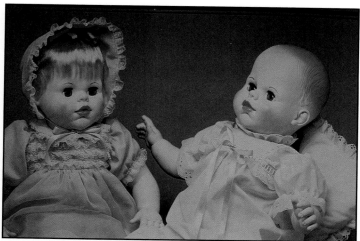

Ideal Catalog.

So-o-o Big Thumbelina® (**1983 – 1985**) (Left) 25" Vinyl head and limbs, soft body, glassene sleep eyes, "mama" voice, rooted hair, wears pink bonnet and dress and booties. Catalog #13078. (Right) Molded hair version wears white long gown. Also came in black version. Catalog #13052. $35.00.

Betsy Wetsy® (**1983 – 1985**) 16" (Left) Light color vinyl, molded hair. Catalog #14241. (Right) Rooted hair, sleep eyes, wears yellow dress and bonnet, comes with bottle; drinks and wets. Catalog #14209. $25.00.

Ideal Catalog.

Ideal Catalog.

Fashion Tressy® (**1983**) 12" All vinyl, jointed, rooted hair, pale vinyl, comes with six packets of curling mixture to turn Tressy's hair curly, rollers, ribbons, applicator, and dish. Three versions: blonde with pink dress, brunette with pink check top and blue skirt, and red head with yellow dress. Also came in black version. Catalog #12716, #12732, #12740. $25.00.

Happi Returns (**1983 – 1984**) 14" Vinyl head, hands, and feet, soft cloth body, in a yellow baby walker, rooted blonde hair, painted eyes, open/closed mouth. Laughing mechanism activated by touch on back. Uses one AA battery. Black version also available. Catalog #12765. $30.00.

Tiny Tears® Limited Production Collector's Doll (1983 – 1985) 14" Porcelain, glass eyes, molded painted or rooted hair, wears antique crocheted outfit, matching booties and pillow, has numbered signed certificate of authenticity. Catalog #10001 and #10002. $75.00.

Shirley Temple™ (1983 – 1985) 16" Porcelain, painted features, seersucker pink dress, embroidered apron and wefted wig with curls, white vinyl shoes with bows. Limited edition of 10,000. Each doll has signed numbered certificate of authenticity. Catalog #14456. Original price $400.00. $250.00.

Thumbelina Limited Production Collector's Doll (1983 – 1985) 18" (shown) and 24" Porcelain, painted eyes, molded painted hair, wears beige crocheted outfit with pillow and booties. Limited edition of 1,000. Comes with numbered certificate of authenticity. Original price 24", $290.00. Catalog #10000. $75.00.

Ideal Catalog.

Shirley Temple Collector's Edition (1983) 8" and 12" Clockwise: Little Colonel, Captain January, The Littlest Rebel, Heidi, Stowaway, Stand Up and Cheer. Ideal wrist-tag that came on doll.

Ideal Catalog.

Shirley Temple Collector's Edition (1983) 8" and 12" All vinyl, glassene eyes, rooted hair, dimples, wearing new series of clothes different from 1982 series: "Suzanna of the Mounties," "Rebecca of Sunny Brook Farm," "Dimples," "Little Miss Marker," "Poor Little Rich Girl," and "Wee Willie Winkie." Catalog Numbers: 8", #10441-10446; 12", #10447-52. 8", $40.00; 12", $50.00.

Courtesy Dorothy Hesner. Photo by Carol Stover.

Shirley Temple Collector's Edition (1983) 12" in Poor Little Rich Girl.

Ideal Catalog.

Victorian Ladies™ Costume Dolls: Charlotte, Emma, Constance, Lydia, Patience, Theresa (1983) 8" and 12" All vinyl, wearing Victorian costumes, light color vinyl, rooted nylon hair, fully jointed, glassene sleep eyes. Emma has green eyes; Charlotte has brown eyes; others have blue eyes. All wear different long gowns with high yokes and set-in sleeves. Catalog 8", #10459-10464; 12", #10453-58. 8", $25.00 each; 12", $35.00 each.

Ideal Catalog.

Nursery Tales™ Character Dolls: Mother Goose, Little Red Riding Hood, Little Bo Peep, Cinderella, Snow White, Alice in Wonderland (1983) 8" All vinyl jointed dolls wearing appropriate fairy tale character outfit. Glassene eyes, rooted hair. Catalog numbers #12849, #12856, #12864, #12872, #12880, #12898. New costumes in 1984. $25.00 each.

Ideal Catalog.

Thumbelina® Collector's Edition (1983 – 1985) (on left) 16" Vinyl, rooted hair, sleep eyes, "mama" voice, wears lace outfit with crochet-trimmed pillow. Catalog #10466. $30.00.

Courtesy Elizabeth Moroch.

Kit 'N Kaboodle™ (1984 – 1985) 14" Vinyl head and hands, soft body, rooted blonde hair, dressed in country and western outfit. Rides a plastic pony who clops along without batteries. Black version also available. Marks: H-288. $30.00.

Ideal Catalog.

Chipettes™ – Jeanette, Brittany, Eleanor (1984 – 1985) 10" Vinyl head, hands, and legs, soft plush body, rooted hair, painted eyes. Girlfriends of the "Chipmunks™." $20.00 each.

Courtesy Laurie's Dollies.

Chipettes™ – Jeanette (1984 – 1985) 10" Vinyl head, hands, and legs, soft plush body, rooted hair, painted eyes. Girlfriend of the "Chipmunks™."

Ideal Catalog.

Betsy Wetsy® (1984 – 1985) 16" All vinyl, molded hair with topknot, sleep eyes, comes with bottle, dressed in green seersucker shirt and shorts with white apron; drinks and wets. Also came with long gown. Black version available. Also came in rooted hair version (both white and black) dressed in coral dress and bonnet. Another version was molded hair with layette. Catalog #14225, #14233, #14209, #14217, #14241, #10080, #10103, #10104. $25.00; black, $30.00.

Courtesy Mary Stuecher.

Ideal Catalog.

Little Women (1984 – 1985) 8" (Beth) and 12" (Meg, Jo, Amy) Rigid pale "bisque-look" vinyl, jointed, sleep eyes with lashes, rooted hair. Costumes are exact replicas of those worn in the 1949 MGM movie "Little Women" starring June Allyson as Jo, Janet Leigh as Meg, Elizabeth Taylor as Amy, and Margaret O'Brien as Beth. Only set authorized by MGM. Marks: ©1978 MGM/CBS INC/1438 (on head); IDEAL (in an oval with a diamond shape around it)/1982. Manufactured by CBS Toys. 8", $30.00; 12", $40.00 each.

Baby Crissy® (1984 – 1985) 18" (Left) All vinyl, jointed, light color vinyl, molded hair with topknot. Catalog #10105. (Right) Rooted hair. Catalog #10109. Both drink, wet, and come with bottle. Black version also available. $35.00.

Ideal Catalog.

Teeni-Tiny Thumbelina (1984) 12" Vinyl head and limbs, soft stuffed body, rooted hair, glassene eyes and lashes, "mama" voice, pink dress with pinafore. Catalog #10160, #10161. $20.00.

Ideal Catalog.

Thumbelina (1984 – 1985) 16" (Left) Rooted hair. Catalog #10162. (Right) Vinyl head and limbs, soft body, molded hair, painted eyes, "mama" voice, pink and white striped dress, looks like newborn. Catalog #10163. Black version also available. $25.00.

Ideal Catalog.

Whoopsie™ (1984 – 1985) 14" Vinyl head and limbs with soft body toddler. Dressed in sailor suit with rooted ponytail. Limited edition version has curls and wears pink striped dress with lace apron. $20.00.

Ideal Catalog.

Tiny Tears (**1984**) 14" Limited production vinyl doll, molded hair, glassene eyes with lashes, wears long eyelet gown in a wicker basket. Porcelain bottle available in 1984. Catalog #14142. $20.00.

Ideal Catalog.

Courtesy Iva Mae M. Jones.

Collector's Edition Shirley Temple™ (**1984 – 85**) 16" All vinyl, rooted hair, wearing three new outfits: "Heidi," "Glad Rags to Riches," and "Stand Up and Cheer." Catalog #10500, #10499, #10501. $45.00.

Collector's Edition Shirley Temple (**1984 – 1985**) 16" Vinyl in Stand Up and Cheer.

Courtesy Iva Mae M. Jones.

Ideal Catalog.

Hara™ (1984) 16" Vinyl head, arms, and legs, light color vinyl, soft body, moving eyes, rooted dark hair, wearing pink striped dress with lace apron. Catalog #10433. $30.00.

Collector's Edition Shirley Temple (1984 – 1985) 16" vinyl in Glad Rags to Riches.

Ideal Catalog.

Nursery Tales™ Character Dolls: Queen of Hearts; Mother Hubbard; Little Miss Muffet; Goldilocks; Mary, Mary; Rapunzel (1984) 8" All vinyl dolls, jointed limbs, glassene eyes, rooted hair, wearing appropriate fairy tale character outfits. Catalog numbers #10252, #10254, #10250, #10255, #10253, #10251. $25.00 each.

Ideal Catalog.

The Wizard of Oz: Tin Man, Lion, Scarecrow, Dorothy, and Toto (1984 – 1985) 9" Vinyl dolls, six piece poseable bodies. Dorothy in white vinyl, thick dark brown braids, painted on shoes and socks, blue check dress, sewn-in white blouse with puff sleeves. Marks on Dorothy: CBS INC/H4-22 (on head); ©1939 LOEW'S REN./1966 MGM/MFG BY CBS INC/B107. $35.00 each.

Victorian Ladies™ Costume Dolls: Leticia, Estelle, Agnes, Guinevere, Rosaly, Lenore, Millicent (1984 – 1985) 8" and 12" All vinyl wearing Victorian costumes, light color vinyl, rooted nylon hair, fully jointed, glassene sleep eyes. Agnes has brown eyes; Guinevere has green eyes; others have blue eyes. All wear different long gowns with high yokes and set-in sleeves. Catalog 8", #10222-10228, 12", #10229-35. 8", $30.00 each; 12", $35.00 each.

Ideal Catalog.

Ideal Catalog.

Abbott and Costello (1984 – 1985) 12" All vinyl character dolls of comedians Bud Abbott and Lou Costello, wearing baseball uniforms. Came with audio tape. $50.00 each.

Tiny Tears (1984 – 1985) 14" Porcelain, limited production, wears crocheted romper set, comes with pillow and booties, porcelain bottle, signed, numbered certificate of authenticity. $45.00.

Ideal Catalog.

Teddy Bear® (1984) 14" Porcelain, limited production 80th Anniversary Teddy Bear. All jointed, comes with signed, numbered certificate of authenticity. $80.00.

Ideal Catalog.

Jim and Dandy (1985) 12" Vinyl head and hands, cloth body, boy and girl twin dolls, painted eyes and open/closed mouth with painted teeth. They play on their Gym Dandy Action Swing Set, which has a slide, swing, teeter-totter, and see-saw. $20.00 each.

Ideal Catalog.

Kindles™ Lap-Size Dolls: Sparkli, Gleami, Flashi, Beami, Glari, Glorali™ (1985) Vinyl heads, soft bodies, necklaces that light up. Catalog #10331. Also came in 8" and smaller figures whose faces light up. $20.00.

Courtesy Marcia Fanta.

Teeny Baby Crissy (1989) from Ideal Nursery Classic Doll Collection vinyl head and limbs, soft body; pull cord and hair grows. Marks: Baby Crissy/1989/ Ideal Inc. Box dated 1991. $35.00.

Courtesy Marcia Fanta.

Teeny Baby Crissy (1989) from Ideal Nursery Classic Doll Collection vinyl head and limbs, soft body; hair grows.

Courtesy Marcia Fanta.

Teeny Baby Crissy (1989) from Ideal Nursery Classic Doll Collection vinyl head and limbs, soft body; hair grows.

Courtesy Dorothy Hesner. Photo Carol Stover.

Ideal Michael's Pets: Cool Bear (circa 1989) Tag says: "Owned by Triumph International Inc. and used by Viewmaster/Ideal Group Inc. under authorization all rights reserved. Dist. by Ideal Inc. Portland, OR 97207. Made in Taiwan R.O.C." Other pets include Ostrich Jeannine. $40.00.

Ideal Dolls Not Photographed

Name	Date Issued	Identifying Characteristics	Current Price
Mr. Hooligan	1910	Composition head, painted features, stuffed plush fur body (white, brown, or blue). Marks: Ideal Art Novelty Co.	$500.00
Dandy Kid	1911	Compo head and body made by skeleton process.	$250.00
Ty Cobb	1911	Compo head and hands, stuffed cloth body and limbs. Famous baseball player.	$350.00
Baby Mine	1911 – 18	28 designs. By special permission of Margaret Mayo, who wrote comedy play, "Baby Mine." Catalog #258. Original price $0.25 to $1.50.	$100.00
Captain Jinks	1912	Molded painted features, compo head and hands, stuffed body and limbs, dressed in khaki uniform trimmed in red, shoes, and stockings. Catalog #220.	$100.00
Baseball Boy	1912	Compo, wears baseball uniform.	$150.00
Naughty Marietta	1912	Compo head and hands, molded painted features, stuffed body.	$100.00
Jack Horner	1912	Compo head, molded hair, painted eyes, wears long tunic with shorts underneath, goes with Naughty Marietta from the nursery rhyme.	$100.00
Russian Boy	1912	Compo head and hands, stuffed body and limbs, Russian-style tunic and pantaloons.	$100.00
Water Baby	1912	12", 14" Celluloid mask baby face, imported sponge body trimmed with ribbon. Original price $0.25.	$50.00
Baby Bettie	1913 – 14	Compo head and hands, soft body, molded painted hair, painted eyes. Catalog #246. Original price $1.00.	$100.00
Artic Boy	1913	Compo head and hands, stuffed cloth body and limbs, wears knit jacket, pants, and bonnet. Catalog #600.	$100.00
Baby Marion	1913	Compo head and hands, cotton body, molded hair, painted eyes, wears knit dress and bonnet, goes with Arctic Boy. Catalog #645. Original price $1.00.	$100.00
Freddie	1913 – 14	"The Country Cousins," compo head and limbs, molded painted features, soft body in bare feet, overalls, and hat. Catalog #221½. Original price $1.00.	$100.00
Flora	1913 – 14	Goes with Freddie, in dress with bow in hair. Catalog #225. Original price $1.00.	$100.00
Tiny Toddler	1913 – 14	Compo head, soft body, long sleeve rompers with belt and hat.	$100.00
Middy Girl	1913	Compo head, hands, and legs, cloth body, painted molded hair, painted eyes, wears ribbon in hair and middy dress.	$125.00
Little Princess	1914	Dressed in knit coat and hat. Catalog #400.	$100.00
Baby Lolo	1914	Wears christening gown and bonnet. Catalog #445.	$110.00
Baby Paula	1914	Wears christening gown and bonnet. Catalog #465.	$110.00
Baby Dada	1914	Wears dress and bonnet. Catalog #245.	$100.00

Name	Date Issued	Identifying Characteristics	Current Price
Sunny Jim	1914	Wears dress (cassock) and hat. Catalog #310. Original price $0.25 to $1.00.	$100.00
Baby Bunting	1914	"Unbreakable" doll with sleep eyes and painted hair. The first Ideal doll with sleep eyes. Compo head, cloth body. Catalog #704.	$150.00
Admiral Dot	1914	Compo head and limbs, cloth body, painted eyes. Sailor Boy wearing middy shirt, pants, and sailor hat, character boy from Barnum and Bailey Circus. Catalog #410.	$200.00
Bulgarian Princess	1914	Wears ethnic clothing.	$75.00
Buster	1915	16" Compo head and hands, stuffed cloth body and legs, jointed limbs, painted mouth, painted or sleep eyes, with or without human hair wigs, wears cotton suit with stripe down front, shoes, and stockings. Original price $2.80.	$100.00
Sanitary Baby	1915	16", 25" Compo head and hands, imitation kid body, painted hair, glass or painted eye.	16", $125.00 / 25", $150.00
Prize Baby (also called Sealect Baby)	1915	Compo head and hands, cloth body and legs, painted eyes, open mouth that holds her pacifier.	$125.00
Dolly Varden	1915	Compo head and limbs, stuffed body, with or without human hair wigs; stationary, painted, or sleep eyes; painted mouth.	$125.00
Jenny Wren	1915	Compo head and hands, painted hair, bow, checked dress with white cuffs and collar.	$100.00
Broncho Bill	1915	Cowboy with compo head and hands, wore white buckskins, red shirt, khaki hat, leather belt, holster, gun, lasso.	$125.00
Baby Talc	1915	Compo head, cloth body, wig, wears one-piece sleeper, bonnet. Licensing tie-in with Talc Baby Powder.	$150.00
Our Pet	1915	Compo head and hands, cloth body and legs, wears knit outfit and hat.	$125.00
Dottie Dimples	1915	Compo head, cloth body, wears long dress and bonnet.	$100.00
Tennis Girl	1915	Compo head, compo arms and legs, open/closed mouth, wears white tennis dress and hat.	$110.00
The Infant	1915	Compo head, wears long christening gown and bonnet.	$100.00
Uneeda Kid	1916	11" Molded-painted hat and painted eyes. 16" Jointed legs and open/closed eyes. Original price $0.75.	11", $165.00 / 16", $425.00
Baby Bi-face	1916	Composition doll whose face twists from smiling to tearful.	$150.00
Mabel	1916	Compo head girl dressed in jacket, skirt, and hat. Catalog #1665.	$75.00
Compo Baby	1916	Five sizes: all composition baby, jointed arms, legs, and neck, stands without support, wigs or painted hair, stationary or moving eyes. Original price starting at $1.00.	$150.00
Cracker Jack Boy	1917	14" Compo head and hands, cloth body, gauntlet hands, molded boots, molded hair, wears a blue or white sailor suit with cap to match, carries a miniature package of Cracker Jack Candy Food by special arrangement with Rueckheim Bros. and Eckstein, manufacturers of Cracker Jacks.	$325.00
Columbia Kids	1917 – 18	Six sizes: 12" – 24" Compo head and hands, with or without wigs; painted, stationary, or sleep eyes. Four styles: Army, Navy, boy, girl. Striped pants or skirt, star shirt, tam.	$175.00
Sweater Boy	1917	Compo baby doll wearing a short sweater and knit hat (no pants).	$150.00

Name	Date Issued	Identifying Characteristics	Current Price
Sleeping Beauty	1917	Same doll as #465 "Baby Paula."	$110.00
Little Princess	1917	Compo head, wears dress, jacket, bonnet, and booties.	$75.00
Peggy (also called Little Princess)	1918	Same doll as "Little Princess."	$75.00
New Columbia Kid	1918	Boy doll wearing red, white, and blue knit wool suit and cap, both with tassels.	$150.00
Elsie	1918	All compo, sleeping eye baby.	$125.00
Baby Mine	1919	All compo, ball-jointed body. New version of doll originally issued in 1911.	$150.00
Matinee Girl	1919		$100.00
Bathing Girl	1919		$100.00
Moving Eye Dolls	1919	200 numbers of baby dolls that come dressed or undressed, fully jointed dolls, molded or curly hair, sleeping eyes, eyelashes. Original price $1.00 up to $30.00.	$110.00
The Little Mother Teaching Dolly to Walk	1920	"Patents Pending"	$125.00
Baby Doll	1920's	Compo head and hands, cloth body and legs, tin sleep eyes, two painted teeth, painted blonde molded hair rather flat on top, wears blue checked rompers	$100.00
Baby Mine	1922	Three sizes, solid cloth head and cloth mask, "Sanitary" feather-weight, long dress and bonnet, walks and talks.	$115.00
Miss Rainshine	1922	Two-headed doll, crying and laughing, wears checked rompers and hat.	$125.00
Mama Doll (Double-Voice)	1922 – 24	12" – 27" Compo head and limbs. Cotton-stuffed body. Human voice says "mama" when bent forward, and cries when tilted backwards. Sleep eyes, socks, and leatherette slippers, comes in both girl and baby doll. 25" had mohair wig, dressed in white organdy dress and cap. 27" had molded hair, dressed in checked percale rompers with Ideal circle tag. Original price $3.00 – 5.00. Marks: Diamond with IDEAL in center, Novelty and Toy Co. Brooklyn New York on outside.	12", $125.00 with wig 12", $145.00 27", $165.00
Papa – Mama doll	1922	Sits, walks, cries, winks, sleeps, calls "mama" and shouts "papa."	$150.00
Nile Queen	1923		$125.00
Egyptian Princess	1923		$125.00
Greenwich Village Vincent (also called Beau Brummel)	1924	Jointed compo, wearing shirt, shorts, and beret (also sold as a companion to Flossie Flirt).	$175.00
Greenwich Village Vivian	1924		$150.00
"Mama" Dolls	1924	15", 20" Compo head and hands, stuffed cotton bodies, painted hair, sleep eyes, "mama" voice, voile bloomer dress, bonnets, loosely jointed at hips, tagged Ideal, 20" had mohair wig. Original price $1.50.	15", $135.00 20", $150.00
Walking Doll	1924	18", 20" Compo head, legs, and hands, human hair wig with long curls, sleep eyes with real lashes, "mama" voice.	18", $150.00 20", $175.00

Name	Date Issued	Identifying Characteristics	Current Price
Sally Singer	1924	20" Compo, sleep eyes, walks, says "mama," sewed wig, Swiss music box inside that plays several tunes.	$200.00
Carrie Joy	1924	Flat-chested Flapper doll. Trademarked Dec. 23, 1924, #208,649.	$180.00
Soozie Smiles Junior	1924	Smaller version of two-headed baby doll, one head with open mouth with pacifier, wears dress and bonnet, patented. Head had painted eyes.	$100.00
Hush-a-Bye Baby	1925	Seven sizes including 20" and 24" Compo one-piece solid head, cloth body, molded painted orange hair, gray sleep eyes, open mouth, rubberized cloth hands, curved legs (some with rubber), crying voice, dressed in long petticoat and flannel diaper, wrapped in blanket and pillow; closes her eyes when rocked to sleep keeping them closed until she was placed upright. In 1926 she was made with rubber hands and some models had both rubber hands and legs. Marks: IDEAL in diamond shape with U.S. Pat. 1621434 outside.	$100.00 $180.00
Suck-A-Thumb Baby	1926 – 31	12", 15" Compo head and legs, rubber arms, molded hair, sleeping eyes, comes in organdy dress with lace trims, slip, shoes, and pacifier. Marks: IDEAL in diamond shape.	12", $75.00 14", $85.00
Ideal Bottle Baby	1926	Rubber arms that move up and down, holding a bottle, wears a dress and bonnet.	$85.00
Handy Andy and Handy Sue	1927	Dressed as farmers.	$80.00
Twinkletoes	1927	Rubber arms and legs, squeeze rubber legs and she cries, flirty eyes, wears romper or white organdy lace-trimmed dress.	$100.00
Baby Smiles (Also called Happy Flossie)	1927	Compo head, soft body, dimpled cheeks, flirty eyes, rubber arms, comes with milk bottle or pacifier, "Smiles" trademark name.	$100.00
Ticklette	1928	13" Smaller version of Tickletoes. Original price $2.00.	$85.00
Curly Tickletoes	1928	13½", 15" Tickletoes with caracul fur wig, nainsook rompers over undershirt and rubber panties. Catalog #F43, #F143. Original price $3.00, $4.00.	13½", $95.00 15", $110.00
Princess Tickletoes	1928	27" Head can turn and tilt, real eyelashes, organdy and lace dress. Catalog #V851. Original price $8.00.	$200.00
Tickletoes De Luxe	1928	13½", 15" Hand crocheted wool and silk coat and bonnet over organdy dress. Catalog #97, #197. Original price $3.00, $4.00.	13½", $95.00 15", $110.00
Peter Pan and Wendy	1928	16½", 18" Compo head, gauntlet hands, cloth body and limbs, molded hair, tin sleep eyes, red and yellow or green felt suit forms body, felt hat with bell. Marks: Peter Pan/ IDEAL in diamond or IDEAL in diamond.	16½", $125.00 18", $165.00
Winsome Winnie	1929	Trademark #285,027, June 4, 1929.	$100.00
Pretty Peggy	1930	22" Compo head and legs, bent compo arms, cloth body, flirty eyes, open/closed smiling mouth, four painted upper teeth, marcelled brown bob human hair wig. Second and third finger molded together. Marks: IDEAL in diamond U S of A on outside four corners (on head).	$135.00
Honey Bunch	1931	Listed in Trademark (tm) list. Also made in 1937.	$125.00
Precious	1931	Composition head, rubber arms and legs, cries when legs are pinched.	$100.00
"Mama" Doll	1931	19" Composition head and arms, cloth body, curly brown wig with bangs.	$150.00

Name	Date Issued	Identifying Characteristics	Current Price
Ideal Baby	1931 – 34	Double action glace eyes, from tm list.	$150.00
Flossie Flirt	1931	Five sizes, including 16", 18", 20", and 22". Compo head, rubber arms and legs, flirty eyes, swivel head that turns and tilts on rubber bust, "mama" voice in cloth body, cry voice in each leg, mohair wig, organdy, voile or batiste, or lawn dress with bloomers. Patented. Original price $2.00, $2.75, $3.25, $3.50.	12", $75.00 22", $135.00
New Tickletoes	1932 – 37	16", 18", 20", 22", 25", 27". Redesigned face, arms and legs of "tru-flesh" rubber, separate fingers and toes, kapok-stuffed cloth body, three voices — cries when you squeeze either leg or when you tip her forward with "mama" voice, blue or brown flirty sleep eyes, silky eyelashes, painted or curly hair. 16" also available in sleep eyes only for $2.00. Catalog #51P (16" sleep eyes only), 1116, 1118, 1120, 1122, 1125, 1127. Original prices: $2.00, $3.50, $4.00, $5.00, $6.00, $7.50, $10.00.	$100.00
Tru-life Rubber dolls	1931 – 34	Compo head, rubber arms and legs, cloth body, molded blonde hair, sleep eyes, open mouth with two painted teeth, organdy dress and bonnet.	$100.00
Smiles	1933	14", 17" Sleeping winking eyes, compo legs, tru-flesh rubber arms, cloth body, wears organdy lace trimmed dress and bonnet, petticoat, rubber panties, leatherette booties and wooly socks; cries, sucks thumb.	$100.00
Bathrobe Baby	1933	12" Compo head, rubber body and limbs, jointed at head, arms and hips, molded painted hair, dressed in flannel bathrobe and diaper.	$100.00
Baby Doll	1930s	8" All compo, painted side glancing eyes, big black pupils, molded hair, wears organdy dress and bonnet. Marks: IDEAL (in circle)/PAT PEND (on body).	$125.00
Ducky Deluxe	1934 – 37	11", 13", 15", 17", 19" All rubber, sleep eyes and lashes or painted eyes (cost less), does not have drinking-wetting feature, patented. Catalog, #411, #413, #415, #417, #419, Sleep eyes. Painted eyes are #311, etc. Original price $2.00, $2.50, $3.50, $4.25, $5.00.	$80.00
Kissable	1934	Baby doll	$95.00
Big Mama Doll (also called Ideal Baby)	1934	36" Double action eyes with eyelashes, human hair wig. Ad for Ideal Baby in *Playthings*.	$200.00
Hush-A-Bye Baby	1935	14" Compo head and arms, cloth body and legs, molded hair, gray celluloid over tin eyes, open mouth, dimples. Marks: Ideal in a diamond.	$100.00
Sunbonnet Sue	1936	From tm list.	$100.00
Jolly Dollies of Many Lands	1937	18 different dolls, cloth, yarn hair, jointed, washable, came in four color box illustrating flags and costumes, designed by Baroness Ilsa Christiane of Sweden. Original price $2.00.	$125.00
Borrah and the Harmonica Rascals: The Cowboy The Cop The Sailor Colored Borrah, himself (Also called Whistlers)	1937	14" All composition, voice in each leg, bounce them up and down and they whistle, harmonica came with each doll. Patterned after Borrah Minnevitch and his famous "Harmonica Rascals." "Borrah" and "Colored" are dressed in check outfits, others are dressed in cowboy, cop or sailor costume. Catalog #1601, #1602, #1603, #1604, #1605. Original price $2.00 each.	$150.00 each

Name	Date Issued	Identifying Characteristics	Current Price
Winnikens	1937	10" All rubber dolls with movable arms and head, molded hair, painted eyes, dressed in six different costumes, including short dresses and sailor suit. Original price $1.00.	$80.00
Little Bo-Peep	1938	15½" All compo, jointed at neck and shoulders, sleep eyes with human lashes, open mouth with six teeth, wearing skirt saying "Bo-Peep" with sheep on it, straw hat. Marks: U.S.A./16 (on back).	$150.00
Charlie McCarthy	1938 – 39	8" Hand puppet with compo head, felt hands molded hat, painted features, wire monocle, cloth body, painted tuxedo, Edgar Bergen's dummy. Original price $0.59. Marks: Edgar Bergen's/©CHARLIE/McCARTHY/Made in U.S.A (on front of body).	$60.00
Sonia	1938	From tm list.	$100.00
Nancy Lee	1930s	13" All compo, mohair wig, sleep eyes, wears red and white checked sunsuit or pink crepe panty-slip combo. Marks: 13 (on body) rubbed out Shirley Temple still visible.	$175.00
Betsy Wetsy®	1939	11" Soft rubber head and body, painted eyes, drinks, and wets, comes with diaper and bottle. Catalog #111. Original price $1.00.	$100.00
Toddling Sue	1939 – 45	14", 17", 20", 23" Compo head and body, movable head, arms and legs, sleeping eyes, open mouth with inset teeth, wig or painted hair, wears dress, coat, and bonnet. Catalog #14TD, #17TD, #20TD, #23TD. Original price $1.50, $2.00, $3.00, $4.00.	14", $100.00 23", $150.00
Baby Smiles	1939	13", 16" Compo head and limbs, soft cloth kapok-stuffed body, sleep eyes with lashes, cry voice, organdy dress and bonnet. Also came in long dress. Catalog #014, #015, #29, #0216. Original price $1.20, $1.20, $1.50, $2.00.	16", $100.00
Superman	1940 – 45	13" Compo head and upper torso, wood ball-jointed body, blue and red painted costume, large S on chest, red cloth cape. Designed by Joseph Kallus. Marks: "DES. and COPYRIGHT BY SUPERMAN INC/ MADE BY IDEAL NOVELTY and TOY CO." (on belt).	$350.00
Gorgeous	1941	From tm list.	$100.00
Magic Squeezee or Squeezums	1941	16", 19", 22" Compo head, plastic Magic Skin arms and legs, kapok-stuffed cotton body, glass-like sleeping eyes and lashes, molded hair, dressed in organdy dress and bonnet, pink slip, white socks and shoes; squeeze either leg and she cries, lay her down and she cries. Patented. #1,793,335, #1,880,109. Not produced during war years. Produced again in 1947 with hard plastic head.	16", $100.00 22", $125.00
Featherweight Dolls	1942		$100.00
Mother Goose Characters: Miss Muffet Little Bo-Peep Mary Had a Little Lamb	1942	14½" All composition girl doll, blue glassene sleep eyes, wig, open mouth with four teeth, dressed in fairytale character costumes. Mary had long dress and pantaloons. Marks: U. S. A. 16.	$175.00
Honey Baby	1943	16", 18", 20" Compo head and limbs, stuffed cotton body, molded painted brown hair, glass-like blue sleep eyes with lashes, rosebud mouth, organdy dress and bonnet. Marks: IDEAL DOLL/MADE IN USA (on head).	$125.00
Lazy Bones	1944	From tm list.	$100.00
Jack and Jill	1945	Soft stuffed dolls, cloth bodies, wearing matching frock (Jill) and shorts (Jack) with big bow and beret. Original price $3.25 each.	$75.00

Name	Date Issued	Identifying Characteristics	Current Price
Sleepy Time Twins – Yawn and Dawn	1945	15" Compo head and limbs, stuffed body, painted features; one sleeping, one yawning, dressed in flannel wrapper and bunting or in lacy dresses and bonnets. Made by Georgene Averill for Ideal. Original price $9.98 per set.	set $220.00
Bit of Heaven	1945	Compo head, arms and limbs, cloth body, sleep eyes with lashes, dressed in organdy dress and bonnet.	$70.00
Continental	1945	From tm list.	$100.00
Baby Beautiful	1945	18", 20", 22", 24", 25", 27" Compo head, arms and legs, soft cotton body, glacé sleep eyes with lashes, closed mouth, molded hair, cry voice, wearing print or organdy dress and bonnet, shoes and socks. 25" and 27" come with composition chest plate on body and full composition arms. Catalog #B964, #B965, #B966, #B967, #B968, #B969. Original price $6.50, $7.50, $8.65, $10.80, $13.50, $16.20. Also came with mohair wig in 1947. 22" and 24" came in short silk coat in 1947. Also came in net party dress in 1947.	18", $100.00 27", $200.00
Plassie	1946	16", 18", 20", 22" Hard plastic head with Magic Skin latex body. Cries when leg is squeezed, sleep eyes with real lashes, separate fingers, cotton-stuffed body, painted molded hair. 18" and 20" only size available in 1947. Catalog #PL965, #PL966. Original price $8.65, $10.80 Marks: IDEAL DOLL/MADE IN USA/PAT.NO 225 2077 (on head).	$125.00
Big Sister	1946	20" Compo head with three faces: sleepy, weepy, and smiling. Head turns by knob on top of head.	$150.00
Oswald the Rabbit	1946	22" Stuffed body, mask face, plastic Magic Skin fingers, character created by Walter Lantz. Original price $3.95.	$175.00
Betsy Wetsy®	1946	12" Hard plastic head, rubber body, oval sleep eyes with lashes, open mouth, molded brown hair, bottle, cries tears, wets. Marks: Made in USA/Pat No 2252077 (on head); IDEAL DOLL (on back).	$75.00
Tickletoes	1947	15" Compo head, rubber latex Magic Skin body. Reissue of 1930s doll. Also sold with a hard plastic head.	$85.00
Baby Squeezy	1947	18", 20", 23", 28" Hard plastic head, latex plastic Magic Skin body and limbs. Reissue of 1941 doll. Catalog #9618, #9620, #9623, #9628. Original price $8.64, $10.80, $12.96, $21.60. Marks: IDEAL DOLL/MADE IN USA. (on head).	18", $75.00 28", $110.00
Smiling Doll Face	1947	29" Soft stuffed cloth body, mask smiling face with two upper painted teeth, yarn wig, sewn fingers, wears solid color overalls, short sleeve check shirt. Catalog #V71. Original price $8.00.	$55.00
Circus Clown	1947	40" Soft stuffed cloth body, mask face, clown suit with ruffles around neck, pointed cap, individual fingers. Catalog #V73. Original price $14.00.	$70.00
Farmer Girl	1947	40" Soft stuffed cloth doll, mask face, yarn wig in braids, individual fingers, wears skirt, apron, check short sleeve blouse, and babushka. Catalog #V72G. Original price $10.00.	$70.00
Farmer Boy	1947	40" Soft stuffed cloth doll, mask face, yarn wig, individual fingers, wears overalls, check short sleeve blouse, and cap. Catalog #V72B. Original price $10.00.	$70.00

Name	Date Issued	Identifying Characteristics	Current Price
Pillow Baby	1947	Composition head, wool plush stuffed body, fleece bonnet and jacket trimmed with net, sleep eyes, lies on tummy in sleeping position on fleece pillow trimmed with ribbon. Catalog #PB8W.	$50.00
Pinafore Girl	1947	27" Soft cloth stuffed doll, mask face, yarn wig in pigtails, wears print dress and striped pinafore. Catalog #V48. Original price $7.00.	$45.00
Bobby Sox Doll	1947		$55.00
Honeyfoam	1947	From tm list.	$60.00
Pinafore Girl	1947	18" Composition head and body, sleep eyes with real lashes, red or brown mohair wig, jointed at neck, shoulders and hips, open mouth with four teeth, eye shadow, pink organdy dress. Marks: 18 (on body).	$200.00
Saucy Lady	1947	27" Soft cotton-stuffed girl doll, mask face, yarn wig with topknot, body made of flesh percale, wears two-tone contrasting color percale dress. Catalog #V51. Original price $7.00.	$55.00
Softy	1947	27" Soft cotton-stuffed girl doll, mask face, yarn wig with top braid, body made of colorful percale, wears pastel colored jumper. Catalog #V50. Original price $7.00.	$55.00
Clarabelle	1947	27" Soft cotton-stuffed girl doll, mask face, wig with braids, wears printed percale slacks outfit. Catalog #V47. Original price $7.00.	$55.00
California Betty	1947	27", 40" Soft cotton-stuffed girl with mask face, mitten hands on 27", sewn fingers on 40", yarn hair in braids, 40" dressed in percale dress, 27" dressed in print overalls, 40" is size of a four-year-old child. Catalog #V45, #V46. Original price $7.00, $10.00.	27", $55.00 40", $70.00
Soft Dolls	1947	Soft cotton dolls with pressed mask faces, wears assorted percale and felt dresses and slacks, yarn wigs, wears berets or ribbons in hair, painted side glancing eyes. Catalog #V31S, #V32S, #V33S, #V34S, #V35S, #V36S. Boys are #V31S and #V34S. Marks: Ideal tag.	$45.00
Full Sized Girl and Boy Magic Skin Dolls	1947	27" Girl, 27" Boy, 27" with layette hard plastic head, Magic Skin stuffed body, sleep eyes, molded hair, girl wears polo shirt, corduroy or velvet jumper, knit shirt and pants, shoes, and socks; boy wears polo shirt, corduroy or velvet long pants, knit shirt and pants, shoes, and socks. Actual one-year-old size. Promoted as display pieces as well as toys. Catalog #9FG, #9FB, #9FLA . Original price $27.00, $27.00, $36.00.	$110.00
Little Eight-Ball	1947	4½" All latex squeeze doll with a "pickaninny" face, spray painted features. Catalog #L8B-1. Original price $60.00.	$25.00
Softies Latex Doll	1947	5½" All latex squeeze doll, spray painted features, molded panties and shoes. Catalog #LDL-1. Original price $0.60. (1948 – tm list)	$25.00
Baby Sox	1948	From tm list.	$45.00
Baby Plassie	1949	16", 19", 22", 24" Hard plastic head (on shoulder plate which tilts and turns), arms, and legs, sleep eyes with lashes, open mouth with teeth, mohair, or molded hair, crying realistic voice; later came in vinyl. Marks: P-50 Ideal/Made in U.S.A. (on head) or Ideal Doll/Made in U.S.A. #2252077	$75.00
Plassie Toddler	1949	14" Hard plastic head, compo arms and legs, cloth body, open mouth with two teeth, felt tongue, mohair wig. Marks: P-50/Made in U.S.A. (on head). Also came with a plastic body, sleep eyes, molded hair or mohair wigs. Marks: MADE IN U.S.A./PAT. NO. 2252077 (on head); IDEAL DOLL/14 (on back).	$80.00

Name	Date Issued	Identifying Characteristics	Current Price
Honeysuckle Baby	1949 – 50	12" Hard plastic head, rubber body, arms, legs, sleep eyes, drinks from bottle, also came in "Negro" version.	$80.00
Musical Doll	1949 – 50s	17" Hard plastic head, stuffed cotton body, latex arms and legs, sleep eyes, open mouth with two upper teeth, Swiss music box in body. Original price $10.00.	$125.00
Snoozie	1949	11", 16", 20" Vinyl head, hands, legs, cotton-stuffed body. 1933 doll reissued with swiss music box inside body. Catalog #0111, #0160, #0200.	$150.00
Roy Rogers	1949	25" Stuffed vinyl head with painted features and hair, vinyl hands, cloth body formed from cowboy outfit and hat with guns in holster, name on hat, Western movie star. Catalog #RR7. Original price $6.98.	$200.00
Magic Squeezums	1949	16", 18", 20", 30" Hard plastic head, latex body with pin jointed arms and legs, or cotton-stuffed body, sleep eyes, mohair or molded hair. Three voices, one in body, and one in each leg, wears dress and bonnet. Reissue of 1941 doll. Marks: IDEAL DOLL/ MADE IN USA.	$80.00
Girl doll	1949	19", 21" Hard plastic, jointed, sleep eyes with lashes, mohair wig, closed mouth, individual fingers in ankle-length dresses. In 1949 Ideal Catalog.	$150.00
Linda Olive	1949	From tm list.	$100.00
Tummy	1950	From tm list.	$100.00
Lovey -Coos	1950	June 6, 1950	$55.00
Mechanical Roy Rogers with Lariat	1950	6½" Plastic cowboy with metal lariat, spring wound clockwork motor twirls simulated rope, packed in acetate window display box. Catalog #MRR100.	$65.00
Fully Painted Plastic Baby Doll	1950	3" Plastic doll jointed at head, arms, and legs, sprayed hair, eyes, and diaper, fits line of plastic furniture made in 1951. Catalog #PBJ10.	$15.00
Itsy Bitsy Baby	1951	Patent 1951	$25.00
Baby Gurgles (also known as Tousle Head in 1953)	1951	19" Hard plastic head, one-piece latex body and legs, latex disc jointed arms, squeeze coo voice, blue sleep eyes, red caracul wig. Baby Gurgles trademarked Oct. 31, 1950 #532,959. Original price $20.00. No trademarks.	$95.00
Cathree	1951	Patent 1951	$35.00
Tumbling Teddy	1951	From tm list.	$35.00
Sister Curly Coos	1951	14", 16", 18", 20" Plastic head, Magic Skin body, sleep eyes, curly saran wig with curlers, organdy dress; cries, sobs, and coos. Catalog #0149, #0169, #0189, #0209.	14", $55.00 20", $85.00
Brother Curly Coos	1951	14", 16", 18", 20" Plastic head, Magic Skin body, sleep eyes, soft curly saran wig with plastic curlers, wears basque-style knit shirt, pants; coos, cries, and sobs. Catalog #0139, #0159, #0179, #0199.	14", $55.00 20", $85.00
Life Size Sister Curly Coos	1951	30" Plastic head, Magic Skin body, curly saran wig, sleep eyes, wears party dress with organdy apron and bonnet, real child's shoes and socks; cries, sobs, and coos. As big as a three-year-old. Catalog #0309.	$100.00
Life Size Brother Curly Coos	1951	30" Plastic head, Magic Skin body, curly saran wig, sleep eyes, wears gray Eton suit with check zipper jacket and polo shirt, gray beret, real child's shoes and socks; cries, sobs, and coos. As big as a three-year-old. Catalog #0299.	$100.00

Name	Date Issued	Identifying Characteristics	Current Price
Betsy Wetsy®	1951	12", 14", 16" Plastic head, vinyl body, sleep eyes, rooted curly hair. Drinks, wets, cries, water also comes out nose, comes with a layette. Catalog #0016, #0026, #0036.	12", $60.00 14", $65.00 16", $70.00
Deluxe Vinyl Head Doll	1951	17", 19", 21", 23", 25", 27" Vinyl head, arms, and legs, cotton-filled body, saran wig with plastic curlers, cry voice, pink flannel or rayon coat, organdy dress, bonnet, baby doll. Catalog #2607, #2617, #2627, #2637, #2647, #2657.	$85.00
Baby Beautiful	1951	15", 20", 22", 24" Plastic head, latex arms and legs, mohair wig or molded hair, sleep eyes, cry voice, organdy dress and bonnet, 15" did not have wig. Catalog #0450, #0500, #0520, #0540.	$85.00
Debutante Dress Girl Doll and Square Dance Girl Doll	1951	15", 17", 19", 21" All plastic full jointed, sleep eyes, saran wig in assorted styles, full length party dress or square dance print dress (not available in 21"). Came with curlers. Catalog #1567, #1767, #1967, #1267.	15", $125.00 21", $200.00
All Plastic Girl Doll	1951	15", 17", 19", 21" Vinyl head, hard plastic body, mohair wig, sleep eyes, wears dress, snap shoes, and hat. Uses Toni body. Catalog #1509, #1709, #1909, #1209.	15", $100.00 21", $175.00
Baby Ruth	1952	16", 18", 20", 22", 24" Geon polyvinyl head, vinyl limbs, stuffed body, saran hair is inserted in her vinyl head, blue sleep eyes, open/closed mouth, cry voice, dress, bonnet, came with plastic curlers. Catalog #2495, #2405, #2415, #2425, #2435. Original price $7.98, $9.98, $11.98, $13.98. Saran wig in 1953.	$85.00
Bonny Braids	1953	11½", 13½" Vinyl head, Magic Skin arms and legs. She's growing up and dressed in organdy dress short or long. Catalog #0009, #0010, #0011.	$70.00
Miss Curity	1953	7½" Hard plastic, blonde wig, sleep eyes, painted eyelashes, painted shoes and stockings, wears white nurses outfit cap with "Miss Curity" on it. Catalog #2810. Original price $2.00. No trademarks.	$65.00
Baby Joanne	1953	Patent 1953	$100.00
Baby Joan	1953	Patent 1953	$100.00
Lalapaluzza	1953	Patent 1953	$100.00
Carol	1954	24" Soft stuffed body, gold wool hair, wearing matching plaid dress and hat, talking doll – phonograph activated by hand crank, plays melodies. Catalog #7733. Original price $3.98.	$75.00
Little Sister	1954	Patent 1954	$90.00
Baby Jo	1955	22" All hard plastic Saucy Walker type body, breather holes in nostrils, closed mouth, light blue sleep eyes, molded hair. Marks: IDEAL DOLL/MADE IN USA/22 (on head).	$90.00
Bonnie Walker	1956	16", 23" Hard plastic walker with pins through hips, open mouth with four upper teeth, blue flirty sleep eyes, lashes, glued-on saran wig. Marks: W-25 OR W-16 (on head); IDEAL DOLL (on body).	16", $75.00 23", $90.00
Lindy	1956	7½" Hard plastic one-piece body and head, gray sleep eyes, molded lashes, curved legs. No trademarks	$20.00
Girl	1957	17" Stuffed vinyl head, one-piece body and limbs, rooted saran hair, blue flirty sleep eyes.	$35.00
Cousin Sue	1957	18" Vinyl head and limbs, cloth body, blue sleep eyes, lashes, open/closed mouth with two upper teeth. No trademarks on body, only on wrist tag.	$35.00

Name	Date Issued	Identifying Characteristics	Current Price
Mountain Boys	1958	29", 48" All cloth percale head and body, wears felt shirt and overalls, wool hair, bears, felt and button eyes, pin with their names: Willie, Luke, and Jake, Paul Webb's cartoon characters from *Esquire* magazine. Catalog #7825, #7830.	29", $50.00 48", $55.00
Snoozie	1958	14", 20" Soft vinyl body, rooted saran curls or pixie cut, blue sleep eyes, open/closed mouth, cry voice, close eyes, flannel pajamas; back knob makes doll wriggle, available through 1965.	14", $30.00 20", $40.00
Dew Drop	1960	12", 16" All vinyl rooted brown hair, brown sleep eyes, wears dress and baby name bracelet. Montgomery Ward exclusive. Marks: ©IDEAL TOY CORP./B-19-1-5.	$55.00
Walking Pattite	1961	18" Plastic body fully jointed, rooted long hair, sleep eyes, closed mouth.	$150.00
Mary Christmas	1961	36" Talking Patti Playpal. A Speigel's exclusive. Same Marks as Patti Playpal: Ideal Doll/G-35 on head and body)	$200.00
Betsy Wetsy® Toddler	1962	16", 19" Vinyl fully jointed, rooted saran hair, sleep eyes, drinks, wets, came with bottle. Original price $6.89, $9.89.	$45.00
New Pos'n Pepper	1965	9¼" Vinyl head, arms and legs, plastic body, new smaller face, poseable arms and legs. Catalog #9355-9. Marks: ©1965/IDEAL TOY CORP./P9-3 (on head); 1964©/IDEAL (in oval)/2 DO-9 (on body)	$30.00
The Munster Family: Herman Lily Grandpa	1964 – 65	Vinyl head, hand puppet, molded features, painted hair and eyes. Come in poly bags and colorful boxes.	set $75.00
Sandy, the Jointed Doll	1964	12½" All cloth, shag wig with bow, oversized head, painted features, striped pink dress. Catalog #7713.	$25.00
Paul and Paulette	1964	Catalog #1030-6. Original price $4.50.	set $40.00
Baby Snoozie	1965	14" Vinyl head and limbs, soft body, rooted straight hair, dressed in two-piece fleece sleeper with cap; turn knob and she moves head and opens and closes her blue eyes. Catalog #0810-2.	$45.00
Betsy® Baby	1965	13½" Vinyl, fully jointed, rooted blonde synthetic hair, blue sleep eyes; drinks and wets. Exclusive eye action: eyes slowly close during feeding. Comes with bottle, diapers, and pins. Catalog #1120-5. Marks: ©1965/IDEAL TOY CORP/TD14-W PAT. PEND (on head); IDEAL TOY CORP./T-D-14 (on body).	$35.00
Betsy Wetsy®	1965 – 73	20" Soft vinyl head and body, rooted synthetic hair, blue sleep eyes with long lashes, open/closed mouth with two teeth. Marks: ©1965/IDEAL TOY CORP./FL20-E-433.	$40.00
Baby Betsy®	1965	18" Vinyl, fully jointed, rooted blonde hair, blue sleep eyes; drinks, and wets. Marks: 1965/IDEAL TOY CORP./TO-18-W2/PAT.PEND.	$40.00
Real Live Lucy	1965	20" Vinyl, jointed arms, legs, and neck, rooted platinum hair, blue sleep eyes, head bobs (on a weight) when touched, offer doll spinach and she doesn't eat, offer bottle and she will eat (magnet in bottle). Catalog #0820-1. Marks: ©1965/ IDEAL TOY CORP./FL20-E-H33.	$40.00
Grown Up Tammy	1965	11¾" Vinyl head and arms, new smaller head with page-boy hairdo, plastic leg and body, rooted blonde hair, painted side glancing blue eyes, high heel feet. Also came in black version. Catalog #9100-9, #9102-5. Marks: ©1964/IDEAL TOY CORP./T-12-E (on head), IDEAL (in oval)/T-12/1 (on back).	$35.00

Name	Date Issued	Identifying Characteristics	Current Price
Bud	1965	12½" Vinyl head and arms, plastic legs and torso, molded painted brown hair, painted eyes, Tammy's boyfriend. Marks: ©1964/IDEAL TOY CORP./T8 12-W-2(on head); ©IDEAL TOY CORP./B12½ /2 (on body).	$50.00
Baby Herman	1965	9" Plastic and vinyl with molded hair, painted features, TV monster. Marks: 1965/IDEAL TOY CORP/M-8 1/4 (on head); MADE IN JAPAN (on back).	$65.00
Soupy Sales	1965	Vinyl head, jointed cloth body, flocked black hair, painted blue eyes, wears bow tie and red sweatshirt. Marks: © 1965/IDEAL TOY CORP./SOUPY SALES - WMC./H9 (on head).	$70.00
Honey Love	1966	21" Vinyl head and limbs, soft body, rooted saran hair, blue sleep eyes, squirms and wiggles, stops when lights go out, has photoelectric cell that deactivates crying and moving mechanism, two D-cell batteries. Catalog #0535-5. Original price $12.00.	$50.00
Girls from Rome: Serefina Lucia Gina	1966	17" Vinyl head, soft jointed vinyl bodies, blue sleep eyes, rooted saran hair, dressed as young teens in mod costumes. Catalog #0900-1. Original price $4.00.	$30.00
Baby Lucy and Little Lucy	1967 – 68	14" Vinyl, fully jointed, rooted platinum hair, painted side glancing eyes with three eyelashes on outer corner, two painted teeth, wears dress and bonnet, head bobs (on a weight) when touched, offer doll spinach and she doesn't eat, offer bottle and she will eat (magnet in bottle), comes with shoofly rocker. Catalog #0825-0. Smaller version of Real Live Lucy (1965). Marks: ©1967/IDEAL TOY CORP./FL18-3532 (on head). Little Lucy Catalog #0826-8 came without shoofly rocker.	Baby Lusy $40.00 Little Lucy $35.00
Playtime Tubsy	1968	18" Vinyl head, vinyl body, open mouth with lower teeth, rooted hair; splashes in bath water, when lies on side closes her eyes, when on her back, she slaps at toy bear and makes music, two D-cell batteries, six separate outfits for Tubsy: romper, creeper, sleeper, velveteen party dress, sailor coat, and organdy party dress outfits. Catalog #0845-8.	$35.00
Posie Dolls: Daisy Petal Lily	1968	18" Vinyl head, soft poseable foam bodies, rooted hair, painted eyes. Daisy has long blonde hair, two painted teeth, and wears shirt with tie and footed pants. Petal has short blonde hair, painted side glancing eyes, open lush mouth, and wears ballerina outfit. Lily has short brown hair, closed longish mouth, and wears striped jumper and leotard outfit. Catalog #1072-8, #1073-6, #1071-0.	$35.00
Flatsy: Dewie Filly Sandy Rally Cookie Bonnie Candy Nancy Baby Flatsy	1969	4½" Vinyl head and body with clip on her back, long rooted hair, poseable flat dolls, also came in "sister sets." Catalog #0201-4. *Dewie* wears a raincoat, boots, panties, and umbrella, comes with a cat in a wagon. *Filly* is a cowgirl with rooted orange hair, chaps and holster, hat, vest, scarf, and Hobby Horse. *Rally* is a car racer with green molded hair, cap, goggles, scarf, slacks, shoes, car coat, and a race car. *Cookie* has rooted pink hair, wears a dress with apron and a chef's hat, comes with a stove and rooster. *Bonnie* is a sailor with two long pink braids, wears sailor cap, slacks, and mid-blouse and has a sailboat on a stand. *Nancy* is a nurse with brown hair, wears cap, cape, leotards, and shoes, and pushes a baby in a carriage. *Candy* has brown hair and is dressed in a party dress, with a table and chairs and a birthday cake.	$10.00
Tearie Betsy Wetsy®	1969	9" "Negro" version. Catalog #1134-6.	$35.00
Little Love	1970	Vinyl head and limbs, cloth body, rooted blonde hair, child can make her suck thumb, open mouth and wave arm with mechanism in her back. Catalog #0541-3. Called Patti Playful in 1973.	$35.00
Flatsy: Trixie Casey Judy Susie	1970	4½" New additions to Flatsy line. *Trixie* is a black doll with black hair, wears a polka dot play outfit with beanie, and came with a bicycle. Catalog #0271-7. *Casey* is a male train conductor with molded red hair and freckles wears a engineer's cap and overalls and comes with a plastic train. Catalog #0272-5. *Judy* wears a terry robe and shower cap comes with a tub and shower. Catalog #0273-3. *Susie* wears shorty pj's and slippers and comes with canopied four-poster folding bed. Catalog #0274-1. *Trixie* Marks: 1968/IDEAL TOY CORP. *Casey* Marks: IDEAL (in oval) 1969/Pat. Pending/Hong Kong.	$15.00

Name	Date Issued	Identifying Characteristics	Current Price
Mini Flatsy	1970 – 71	2½" Poseable vinyl with rooted hair, comes in oval which can be worn as locket. Has a clip so she can be worn as an ornament. Catalog #0315-2.	$12.00
Velvet	1970	15" Vinyl head and jointed body, rooted blond hair that grows, violet sleep eyes, Crissy®'s cousin, also came in "Negro" version, four outfits sold separately. Catalog #1035-5.	$40.00 Black, $65.00
Flatsy: Sleepy Keely Munchie Kookie Nana Carrie Shaina Fizzie	1971	4½" New additions to the Flatsy line. Catalog #0159-4.	$15.00
Candy Mountain Flatsy: Scoop Cornball Creamy	1971	Scoop rides in an Ice Cream Cone Car, Cornball rides in a Lollipop Car, and Creamy rides in an Ice Cream Truck. Catalog #0169-3, #0170-1, #0171-9.	$15.00
Spinderella Flatsy	1971	4½" Flatsy mounted on a stage; pull string and she pirouettes. Catalog #0154-5. Marks: IDEAL (in oval)/1969/Pat.Pend./Hong Kong (on back). 1970/IDEAL TOY CORP./HONG KONG (on stage).	$30.00
Black Movin' Groovin' Crissy®	1971	17½" Vinyl head and body, swivel waist, growing hair. Catalog #1082-7.	$40.00
Movin' Grovin' Cricket	1971	15½" Vinyl head and body, red growing hair, sleep eyes. Marks: ©1971/IDEAL TOY CORP./MO-15/U.S. Pat. 3,162, 976/OTHER PAT.PEND./HONG KONG P. (on shoulder); ©1971/IDEAL TOY CORP./MO15/HONG KONG P (on waist).	$55.00
Black Look Around™ Crissy®	1972	Vinyl head and body, wears long plaid dress; pull string in back and her head turns, hair grows. Catalog #1092-6.	$45.00
Look Around™ Velvet®	1972	Vinyl head and body, wears short plaid dress; pull string and her head turns, hair grows. Also came in a black version. Catalog #10093-4.	$40.00 Black, $45.00
Tiny Tears	1972	13½" Vinyl head and one-piece non-jointed body, molded or rooted blonde hair, blue glassene sleep eyes; lay her down and she cries real tears, pick her up she stops. Catalog #1141-1. Original price $5.25. Marks: ©1972/ Ideal Toy Corp/TNT-14-R-210 (on head); ©1971/Ideal Toy Corp/TNT-14-8-24.	$30.00
Scribbles	1972	8" Cloth head and body, molded vinyl hands, orange, yellow, or hot pink hair; holds chalk in her fingers and writes on blackboard. Catalog #0502-5. Original price $1.99.	$30.00
What's His Face and What's Her Face	1972	Cloth stuffed face and body with separate features to make them change expressions. He is dressed like a clown, she wears polka dot dress. Catalog #1167-6. Original price $5.55.	$20.00
Foam Soft "Magic Skin" Tiny Tears	1973	13½" Vinyl head, foam-filled, soft Magic Skin body, rooted blonde hair, "rock-a-bye" eyes that close slowly as she's rocked to sleep; cries when laid down. Also came in black version. Catalog #1141-1. Original price $5.25.	$30.00
Just -To-Love Babies	1973	All foam with stocking material covering, come in three different outfits. Catalog #1179-1. Original price $4.75.	$25.00
T.V. Favorite Hand Puppets: Fat Albert Weird Harold Archie Betty Charlie Chan No. 1 Son, Henry	1973	Vinyl molded head on vinyl glove with painted bodies, hand puppets. Catalog #1191-6. Original price $1.20.	each, $20.00

Ideal Dolls Not Photographed

Name	Date Issued	Identifying Characteristics	Current Price
Stretchie	1973	8" Vinyl head, accordion-pleated plastic arms and legs, painted faces, rooted hair in six colors: green, yellow, pink, aqua, blonde, and brunette. Packaged in plastic pocketbook. Catalog #0865-6. Original price $2.55.	$10.00
Peanuts Gang: Charlie Brown Lucy Linus Peppermint Patty Snoopy	1976 – 78	7", 14" All cloth stuffed printed dolls from "Peanuts" cartoon strip by Charles Schultz. Catalog #1409-2.	7", $15.00 14", $20.00
Dennis the Menace	1976	7", 14" All cloth stuffed printed doll from comic strip by Hank Ketcham, blonde hair and freckles wearing overalls and striped shirt. Catalog #1430-8.	7", $15.00 14", $20.00
Robbie Knievel	1976	6" All plastic figure stunt man, 13-year-old son of Evil Knievel.	$35.00
Baby Tickle Tickle	1978	15" Vinyl head, soft foam-filled body, rooted blonde hair, open mouth, painted eyes, move arm up and down and she turns head and giggles, move arms faster and she'll bob head and laugh, dressed in pink rompers, also came in "Black" version. Catalog #1175-9.	$35.00
Newborn Snuggles	1980	12½" Vinyl head, cloth body, rooted blonde hair, painted eyes, snuggles a cat. Also came in "black" version. Catalog #1485-2.	$30.00
Baby Sees All	1981	13" Vinyl head, soft cloth body, blue eyes that dart from side to side when body is pressed, her head then turns side to side. Also came in "black" version. Catalog #1040-5.	$30.00
Velvet	1981	Reissue from original 1971 mold.	$20.00
Tiny Tears	1981 – 85	13½" All vinyl, blue glassene eyes, curly blonde hair, drinks and cries tears, and comes with bottle. Wears short romper. Came in molded or rooted hair. "Black" version also available. Catalog #8533-2.	$25.00
Tiny Tears	1982	14" Vinyl head with soft body. Drinks and cries only. Rooted blonde or molded hair, glassene eyes with lashes. Dressed in dress with apron. First time a tearing mechanism in soft bodied doll. Also came with a layette. Catalog #1384-7, #1386-2.	$25.00
Thumbelina	1983	18" Collector's edition. Vinyl head, arms and legs, soft body, painted eyes, open/closed mouth, violet eyelet long gown and pillow. Catalog #13193.	$25.00
Chipmunks: Simon Alvin Theodore	1984	18" Plush body, vinyl face, talking chipmunks.	set of three, $80.00
Tiny Tears	1984	14" All vinyl, rooted hair, glassene eyes and lashes, wears a short dress and bloomers or long gown. Came with bottle. Also came in black version. Another verson came with a layette. Molded hair doll came in black and white versions, (same doll as 1983). Catalog #13672, #13680, #10202, #10203, #13862, #14001, #13649, #13600.	$20.00
Talking Patti Playpal	1987	35" All vinyl, with tape player and four batteries inside. Marks: ©1987 IDEAL INC. Clothing available: 1) Short red dress with white collar, white strip from neck to waist with little flower on it, big white bow for belt, attached red hair bow, matching red shoes. 2) Long pale blue dress with white lace collar, gold thread running through it, small white bow at waist and bottom, lace with gold trim around hem, matching hair ribbon and shoes. 3) Red pleated skirt, white shirt with a P on the front, two strips of red and blue on arm and across waist, red socks, cotton-type material. Tagged: "IDEAL PATTY PLAY PAL 1987 Ideal Inc./ A Subsidiary of View-Master Ideal Group Inc./ Portland Ore. 97207/ Made in Macao." Also tapes available: A Funtime Party, A Fairytale Fantasy.	$150.00
Baby Bubbles	1989	Vinyl head and limbs, cloth body, sleep eyes, blonde hair. Marks: 1989/IDEAL BABY BUBBLES/ PORTLAND OREGON.	$30.00

Ideal's Shirley Temple Dolls (1934 – 1985)

1934 – 1939 Composition Doll

Markings Seen on Doll

- •Shirley Temple name arched with a size number underneath:

- • Shirley Temple Name arched followed by Ideal name

- • Shirley Temple Name straight letters followed by Ideal name in diamond

- •No markings

These markings seen in these variations on both head and body. Sometimes there were size markings on the arms and legs at the socket

Wigs came in pale golden blonde, ash blonde, and strawberry blonde. Eye color varied from pale honey brown to regular brown to some rare ones in blue. Some came in brown or blue tin.

She came in either Sleep or Flirty Eyes. Flirty eyes (eyes that moved side to side as well as closing) could be found on dolls from 13" up

Tongues made of either soft felt or smooth hard material

Labels on clothing: white rayon label with Shirley's name printed on blue. Shirley's name printed in red. Shirley's name, a blue eagle, and N.R.A. imprint

Background

The 1934 – 1939 Shirley Temple (ST) dolls were designed by Bernard Lipfert. They are marked on the head and body "Shirley Temple" and come in sizes between 11" and 27". Most common sizes are 13" and 18". Over one and a half million STs were sold in the 1930s.

The first announcement of the Shirley Temple doll came in the September 1934 *Playthings Magazine*: " 'Shirley Doll' has the same well-shaped body, legs and arms as 'Ginger.' New Ideal double action glacé eyes and lashes, has wig in choice of brunette, blonde, or auburn. Variety of costumes in pink, blue, maize, green, or white." The name Shirley Temple was not mentioned or that she was a film star.

First ad in *Playthings*: October 1934 – Shirley Temple was so popular Ideal didn't have time to send out samples. Fox Films is helping to promote doll with display material and admission tickets for stores to use for promotions such as contests for girl who best resembles ST. Four sizes of new doll retailing at $3.00, $5.00, $6.00, $7.00.

In December 1934 *Playthings* – Now Shirley Temple outfits, exact replicas of dresses worn in movies retail from $1.00 up. Each box has photo of Shirley with signature. Each dress has woven label featuring her signature. 1934 Outfits: "Littlest Rebel," "Curly Top," "Our Little Girl."

1935 *Playthings* ad for Shirley Temple Wardrobe Trunk – three sizes, retail $5.00, $8.00, $11.00. Have stickers of Shirley's name and pictures on all sides. Factories from many countries licensed by Ideal to make ST include: Spain - Hijos Francisco Merin Perez; Canada - Reliable; England – Richards, Son and Allwin; Paris - Printemps Sapac; Australia - S. Hoffnung and Company. Contracts were pending with factories in Poland and Holland to produce ST.

1936 – The ST mold was changed. Information from *Playthings* includes Cape Cod Slicker (featured in "Captain January") sold separately. Four styles. All sizes. "Littlest Rebel" doll costumes were ready. Coming was a new ST doll at a new price to celebrate her birthday, April 23rd (she'll be 7).

A March 1936 article in *Playthings* quoted Morris Michtom, who had returned from 18 days in Hollywood visiting ST. He was most impressed by "the natural sweetness and happiness of the child." "She is intelligent, too. Acting is not work with Shirley Temple, in fact she regards it as so much play. An incident which showed her intelligence and judgment occurred one night when I was at dinner with the Temples. I turned to Shirley and asked her a question which has often been put to me, 'How is it, darling, when you are acting you are never pictured with a Shirley Temple doll like yourself?' Quick as a flash she answered, 'Oh, Mr. Michtom, you wouldn't want me to do that; it wouldn't be nice — it would be too much like advertising, and you can't do that in a picture.' I had to agree she had me there."

In a April 1936 ad – ST in new cowgirl costume-special summer item. Official Doll of the Texas Centennial comes in three sizes, 11", 13", 16," retails for $2.98, $3.98, $5.98. Plaid shirt, khaki shorts, brown stockings, high brown boots, sleeveless vest, leather chaps, red bandana, studs, real Western metal ornaments, and Stetson hat. Still sold in 1937. Also 27" available for $15. Also new developments in ST accessories and costumes including new doll handbags.

In a May 1936 ad – ST doll came in these dresses for 16", 20", 27" priced at $3.96, $5.92, 12.18. Outfits included "Captain January," "Baby Take A Bow," "Curly Top," "Bright Eyes," "Littlest Rebel." 11" doll came in "Curly Top" or "Baby Take a Bow," only $2.19. Costumes could be bought separately for $0.94 for 11" up to $2.49 for 27" doll.

As of June 36 – Promotional material available by Ideal to help dealers sell Shirley dolls are pictures in many poses; mirrors with her picture on the back; flip books showing her changing expressions; a booklet by Shirley called "The Story of My Life;" balloons; and cutouts. Also available for dealers were newspaper mats of ads and publicity releases; life-size cut-out figures with easel; 18" counter standees; 16" head hangers; enlarged photos and other aids for arranging ST displays. August, 1936 story: Available outfits for ST included: party dresses, play dresses, pajamas, coats, hats, raincoats, Cape Cod slicker, and sailor suit. Outfit "Poor Little Rich Girl" has coat and beret. Sales were up 14% in 1936 over 1935 of ST for Ideal.

April 1937 – New product Shirley Temple Doll Hair Curler "to keep Shirley Curly." Will be packed with curlers and instructions in each doll sold.

Cowgirl #2011/18 in 11" sold for $3.00; #2017/181 in 17" sold for $5.00; #2027/181 in 27" sold $15.00. "Wee Willie Winkie" #2018/350 in 18" sold for $6.00; #2022/350 in 22" sold for $9.00; #2027/350 in 27" sold for $15.00. ST "Heidi" outfit sold. A special store display was designed with Shirley playing a pipe organ. Shirley was synchronized to transcribed organ music. She was mechanically animated with 5" speakers behind organ pipes. The display was 4' wide x 5½' high x 3' deep. It must have been quite a sight!

1938 Shirley Temple at Nine – a new model Shirley with curls close to the head and side part.

February 1940 – Costume from film "The Blue Bird" available.

Shirley Temple Baby

Designed to look like Shirley at age 2. Came in either molded hair or mohair wig. Two types of wigs, thin realistic baby style or Shirley-type curls. Composition head was attached to composition neckpiece, glued to kapok-stuffed cloth body. Some arms and legs were composition, some hard rubber. Some arms were solid to shoulder or some had gauntlet construction: cloth upper arms. She cried ma-ma. The doll did not have a wardrobe to be purchased separately but came in a variety of outfits, including dress in puffed and cap sleeve styles with matching bonnet, pink silk coat and bonnet, or dress with knitted sweater and hat. A special robe and pillow outfit came with the Shirley Temple carriage. Most babies had flirty eyes.

Marks: number, SHIRLEY TEMPLE (curved) (on head); body unmarked.

Prices

Prices for Shirley depend on condition and rarity of outfit. Higher if original box and button are present. Current prices, except where noted for excellent condition

11" (rare size)	$650.00
13"	$600.00
15" – 16"	$600.00
17" – 18"	$700.00
20"	$800.00
22"	$800.00
25"	$850.00
27"	$900.00

Rarer outfits include Little Colonel, Texas Ranger, Blue Bird, and Hawaiian.

Baby Shirley Temple
16" $600.00
18" $700.00
20" $900.00
22" $1,000.00
25" (rare) $1,500.00

1958 – 1963 Vinyl and Plastic Doll

3/18/58 from *Long Island Daily Press* "SHIRLEY TEMPLE visits Ideal's Hollis, NY, plant to introduce the new version of the doll that bears her name. Age 29, she is star and hostess of NBC's Storybook children's television show [See photo section]. New doll will be made in three sizes, has saran hair, vinyl plastic body, and wears a nylon dress."

Doll is marked IDEAL DOLL ST and size. Walking 19" ST in 1961; 17" and 19" sold through 1961; 12" sold through 1962; 15" sold through 1963.

Prices

1958 – 1963 Vinyl and plastic current prices:
12" $175.00
15" $225.00
17" $250.00
19" $325.00
36" $1,200.00

1972 Montgomery Ward "Yesterday's Darling" reissue of 1958 doll

15" Vinyl Marks: IDEAL DOLL/ST-19-1 (on head); IDEAL ST-15/HONG KONG (on back).
Current price $150.00

1973 – 1975 16½" Vinyl Doll

16½" Vinyl, rooted blonde nylon hair, and stationary brown eyes. In 1974 came in four costumes including "Little Colonel" costume of pink taffeta, "Rebecca of Sunnybrook Farm," "Heidi," and "Captain January."
Current price $135.00
Boxed outfits $35.00

1982 – 1983 8" and 12" Vinyl Doll

8" and 12" All vinyl, rooted nylon curls and hazel sleep eyes. Six dolls available. 1982 outfits included: "Stand up and Cheer," "Heidi," "Littlest Rebel," "Little Colonel," "Stowaway," "Captain January." 1983 outfits: "Suzanna of the Mounties," "Rebecca of Sunnybrook Farm," "Dimples," "Little Miss Marker," "Poor Little Rich Girl," and "Wee Willie Winkie." Original price: 8", $20.00; 12", $30.00.
Current price:
8" ....$40.00 each
12" ....$50.00 each

1983 – 1985 16" Porcelain

Marketed but not manufactured by Ideal. 16" porcelain, limited production collector's doll. Painted features, seersucker pink dress, embroidered apron and wefted wig with curls, white vinyl shoes with bows. Advertised as design personally supervised by Shirley Temple Black. Ten thousand produced. Each doll has signed, numbered certificate of authenticity. Catalog #14456. Original price $500.00. Was not successful.

Current price $150.00

1984 – 1985 16" Vinyl

Collector's Edition Shirley Temple™. 16" all vinyl, rooted hair, wearing three new outfits, "Heidi," "Glad Rags to Riches," and "Stand Up and Cheer." Catalog #10500, #10499, #10501. Original price $70.00. Re-issue of 1973 – 1975 doll.
Current price $45.00

Betsy Wetsy®

Name	Date Issued	Identifying Characteristics	Current Price
Betsy Wetsy®	1937 – 38	10½", 11", 13", 15", 17", 19" "Idenite" hard rubber head, soft rubber body, wavy brown molded hair, glassene or painted tin sleep eyes with lashes. Sold in boxes or suitcases with layettes. The doll was offered as a premium for subscription to *Child Life* magazine in Jan. 1938. Her airplane suitcase had hat, dress, slip, socks, moccasins, diaper, bottle, soap, sponge, powder puff, safety pins, clothespins. Catalog numbers: #211/3, #811, #813/3, #815/3, #817/3, #819/3. Original price, $1.75, $2.00, $3.00, $4.00, $5.00, $6.00. Marks: IDEAL(on head and back).	10½" – 11", $85.00 13", $100.00 15", $125.00 17", $125.00 19", $150.00
Betsy Wetsy®	1939	11" Soft rubber head and body, painted eyes, comes with diaper and bottle; drinks, and wets. Catalog #111. Original price $1.00.	$125.00
Betsy Wetsy®	1946	Hard plastic head, rubber body (dark color under flesh pink rubber coating), sleep eyes with lashes, molded painted hair. Marks: MADE IN USA/PAT NO 2252077 (on head); IDEAL DOLL (on back).	$75.00
Betsy Wetsy®	1951 – 54	12", 14", 16" Hard plastic head, vinyl body, sleep eyes; cries when squeezed (tear holes inner corner of eye). Molded painted hair or lamb's wool wig. Catalog #0016, #0026, #0036.	12", $100.00 14", $135.00 16", $150.00
Betsy Wetsy®	1954 – 56	11½", 13½", 16", 20" Hard Celanese acetate plastic head, vinyl body and limbs. Molded or rooted curly wool hair; drinks, wets, and cries when squeezed, water came through tear holes. Some had pierced nostrils so water came through nose. Dressed in shirt and diaper. Comes with nine-piece layette. 20" dressed in romper. Catalog #1001, #1006, #1011. Original price $5.98, $7.98, $9.98. Marks: MADE IN U.S.A./PAT.NO.2252077 (on head); IDEAL DOLL (on back).	11½", $100.00 13½", $135.00 16", $150.00
Betsy Wetsy®	1956	11½", 13½", 16", 20" Soft vinyl head, vinyl body, rooted saran hair, sleep eyes; drinks, wets, and cries. Came in layette or suitcase. 20" came in romper. Catalog #1025, #1026, #1027, #1020. Original price $5.98, $7.98, $9.98.	11½", $50.00 13½", $55.00 16", $65.00 20", $75.00
Little Betsy Wetsy®	1957	8" All vinyl, rooted saran hair, sleep eyes; drinks and wets. Twelve outfits available separately. Catalog #9600. Marks: IDEAL TOY CO/BW 9-4.	$30.00 MIB $55.00
Betsy Wetsy®	1959 – 62	11", 13", 16" All vinyl, rooted saran or molded hair. Catalog #1103, #1026. Marks: IDEAL DOLLS/B-23.	11", $40.00 MIB $65.00 13", $45.00 16" $50.00
Big Baby Betsy Wetsy®	1959	21" All vinyl, rooted saran or molded hair. Hole in upper back. Catalog #1151. Marks: IDEAL DOLL/VC-22.	21", $65.00 23", $85.00
Betsy Wetsy® with Bath® and Betsy Wetsy in her Automatic Swing®	1960 – 62	16", 23" All vinyl, redesigned face, rooted hair; drinks, wets, and cries. Wears a romper with name on the bib, has 10-piece layette. Comes with 20" plastic bathtub. Catalog #1230-2, #1240-1. Or could be bought with 28" automatic swing and 10-piece layette. Catalog #1231-0, #1241-923. Original price $17.00. Marks: 12", IDEAL DOLL/WC-11; 16", IDEAL DOLL/VW-3.	16", $60.00 23", $70.00 Swing, $100.00
Betsy Wetsy®	1961 – 62	13", 15", 16", 17" All vinyl, molded or rooted hair, in bath with layette. Catalog #1251-8, #1261-7, #1271-6, #1230-2. 13", 15", 17" still available in 1962.	13", $35.00 15", $37.00 16", $40.00 17", $40.00
Betsy Wetsy®	1961 – 63	11½", 13½", 16" All vinyl, different head than other 1961 doll, molded or rooted hair, came in layette set; drinks, wets, cries. Catalog #1103-1, #1104-9, #1105-6. 11½" available in molded hair, and all sizes available in rooted hair in 1962. 11½", 13½" and 17½" still available in 1963.	11", $30.00 13", $35.00

Name	Date Issued	Identifying Characteristics	Current Price
Betsy® Baby	1964	13½" All vinyl, rooted hair, new action eyes, wears romper apron that ties under arms; her eyes slowly close during feeding. Drinks, wets, and cries. Catalog #1120-5.	11", $30.00 13", $35.00 17", $40.00
Tiny Betsy Wetsy®	1964	13½" All vinyl, rooted hair, sleep eyes with lashes, outfits available separately. Catalog #1110-6.	11", $30.00 13", $30.00 17", $40.00
Betsy Wetsy®	1965	13½", 25" All vinyl, rooted hair. Eyes slowly close during feeding. 13½" doll wears seersucker play dress. Marks: 13½", IDEAL TOY CORP/TD 12-W.PAT.PEND. (on head); 1965 IDEAL TOY CORP./TD-12 (on body). 25", IDEAL TOY CORP./OBW 20-5 (on head); BW 20 (on body).	13½", $30.00 25", $40.00
Tearie Betsy Wetsy®	1968	9", 11½", 17" Vinyl head and body, rooted blonde hair, sleep eyes; drinks, wets, and cries. 9", painted eye. Catalog #1130-4.	9", $20.00 11½", $25.00 17", $30.00
Tearie Betsy Wetsy®	1969	9" "Negro" version. Catalog #1134-6	$25.00
Betsy Wetsy®	1983 – 85	16" All vinyl, molded hair with topknot, sleep eyes, comes with bottle, dressed in green seersucker shirt and shorts with white apron; drinks and wets. Black version available. Both black and white dolls came in rooted hair version dressed in coral dress and bonnet. Also came with long gown. Another version had molded hair and layette. Catalog #14225, #14233, #14209, #14217, #14241, #10080, #10103, #10104.	$25.00 Black, $30.00

Little Betsy Wetsy® Fashions

Available 1957

Little Betsy Wetsy® has 8" rooted saran hair, sleep eyes, came with bottle; drinks and wets. Original price $2.98.

Number	Description
9610	Yellow romper and bonnet, booties
9611	Flannel robe and nightie
9612	Cotton print dress
9614	Denton sleeper
9630	Blue playsuit, bonnet, booties
9631	Yellow dress, bonnet, slip, booties
9632	Corduroy overalls, shirt, booties
9633	Aqua dress, bonnet, slip, booties
9634	Coat and bonnet
9650	Yellow pinafore dress, bonnet, slip
9651	Red checked dress, bonnet, slip
9652	Pink organdy dress, bonnet, slip
9653	Blue flocked organdy dress, bonnet, slip
9654	Organdy christening dress, bonnet
9600	Doll dressed in diaper with bottle
9680	Vinyl travel case with wardrobe: Denton sleeper, cotton print dress, bottle, booties, and 8" doll
9689	Travel case only

Dolls with Toni P-90 Hard Plastic Bodies

Toni (1949 – 1953)

Description: Hard plastic, nylon hair

Size	Body marks	Current value
14"	P-90	$200.00
16"	P-91	$250.00
19"	P-92	$275.00
21"	P-93	$300.00
22½" (rare size)	P-94	$800.00

Toni Walker (1954 – 1956)

Description: Hard plastic with walker body

Size	Body marks	Current value
14½	P-90W	$200.00
16½	IDEAL DOLL/16 or P-91W	$250.00
19½"	P-92W	$275.00
21½"	P-93W	$300.00

Sara Ann or All Plastic Girl Doll with Saran Wig (1951)

Description: Hard plastic, saran hair which is easier to curl and style than nylon

Size	Body marks	Current value
15"	P-90	$175.00
21"	P3 on head, P3 or P93 on back	$275.00
24"	P-4 on head, P-4 or P-94 on back	$500.00
17" (not seen)		
19" (not seen)		

Miss Curity (1953)

Description: Hard plastic, black eye shadow over and sometimes under eye. Center part hair is pulled off face.

Size	Body marks	Current value
14½"	P-90, some just marked IDEAL DOLL on head	$300.00

Mary Hartline (1952)

Description: Hard plastic, strung. Hair has side part. Dark eye shadow

Size	Body marks	Current value
16"	P-91 on head, P-91 or P-16 on back	$350.00
22½"	P-94 on back	$700.00

Mary Hartline Walker (1953)

Description: Vinyl head, hard plastic walker body

Size	Body marks	Current value
16"	V/91 (on head); IDEAL 16 (on body)	$300.00

Harriet Hubbard Ayer (1953)

Description: Stuffed vinyl head, hard plastic body with glued on wigs of various hair colors, arms are also vinyl with red fingernails.

Size	Body marks	Current value
14"	P-90MK or 14/IDEAL DOLL	$150.00
16"	MK16 on head, P-91 on body	$175.00
19"		$250.00
21" (not seen)		

Betsy McCall (1952 – 1953)

Description: Vinyl head, hard plastic walker body, glued-on dark wig, and brown sleep eyes. Came with apron pattern showing pictures of paperdoll.

Size	Body marks	Current value
14"	P-90 on body, MCCALL CORP.® on head	$200.00

Ruth (1953)

Description: Vinyl head, hard plastic body, saran hair inserted into head.

Size	Body marks	Current value
17"		$125.00
19"	Ideal DOLL/V-92 (on head); IDEAL DOLL/P-19	$150.00
21"		$175.00

Princess Mary (1955 – 1956)

Description: Stuffed vinyl head, walker body, rooted hair.

Size	Body marks	Current value
16"	V-87 or V-91 on head, 16 or P-91 on back	$200.00
19"	P-92	$225.00
21" (not seen)	P-93	$250.00

All Plastic Girl Doll (1951)

Description: Vinyl head, hard plastic body, mohair wig

Size	Body marks	Current value
15"	P-90	$125.00
17"	P-91	$125.00
19"	P-92	$125.00
21" (not seen)	P-93	

Walking Bride Doll (1955 – 1956)

Size	Body marks	Current value
14"	IDEAL DOLL/W90 (on head and body)	$125.00
19"	IDEAL DOLL/V92 (on head); IDEAL DOLL/19 (on back)	$150.00

Hard Plastic Bodies and Heads with Mohair Wigs (late 1940s – early 1950s)

Size	Body marks	Current value
14"	P-90	$250.00
16"	P-91	$275.00
19"	P-92	$300.00

The Toni home permanent could be used on the doll's Nylon™ wigs.

The Toni dolls came in a wide range of clothes from bridal gowns to school dresses; there are at least 100 separate outfts. Many dresses were made of Nylon,™ a new miracle fiber from the Dupont Company. Full page ads in magazines touted Toni as having both Nylon™ wigs and dresses.

Dress labels on some Toni clothing said "GENUINE TONI DOLL/WITH NYLON™ WIG/MADE BY IDEAL TOY CORPORATION." Even the vinyl shoes were marked "IDEAL TOY CORPORATION/MADE IN U.S.A."

Toni was a high priced doll in her era, and she was heavily promoted in order to market her at the higher prices.

There was a series of dolls with mohair wigs before Toni was introduced in the late 1940s whose marks were similar: P-92/ IDEAL TOY CO./MADE IN U.S.A. (on head) and IDEAL DOLL/P-91 (on back).

Miss Revlon and Her Outfits (1956 – 1959)

26" most rare sold only in 1957
23" sold only in 1956 – 1958
15" sold only in 1958 – 1959
20" most common sold in 1956 – 1959
18" most common sold in 1956 – 1959

First brochure to mention the Revlons is 1956.

In brochures packed with the dolls, the emphasis was on hair play, stating that Revlon Satin Set hair spray would keep your doll's hair in place.

Extra boxed outfits, cotton dresses and slips were available for the 18" size dolls . The basic 18" dolls were also sold in black chemises in striped boxes; most were sold dressed.

Miss Revlon was advertised as a girl's teenaged "Big Sister."

Miss Revlons usually are strung and fully flanged (kept on by plastic inside body that is part of the limb or neck). Miss Revlons in 18" and 20" sizes had bodies similar to the 15" and 10½" Miss Revlon Crown Princess. The flanged 18" is marked VT-18 on top of the neck flange (have to take the head off to see it).

The walkers and fully flanged dolls are rare versions of the 18" and 20" dolls made in 1959.

18" and 20" walkers came in both straight leg and bent-knee version. Bent-knee sold in slacks outfit. Straight legs sold in dresses, usually gowns.

Very few 17" dolls seen. The 17" is marked VT-18 but has a more pixieish face, bubble cut hair, and shorter arms and legs which do not have size markings.

Most Revlons have size markings on arms and legs. Marks on right inside arm near armpit, "18".

So-called Flat Faced VT-18 and 20 dolls are actually from the same head mold as other Revlons; they simply lack the metal front-to-back stretcher which was normally installed in the head. When the factory ran out of parts, they just left it out.

Earliest dolls from 1956 came in the red and white diamond boxes.

26" made only in 1957 is the Revlon Glamour doll collection wearing three of the versions of the glamorous dresses and gown.

Sears had several versions of fashions that were not available elsewhere in 1958:
Happi-Time Modiste, a fake fur coat in plush with matching hat, rayon blouse with metallic thread trim, pleated cotton skirt, lace trimmmed panties, shoes, nylons, pearl earrings. Available in 1958, 20" size.
Queen of Diamonds variation had a dress with gold lamé bodice, print skirt, lined velvet coat, and lamé scarf. Sewn-in slip, panties, nylons, shoes, rhinestone earrings, necklace, and ring. Available in 18" and 20" sizes.
Kissing Pink version is a print dress with net and ruffled crinoline; bodice has imitation rhinestone buttons. Pearl necklace and earrings.
Fifth Avenue, 20", has jointed knees and is a walker. Lounging ensemble of cotton blouse, slacks, and high heel shoes, ear-rings, flower spray, and cotton fleece jacket.

15" Miss Revlon has an hourglass silhouette in contrast to thick waist on other Miss Revlons. Head is molded differently with smoother transition from neck to head, jawline less jutting. Several dresses unique to 15" doll: floral print dress with nylon organdy cowl collars in blue and yellow/orange. Brunette doll was sold without earrings or fingernail polish. Also seen was a strapless pink gown with silver overlay. Pink or blue nylon organdy flocked with baby blue butterflies has cowl collar or puffy sleeves with round collar. Also seen is a Kissing Pink dress with navy blue fabric variation.

Princess Mary marked "V-22" has the exact mold marks as the 22" Revlon except that the "T" on the VT is not clearly seen.

Miss Revlon shoes had the criss-cross elastic or the elastic across the toe. The criss-cross ones were most common and were made only in black.

Kissing Pink (1956 – 1959)

Striped dress with bow in front and an assortment of cotton dresses with crinoline slip, high heel shoes, nylon hosiery, and pearl necklace.

#0940   18"   #0960   20"   #0980   23"

In 1958 15" available in Sears catalog wearing print dress with imitation rhinestone buttons, pearl necklace and earrings. In 1959 only 18" and 20" available.

Cherries A La Mode (1956 – 1959)

Dress with cherries and assortment of nylon dresses with crinoline slip, high heel shoes, nylon hosiery, pearl necklace, pearl earrings, and hat.

#0945   18"   #0965   20"   #0985   23"

In 1959 only #0935-15" available.

Queen of Diamonds (1956 – 1958)

Velvet dress with fur stole, an assortment of styles with high heel shoes, nylon hosiery, rhinestone earrings, necklace, and ring.

#0950   18"   #0970   20"   #0990   23"

1959 Queen of Diamonds 18" and 20" advertised in Sears catalog had velvet coat lined with lamé, a lamé scarf, and a dress with lamé bodice with rhinestone jewelry.

New in 1957

Snow Peach Bride floor-length bridal gown, long sleeved and jewel necked with lace bodice and lace overlay skirt. Floor-length tulle veil trimmed in lace with crown of orange blossoms. Holds wedding bouquet with trailing white satin streamers. Teardrop pearl earrings, necklace, and ring.

#0955   18"   #0975   20"   #0995   23"

Revlon Glamour doll (1957)

Only in 23", all with earrings, necklace, and rings.   Revlon Glamour doll in 26":

#0921	Net and lace dress with matching stole	#0931	Net and lace dress with matching stole
#0922	Strapless gown with tiers of ruffles	#0932	Strapless gown with tiers of ruffles
#0923	Velvet dress with lace	#0933	Navy dress with lace trim
#0924	Velvet ball gown with lace sidesweep		
#0925	Velvet dress with tulle side panel		
#0926	Lace over taffeta with long sleeves		
#0927	Bride		
#0928	Taffeta dress with net side panel		
#0929	Navy dress with lace trim		
#0930	Strapless taffeta with petal skirt, short cape, and gauntlets		

Little Miss Revlon Outfits

46 Different Outfits Available
From Ideal Booklet #21-757-LMRC

#900 Basic Little Miss Revlon Doll — Original Price $2.98

Outfits marked on tag inside outfit: IDEAL (in oval) Toy Corp./HOLLIS, N.Y. Trademarks on box: Doll clothes by IDEAL (in oval) for Little Miss Revlon. Made in U.S.A. by Ideal Toy Corp./Hollis 23, N.Y. Numbered without the nine in front, so in brochure #9177 would say 177 on box. Current prices for MIB outfits in $35.00 range.

Night Time Series   Original Price

9177	Shorty Nightgown	$1.00
9178	Pajamas (short sleeve check with long pants)	$1.50
9179	Lounging Pajamas (snap front patterned jacket with solid pants)	$2.00
9207	TV Lounging Outfit w/sun glasses (diamond shape pull-over with solid red ribbed pants	$2.50
9249	Negligee Set with shoes, curlers	$3.00
9176	Hostess Gown with mirror (long gown with tie around waist)	$3.50

School Series

9105	Torso Dress (daisy print dress with cowl collar)	$1.50
9114	School Dress (solid dress with design across chest)	$1.50
9115	Polka Dot Dress	$1.50
9119	Jumper (with blouse underneath)	$1.50
9120	Striped Dress with shoes, stockings, purse	$2.00
9121	Gay Stripe Dress with shoes, stockings, purse (plaid skirt, solid jewelry, long sleeve blouse)	$2.00
9122	Party Dress with shoes, stockings, purse (solid color short sleeve dress with ribbon around edge of shirt and bodice)	$2.00
9123	School Dress with shoes, stockings, purse (striped long sleeve dress with tie)	$2.50

Playtime Series

9215	Two-Piece Playsuit (shorts with short sleeve skirt)	$1.00
9216	Sun Dress and Bonnet	$1.50
9208	Pedal Pusher Outfit with sunglasses	$2.50
9209	Jeans and Shirt with hat	$2.50
9211	Sunsuit with hat (shorts with shirt over with coolie hat)	$2.50
9205	Coolie Beach Outfit with hat, sunglasses (Playsuit with sleeveless wrapper and cloth coolie hat with dark border)	$3.00

Junior Miss Series

9210	Skirt and Blouse with shoes, stockings, and purse (print skirt with white blouse)	$2.50
9212	Sweater, Skirt Outfit with shoes, stockings, purse (felt skirt)	$3.00
9213	Pinafore with shoes, stockings, purse (white pinafore over print dress)	$3.00
9127	Pinafore with shoes, stockings, purse (clear net pinafore over solid dress)	$3.00

Novelty Series

9130	Sailor Outfit with hat (solid color dress with snaps on left side, with middy collar)	$2.00
9258	Ballerina Outfit with shoes, flowers	$2.00

Novelty Series (continued)   Original Price

9116	Calypso Blouse and Skirt with crinoline, flowers (white blouse and a solid color skirt with rick-rack)	$3.00
9256	Nurse Outfit with cap, shoes, stockings	$3.00
9257	Artist's Outfit with shoes (with beret, pedal pushers, and smock)	$3.00

Visiting Outfits

9117	Visiting Outfit with crinoline, hat (Solid white ruffled blouse with striped skirt)	$3.50
9118	Traveling Outfit with crinoline, hat (Polka dot dress with rick-rack)	$3.50
9141	Sunday Outfit with crinoline, hat (striped skirt with solid top and tie, hat with netting)	$3.50
9143	Velvet Sheath with hat, purse	$3.50
9255	5-Piece Redingote* Outfit with hat, purse (polka-dot sheath with coat lined with polka-dots, belt, hat)	$3.50
9142	Princess Style Outfit with crinoline, hat, purse	$4.00
9254	5-Piece Striped Suit with hat (striped car coat, straight skirt)	$4.00

Formal Series

9157	Lace Formal with shoes, stockings (light color bodice with dark lace skirt)	$4.00
9160	Taffeta Formal with shoes, stockings	$4.00
9158	Nylon Formal (print skirt)	$4.00
9159	Debutante Gown with crinoline, flowers (with black lace apron)	$4.50

Bridal Series

9172	Bridal with shoes, stockings (with hair netting)	$4.50
9171	Bridesmaid Outfit with hat, flowers, shoes, stockings	$4.50
9170	Debutante Bridal Gown with flowers, pearls, crinoline	$5.00

Coats

9241	Flared Woolen Coat	$2.00
9252	Raincoat, Boots, Tote Bag	$2.00
9240	Checked Coat, Hat, Purse	$3.00

Boxed Sets

9010	Little Miss Revlon Gift Box, doll and four outfits (in style shop box)	$10.00
9289	Little Miss Revlon Travel Case (11" x 11¾")	$3.00

Accessories

9280	Crinoline (set of two)	$1.00
9284	Shoes and Stockings (two pair each)	$1.00
9285	Eyeglasses (assorted colors)	$0.25
9286	Set of six hangers (assorted colors)	$0.30
9287	Hat in hat box	$1.00
9299	Little Miss Revlon Doll Stand	$0.60

*Redingote = A woman's lightweight coat open at front

Shirley Temple Doll Fashions
(1959 – 1963)

Year	Size	Number	Description
1959	12"	9520	TV Wardrobe Package – Shirley wears slip, panties, black slip-on shoes, and socks; comes with play outfit, school dress, party dress, purse, raincoat, hat, tote bag, glasses and necklace
	15"	1400	Velvet dress with organdy pinafore with pocketbook
	17"	1410	Yellow dress with slip, purse, ST pin, side-fastening shoes
	19"	1420	Plaid skirt with velvet top, slip, purse, side-fastening shoes, ST pin
1960	12"	9500-0	Slip, panties, slip-on black shoes, socks, and hair bow
		9715-4	Velvet dropped shoulder dress
		9724-6	Sailor Girl outfit, white pleated skirt, navy middy jacket
		9713-9	Cotton School dress, embossed blouse
		9716-2	Flowered pinafore on embossed dress
		9718-8	Cowgirl outfit, boots, sombrero
		9720-4	Nylon Party dress, straw hat
		9712-1	Rickrack school dress
		9714-7	Felt jumper with dog, blouse, headband
		9710-5	Flannelette nightgown with matching cap
		9717-0	Nylon visiting dress
		9721-2	Taffeta coat, straw hat
		9711-3	Plastic raincoat, hat, tote bag
		9722-0	"Heidi" outfit – polka dot skirt, organdy apron, laced bodice
		9560-4	"Wee Willie Winkie" outfit, pleated kilt, jacket, matching cap
		9719-6	"Rebecca of Sunnybrook Farm" outfit, plaid overalls, shirt
		9564-6	"Captain January" outfit, white or navy sailor suit with bow and white cap
		9520-9	TV Wardrobe Package with two dresses, nightgown, raincoat, purse, hat, tote bag.
For sizes	15"	1400-1	Doll came in a window box along with five outfits Shirley wore in her movie classics:
	17"	1410-0	"Stand Up and Cheer," polka dot nylon dress with ruffle
	19"	1420-9	"Captain January," navy middy dress and hat
			"Heidi," polka dot skirt, white apron, laced bodice, white blouse, hat
			"Rebecca," navy jumper with plaid pockets, shirt, and scarf
			"Wee Willie Winkie," Scotch kilt outfit
1961	12"	9500-0	Pink romper comes with name pin
		9750-1	Plaid short sleeve shirt and shorts
		9755-0	Clown flannelette pajama and stocking hat
		9756-8	Pique school dress with striped trim
		9757-6	Dress with v-shaped front bib
		9760-0	Pedal pusher and print blouse, straw hat
		9765-9	Flocked nylon dress with shoulder ties
		9766-7	Felt coat and beret
		9767-5	Ballerina pleated outfit with ruffled collar, headband
		9768-3	Cotton school dress with striped blouse and solid pinafore
		9770-9	Dropped shoulder nylon party dress with velveteen bodice and hat
		9771-7	Three-piece cardigan suit, pleated check skirt
		9775-8	Leatherette car coat with fur collar, and felt slacks, and cap
	15"	1403-5	Cinderella-long gown with white skirt, lace trim on dark bodice
		1405-0	Alice in Wonderland – dress with white organdy pinafore
		1407-6	Little Red Riding Hood – cape with hood and print dress with white apron
		1404-3	Little Bo-Peep – ¾-length dress with print skirt, dark bodice and puff sleeves, straw hat
		1408-4	Party dress – short sleeveless dress with flower at waist
	17"	1410-0	Plaid party dress with lace trim, straw hat

Year	Size	Number	Description
	19"	1425-8	Walking doll wearing plaid party dress with lace trim, straw hat
1962	12"	9500-0	Basic doll wears one-piece playsuit, shoes, socks, and name pin
		9782-4	Nightgown
		9783-2	School dress with solid top, striped skirt
		9784-0	Raincoat and hat
		9785-7	Two-piece playsuit of knit sweater and shorts
		9786-5	Felt coat with fur collar, fur hat
		9787-3	Party dress with velvet top, nylon skirt
		9788-1	Party dress with nylon top, velvet skirt, straw hat
		9775-8	Leatherette car coat, felt slacks, scarf
		9520-8	TV package with two dresses, red leather coat, tote bag, sunglasses, wearing one-piece check playsuit, name pin
	15"	1415-9	Party dress with cut-out decoration on bodice
		"	Jumper with white blouse
		"	Dress with buttons on solid bodice, white skirt with dark ribbon trim
		"	Dress with three tiers of ruffles on sleeve, solid color bodice and skirt
1963	15"	1415-9	Redesigned face and hair-do with bangs, wears assorted dresses

Tammy Family Fashions
(1962 – 1964)

Number	Outfit	Description
Tammy Clothes		**1962**
9091-0	Underwear	Nylon petticoat, panties, bra, comb, brush, mirror, and slippers
9092-8	Sleepytime	Pink check shortie pajamas, slippers, comb, curlers, and glass of milk
9093-6	Fun in the Sun	Red bathing suit with white terry cover-up, bathing cap, and mat
9111-6	Puddle Jumper	Blue Chesterfield raincoat, scarf, white boots, and red shoulder bag
9113-2	Tennis the Menace	Print overblouse with cord belt, yellow shorts, tennis socks, shoes, sunglasses, tennis racquet and press, and hair band
9114-0	Walking her Pet	Leather skirt, wool plaid top, red scarf, gold heart chain, red shoulder bag
9115-7	Pizza Party	Harlequin top, red leotard, wedgies, glasses, pizza, and newspaper
9117-3	Beau and Arrow	Red hooded sweatshirt, dungarees, bow and arrow, and sneakers
9131-4	Cheerleader	White sweater with letter T, red short felt skirt and matching cap, white socks, sneakers, baton, and megaphone
9132-2	Cutie Co-ed	Blue corduroy jumper, red turtleneck, red leotards, red bag, radio, gold heart necklace, and red sneakers
9133-0	School Daze	Red top dress with plaid skirt, gold belt, typewriter, phone, phone book, zippered red portfolio, and red heels
9131-4	Picnic Party	Blue striped knit shirt, white clamdiggers, sneakers, sunglasses, headband, picnic basket, tablecloth, and transistor radio
9135-5	Sweater Girl	Red cardigan sweater, gray skirt, pearl necklace, camera, red and black purse, eyeglasses, and date book
9152-0	Ring-A-Ding	Pink overblouse, black velvet pants, wedgies, phone book, bowl of fruit, and TV
9153-8	Dream Boat	Blue satin and brocade party dress, silk jacket, flowered headband, gold purse, date book, and camera
9172-8	Travel Along	Blue and white check dress, gold chain belt, red kerchief, nylons, white pumps, eyeglasses, vinyl shoulder bag, newspaper, and hat box
9173-6	Model Miss	Blue wool lined coat, pocketbook, pearl bracelet, model's hat box, cap, red shoes, nylons, and date book
9174-4	Sorority Sweetheart	Wool jerkin with sorority emblem, check blouse, blue wool skirt, nylons, red ribbon and red pumps, TV, phone, eyeglasses, and phone directory

9175-1	CheckMate	Red check blouse, white pleated skirt, blue wool blazer, camera, shoulder bag, pearl necklace, hair bow, nylons, news, and white shoes
9211-4	Snow Bunny	Red wool jacket with fur trim, black pants, white fur-topped boots, skis, poles, and white mittens

1963

9094-4	Knit Knack	Crocheted and knitted square neck dress, beret, and shoes
9118-1	Tee Time	Aqua panty-blouse and golf skirt, sun hat, plastic golf bag, golf belt with three tees, sneakers, and score card
9119-9	Purl One	Blue sleeveless shirtwaist dress, red and black shoulder bag, hanky, knitting bag with wool, two knitting needles, and shoes
9176-9	Fur and Formal	Gold metallic brocade dress, fur-stole, pearl necklace and bracelet, long white gloves, gold bag, flowered headband, nylons, and red shoes
9177-7	Skate Date	Gold brocade top and velvet skirt, roller skates, shoes, stretch panties, nylons, gold headband, and plastic skating bag
9212-2	Figure 8	Wool pants, white knit jacket, wool scarf and hat, gloves, ice skates, shoes, and carrying strap

1964

Spring

9051-4	Garden Party	Sleeveless dress with straw hat
9052-2	Racket Club	Sleeveless tennis dress
9053-0	Sweet Dreams	Shorty pajamas
9054-8	Sunny Stroller	Sleeveless yellow and white striped dress
9055-5	Dance Date	Sleeveless dress with printed flower skirt
9056-3	Beach Party	Two-piece bathing suit with bathing cap
9061-3	Flared and Fitted	Sleeveless party dress
9062-1	Spring Topper	Coat
9063-9	Pretty Precious	Two-piece sleeveless dress
9120-7	Nurse's Aide	Red and white candy-striper outfit with stethoscope
9134-8	Picnic Party	White clamdiggers, striped shirt, and picnic basket
9136-3	Miss Ballerina	Gold and white tutu, tulle skirt, tights, ballet slippers, and bag
9137-1	Fraternity Hop	Red sleeveless top, gold brocade short gown, and red velvet wrap
9155-3	Jet Set	Car coat with toggles, plaid pants, and kerchief
9168-6	On the Town	Velvet fur-trimmed matching jacket and dress
9169-4	Beauty Queen	Long gown of gold brocade skirt and red velvet sleeveless top, loving cup, flowers and tiara
9213-0	Wedding Belle	White long wedding gown, veil, tiara, and fur-stole

Pepper Clothes

9306-2	Budding Ballerina	Tutu, ballet slippers, and bag
9308-8	Teacher's Pet	Plaid school dress with bookbag
9317-9	Happy Holiday	Pink and white striped short sleeve dress with shuffleboard game
9318-7	After School	Cotton hooded sweatshirt, dungarees, and ping-pong paddles
9326-0	Birthday Party	Sleeveless party dress and record player
9327-8	Cat's Meow	Check long sleeve shirt and solid pants
9331-0	Miss Gadabout	Two-piece suit, skirt, and hat
9339-3	Snow Flake	Hooded spotted coat, pants, and sled
9332-8	Flower Girl	Long sleeveless gown and flowers

Clothes on cards

9401-1	Nylon Undies	Nylon petticoat and panties
9403-7	Bed Time	Flannel two-piece pajamas and slippers
9404-5	Classroom Caper	Sleeveless school dress and lace trimmed panties
9406-0	After School Fun	Knit wool short sleeve sweater and gray flannel pants
9408-6	Frosty Frolics	Blue flannel winter coat with fur collar and headband
9409-4	Party Time	Nylon and velvet sleeveless dress

Mom — Clothes all on cards

9415-1	Nighty Nite	Printed lawn cotton sleeveless nightgown
9417-7	Hidden Glamour	Black lace lingerie: bra, panty, and half slip
9418-5	Lazy Days	Fleece bathrobe
9419-3	Shopping Topping	Sleeveless dress, blue pattern top, and solid skirt
9421-9	Evening in Paris	Sleeveless gold brocade sheath
9422-7	Lounging Luxury	Short sleeve print top, rayon brocade pants, and wedgies

Dad and Ted — Clothes all on cards

9451-6	Broadcloth shirt	Assorted colors
9452-4	Slacks	Assorted colors
9453-2	Bermuda shorts and knee socks	
9456-5	Pajamas and slippers	
9457-3	Bathrobe and slippers	
9458-1	Pull-over sweater	
9461-5	Blazer jacket	
9462-3	Cardigan sweater	With matching knee socks
9463-1	Sports vest	With tie and shoes
9466-4	Sweater and slacks	
9467-2	Sports carcoat	With cap
9468-0	Suit	Suit, jacket, trousers, and shoes

Crissy® Family of Grow-Hair Dolls
(1969 – 1977)

Doll	Year	Value	Description
Crissy®			
Beautiful Crissy®	1969	17½", $45.00	All vinyl, dark brown eyes, long auburn grow-hair, wears orange lace dress. First year hair grew to floor length.
Beautiful Negro	1969	17½", $65.00	
Movin' Groovin'	1971	$35.00	
Black Movin' Groovin'	1971	$40.00	
Talky	1971 – 1973	$55.00	
Spanish Speaking Talky	1972	$65.00	
Look Around	1972	$40.00	
Black Look Around	1972	$45.00	
Swirlacurler	1973	$35.00	
Black Swirlacurler	1973	$45.00	
Twirly Beads	1974	$35.00	
Black Twirly Beads	1974	$45.00	
Beautiful Crissy Reissued	1982 – 1983	$25.00	
"Country Fashion"	1982 – 1983	$25.00	
Reissued Black	1982 – 1983	$30.00	

Doll	Year	Value	Description
Velvet	1970 – 1971	15½", $55.00 Black, $65.00	Crissy®'s younger cousin. Blonde grow-hair, violet sleep eyes, wears purple dress. First Velvet in lavender corduroy is harder to find.
Movin' Groovin'	1971	$35.00	
Black Movin' Groovin'	1971	$55.00	
Look Around	1972	$35.00	
Black Look Around	1972	$75.00	
Talky	1971 – 1973	$45.00	
Beauty Braider	1973	$35.00	
Black Beauty Braider	1973	$45.00	
Swirly Daisies	1974	$35.00	
Black Swirly Daisies	1974	$45.00	
Tressy	1970	17½", $65.00	Black grow-hair, blue sleep eyes, closed smiling mouthpale skin tone, wears Hawaiian print mini dress. Sears exclusive.
Black Tressy	1970	$80.00	
Posin' Tressy	1972	$75.00	Darker complexion, swivel waist. Called Movin' Groovin' in Sears catalog. Wears aqua satin mini dress with blue shoes. Also came with wedding dress.
Mia	1971	15½", $50.00	Velvet's friend. Dark brown hair, blue sleep eyes, wears turquoise romper.
Kerry	1971	17½", $55.00	Crissy®'s friend. Blonde hair, green sleep eyes, green romper, green shoes.
Cricket			
Posin' Cricket also called Movin' Groovin'	1971 – 72	15½", $65.00	Vinyl head and body, tosca rooted hair, brown sleep eyes. Open smiling mouth. Sears exclusive. In 1972 came in bridesmaid dress that matched Tressy's bridal gown.
Cinnamon	1972 – 74	13½", $60.00	Velvet's little sister. Auburn hair, blue painted eyes.
Black Cinnamon	1974	$70.00	
Hairdoodler	1973	$40.00	
Black Hairdoodler	1973	$70.00	
Curly Ribbons	1974	$45.00	
Black Curly Ribbons	1974	$70.00	
Brandi	1972 – 73	17½", $55.00	Crissy®'s friend. Golden blonde hair, blue painted eyes, orange bathing suit, glowing tan, swivel waist, heart tattoo on cheek.
Dina	1972 – 73	15", $50.00	Velvet's friend. Platinum blonde hair, blue painted eyes, purple playsuit, butterfly tattoo on leg, tan, swivel waist.

Doll	Year	Value	Description
Baby Crissy®	1973 – 76	24", $75.00	Soft vinyl, wears pink dress; pull string to make hair grow.
Black Baby Crissy®	1973 – 76	$85.00	
Reissued	1981	24", $35.00	1981 reissue, no grow hair.
Baby Velvet	1974	20" $85.00	20" foam body, lavender sleep eyes, blonde grow hair.
Tara	1976	15½", $75.00	Authentic black doll wears yellow gingham pants outfit.
Magic Hair Crissy®	1977	19", $35.00	Teen doll with Velcro add-on hairpieces.
Black Magic Hair Crissy®	1977	$40.00	

All dolls ™ Ideal Toy Corp.

Petite Princess and Princess Patti Furniture (1964 – 1965)

Petite Princess

Number	Item	Price
4407-3	Salon Curved Sofa	$35.00
4408-1	Boudoir Chair Lounge	$35.00
4409-9	Guest Chair	$35.00
4410-7	Salon Wing Chair	$35.00
4411-4	Salon Drum Chair	$35.00
4412-3	Occasional Chair/Ottoman	$35.00
4413-1	Host Dining Chairs	$25.00
4414-9	Guest Dining Chairs	$25.00
4415-6	Hostess Dining Chairs	$25.00
4416-4	Little Princess Bed	$45.00
4417-2	Royal Dressing Table/Stool	$45.00
4418-0	Treasure Trove Cabinet	$35.00
4419-8	Royal Buffet	$45.00
4420-6	Palace Chest	$25.00
4421-4	Dining Room Table	$35.00
4422-2	Regency Hearth Place	$45.00
4423-0	Grandfather Clock & Folding Screen	$45.00
4424-8	Rolling Tea Cart	$25.00
4425-5	Royal Grand Piano	$75.00
4426-3	Lyre Table Set	$25.00
4427-1	Pedestal Table Set	$25.00
4428-9	Heirloom Table Set	$25.00
4429-7	Tier Table Set	$25.00
4431-3	Palace Table Set	$25.00
4437-0	Occasional Table Set	$25.00
4432-1	Fantasy Telephone Set	$25.00
4433-9	Salon Coffee Table Set	$25.00
4439-6	Royal Candelabra	$15.00
4438-8	Fantasia Candelabra	$35.00
4440-4	Salon Planter	$25.00
4450-3	Fantasy Room	$35.00
9710-3	Fantasy Family	$45.00

Princess Patti

Room	Item	Price
Bathroom	Waste basket, stool, mirror	$55.00
	Hamper	$15.00
	Oval tub with swans	$55.00
	Sink w/ attached mirror	$45.00
	Toilet	$45.00
	Linen cabinet with four towels	$85.00
Kitchen	Round kitchen table w/ flowers	$55.00
	Four kitchen chairs	$60.00
	Range w/ four utensils	$85.00
	Refrigerator	$200.00
	Sink & dishwasher	$75.00
	Hutch with plates	$55.00
Other	Television with stand	$225.00
	Dollhouse	$150.00
	Vinyl carrying case	$75.00
	Retail Display Dollhouse	$700.00

Mysteries Solved

This section corrects information that has previously appeared in print or thought by collectors about Ideal dolls.

There was **not** a 9" **Shirley Temple** doll; she is, in fact, **Coquette (1939)**. All composition, painted molded hair, painted blue side glancing eyes. She came dressed in long gown and was also available with a carrying case with a layette and other outfit. She appears in the 1939 Ideal catalog. Marks: 9 (backwards 9)/IDEAL/DOLL (on back).

According to Pat Schoonmaker in *Doll Reader* magazine, if you want to know how to differentiate between a **Shirley Temple** doll and other dolls from the same era, keep these facts in mind: Cinderella (1938) doll had the same head mold as Ginger (**1934 – 1927**), Snow White (**1938**), and Mary Jane (**1941**). They all had dimples in their chins, while Shirley did **not** have a dimple in her chin but had a dimple in each cheek..

The **Crown Princess (1957)** 10½" vinyl is basically the same doll later called **Little Miss Revlon**. She was offered in the 1957 catalog. According to Ruth Leif, her limbs were flanged vinyl while **Little Miss Revlon** is strung. For identification purposes, Crown Princess does **not** have pierced ears and earrings. **Little Miss Revlon** has pierced ears.

There was **not** a **teen Shirley Temple** doll (**circa 1957**). Apparently preliminary plans were made for one including having a prototype sculpted by Bernard Lipfert, but Shirley Temple Black did not agree to a teen doll in her image. The doll that has appeared in print as a "Teen Shirley Temple" is, in fact, a Crown Princess. Her ears are unpierced.

The **Loni Anderson doll** was never produced. According to television star Loni Anderson's publicist, Ms. Anderson herself has said a doll was not produced in 1981; only a prototype was made that appeared in the catalog.

The 15" **Trudy** doll was made by Three-in-One Doll Co. However, Ideal made a larger (20") version called **Big Sister** in the 1940s. She has a composition head and a felt stuffed body This is the three-faced doll whose head rotates when a knob on the top of her head is turned. It is unclear who "knocked-off" whom in this instance. However, since Ideal had made an earlier three-headed doll (Soozie Smiles in 1923 and an even earlier two-headed doll Baby Bi-Face in 1916), it is probable that Ideal was the first on the market.

As prices approach $3,000 for the **Comic Heroine** dolls, and $4,500 for **Samantha, the Betwitching Doll,** I'd like to try to clear up confusion between these dolls and **Misty,** another 12" doll also produced by Ideal in the mid-1960s. There were two versions of Misty: the early straight ahead "center eye" doll with blue eyes and blonde hair with bangs and a straight leg body. This doll is currently worth $150 nude. This doll has erroneously been called the Elizabeth Montgomery doll. There **was never** an **Elizabeth Montgomery doll.** Ideal thought this first version of Misty looked too harsh according to a former Ideal employee, so they made the more commonly found side glancing blue-eyed Misty doll with light blonde hair and bangs with a straight leg body. She is marked ©1965/IDEAL TOY CORP/W-12-3 (on head); ©IDEAL (in oval); 12M-12 (on hip). She was available in 1965 – 1966. This Misty is worth $25 nude. Then there was a **Pos'n Misty** doll also available from 1965 – 1966. She has blonde hair with bangs swept to the side. She has posing arms and legs. Her marks are: ©1965/IDEAL TOY CORP./W12-3 (on head); body unmarked. The highly sought-after **Samantha: The Bewitched Posing** doll is from the ABC television show "Bewitched" starring Elizabeth Montgomery. 12" Samantha, made in 1966, is all vinyl; however, she has khaki green/brown side-glancing eyes. Two versions have been seen: with bending knees and without bending knees. Samantha whose legs do not bend is marked: IDEAL DOLL/M-12-E-2 (on head); IDEAL in oval/1965 (on body). Samantha has been seen with legs that can be posed has the same body as Pos'n Misty. Her marks are: IDEAL DOLL/M-12-E-2 (on head and body). Both dolls have dark blonde hair pulled back off their face and no bangs.

The **Comic Heroine** dolls are 11½" with an all vinyl poseable body. They were sold from 1967 – 1968. They all had the same Pos'n Misty head but had pink lips, green side-glancing eyes with green eye shadow, and rounded black eyebrows. They have the Pos'n Misty body with wires in the arms and legs. They can be identified by the fact that their hair does not have bangs, the hair is rooted in a line from front to back and will fall long on either side of the part and have a flipped curl at the end. Some have small bobby pins or what looks like a baggie tie holding hair in place. Their dentity can be determined by the hair color. **Mera-Princess of the Deep** has red hair; **Wonder Woman** is dark burnette; **Supergirl** is a blonde; **Batgirl** has black hair. However, the Sears version of Batgirl was blonde. They are all marked: 1965/Ideal Toy Corp.W-12-3 (on head); 1965/Ideal (in oval)/2 M-12 (on hip).

Tabatha or Tiny Thumbelina – There has been confusion between a doll called Tiny Thumbelina (1968) #0406-9 and Tabatha (1966) #1150-2. Both look very much alike since they have the same head and are 14" baby dolls. Both have a vinyl head and painted side glancing eyes, and rooted pixie cut platinum hair. However, Tabatha is worth more than Tiny Thumbelina. At a recent auction, Tabatha sold for $1,400. The differences between the dolls are that Thumbelina's painted blue eyes have irises painted to the left side. She has a soft cloth body and most importantly, she has a knob in back of her body to make her move. She wears a knit set. Her marks are: ©1966/IDEAL TOY CORP./TAT-14-H-62. Tabatha's irises are painted to the right, and she has a soft squeezable body, unclear if cloth or not, short shiny silver hair, and wears a two-piece shortie pj set. Her legs also do not appear to be as bent as Tiny Thumbelina.

Laura and Robin: According to a 1981 published Toy Fair report, Laura and Robin (her black counterpart) were supposed to be released in 1981 wearing a wardrobe designed by Calvin Klein. They came with a soft bosom and derriere and dressed in a bra and panties. The doll was designed by Judy Albert. A complete wardrobe for them appears in the 1981 catalog. However, the author has never seen any of these dolls. It is likely they were never produced.

Mysteries Remaining

It is unclear whether there was a **Marilyn Knowlden** doll. According to Pat Smith, the doll was a Shirley Temple doll with a black wig. Marilyn Knowlden was a child star of the 1930s but never attained as great film success as Shirley Temple. Thus, her dolls did not sell very well, and they are now rare. Pat says the doll was advertised in the John Plain Wholesale catalog.

It is unclear whether Ideal manufactured a 10" vinyl doll called **Shirley Ann** in the 1950s trademarked 10. She has a pre-teen girl's body and straight blonde or brown hair. Ruth Leif says her clothes have the Ideal snap but the dress is a cheaper rayon in a style than Ideal is known for. It is possible the doll was made for another doll company to sell.

Pictured in the photo section is a 17½" doll that looks the same as **Black Magic Hair Crissy®** (**1977**) but there is no Velcro on her head to attach the five hair pieces that come with her. The doll without Velcro on her head is wearing an ElectroMan outfit. The ElectroMan doll (1977), a boy's toy that sensed light, was unsuccessful. So, it is likely that Ideal had extra outfits available. It is unclear what name Ideal gave this doll.

This author has seen no proof that there was a hard plastic version of **Judy Garland as Dorothy of Oz** produced by Ideal in the 1950s (as reported in a 1989 article on Judy in *Doll Reader*).

3½" **Angel Babies** (1982) may not have seen widespread production.

Chronology of Plants

1903	Thompson Ave. Store	Brooklyn, NY
1906	Small shop	Brooklyn, NY
1907	50' x 50' Loft	Brooklyn, NY
1908	311-17 Christopher Ave.	Brooklyn, NY
1911	233-35 Powell St.	Brooklyn, NY
1913	273-299 Van Sinderen Avenue	Brooklyn, NY
	468 Broadway-Show Rooms	
1935	23-10 43rd Ave	Long Island City, NY
	Salesroom: 872 Broadway	
1949	184-10 Jamaica Ave	Hollis, NY (Queens, L.I.)
1973		Newark, NJ
before 1981	500 Harmon Meadow Blvd.	Secaucus, NJ
1960s on		Caribbean
		Dominican Republic
		Hong Kong
		Haiti
1982		China

Major Company Trademarks

(Date Indicated is Date First Used)

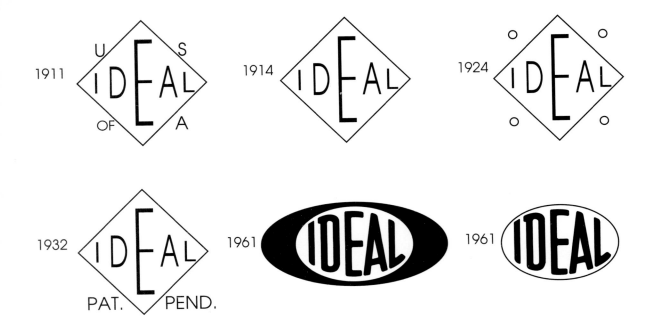

1911   1914   1924

1932   1961   1961

References

Primary Research Materials

Butler Brothers Catalog 1908, 1916, 1924. Courtesy Margaret Strong Museum, Rochester, NY.

Ideal Company Catalogs: 1937 – 1939, 1947, 1951 – 1985.

Playthings Magazine, Ideal Ads from 1908 – 1955. Courtesy Mrs. Sig Halpern

Sears Company Catalogs. 1920 – 1930.

Toys and Novelties Magazine. 1930 – 1963.

Books

Anderton, Joanne: *Twentieth Century Dolls*. Trojan Press, N. Kansas City MO, 1971.

———*More Twentieth Century Dolls*. Wallace-Homestead, Des Moines, IA , 1983.

Axe, John: *Tammy and the Dolls You Love to Dress*. Hobby House Press, 1979.

Coleman, Dorothy, Elizabeth, and Evelyn: *The Collector's Encyclopedia of Dolls. Volume I and II*. Crown Publishers, NY, 1968 and 1986.

Foulke, Jan: *10th Blue Book: Dolls and Values*. Hobby House Press, Cumberland MD, 1991.

Hart, Luella: *List of Doll Trademarks*.

Judd, Pam and Polly: *Compo Dolls: 1928 – 1955*. Hobby House Press, 1991.

———*Hard Plastic Dolls, Vol. I and II*. Hobby House Press, 1987 and 1989.

Mandeville, A. Glenn: *Golden Age of Collectible Dolls*. Hobby House Press, 1990.

O'Brien, Richard : *American Toys: From Puritans to the Present*. Abbeville Publishing, NY, 1990.

Smith, Patricia: *Doll Values: Antique to Modern*. Collector Books, Paducah, KY, 1992.

Waugh, Carol-Lynn: *Petite Portraits*. Hobby House Press, 1982.

Ideal Doll Index

COLLECTOR BOOKS

Informing Today's Collector

For over two decades we have been keeping collectors informed on trends and values in all fields of antiques and collectibles.

BOOKS ON DOLLS

4631	**Barbie Doll** Boom, 1986–1995, Augustyniak	$18.95
2079	**Barbie Doll Fashion,** Vol. I, Eames	$24.95
4846	**Barbie Doll Fashion,** Vol. II, 1968–1974, Eames	$24.95
4847	The **Barbie Doll Years,** 2nd. Ed., 1959–1996, Olds	$17.95
3957	**Barbie Exclusives,** Rana	$18.95
4632	**Barbie Exclusives,** Book II, Rana	$18.95
4557	**Barbie,** The First 30 Years, 1959–1989, Deutsch	$24.95
3873	**Black Dolls,** Book II, Perkins	$17.95
1529	Collector's Ency. of **Barbie Dolls,** DeWein/Ashabraner	$19.95
4882	Coll. Encyc. of **Barbie Doll Exclusives & More,** Augustyniak	$19.95
2211	Collector's Encyclopedia of **Madame Alexander Dolls,** Smith	$24.95
4859	Collector's Guide to **Barbie Doll Paper Dolls,** Mieszala	$16.95
4861	Collector's Guide to **Tammy,** Sabulis/Weglewski	$18.95
4863	Collector's Guide to **Vogue Dolls,** Izen/Stover	$29.95
4707	Decade of **Barbie Dolls** & Collectibles, 1981–1991, Summers	$19.95
5039	**Doll Values,** Antique to Modern, 2nd Ed., Moyer	$12.95
1799	**Effanbee Doll** Encyclopedia, Smith	$19.95
4571	**Liddle Kiddles,** Identification & Value Guide, Langford	$18.95
5047	**Madame Alexander** Collector's Dolls Price Guide #23, Crowsey	$9.95
4873	**Modern Collectible Dolls,** Id. & Value Guide, Moyer	$19.95
3826	Story of **Barbie,** Westenhouser	$19.95
1513	**Teddy Bears & Steiff** Animals, Mandel	$9.95
1817	**Teddy Bears & Steiff** Animals, 2nd Series, Mandel	$19.95
2084	**Teddy Bears, Annalees's & Steiff** Animals, 3rd Series, Mandel	$19.95
1808	Wonder of **Barbie,** Manos	$9.95
4880	The World of **Raggedy Ann** Collectibles, Avery	$24.95
1430	World of **Barbie Dolls,** Manos	$9.95

BOOKS ON TOYS, MARBLES & CHRISTMAS COLLECTIBLES

3427	**Advertising Character** Collectibles, Dotz	$17.95
2333	Antique & Collectible **Marbles,** 3rd Ed., Grist	$9.95
3827	Antique & Collectible **Toys,** 1870–1950, Longest	$24.95
3956	**Baby Boomer Games,** Polizzi	$24.95
3717	**Christmas Collectibles,** 2nd Edition, Whitmyer	$24.95
4976	**Christmas Ornaments,** Lights & Decorations, Johnson	$24.95
4737	**Christmas Ornaments,** Lights & Decorations, Vol. II, Johnson	$24.95
4739	**Christmas Ornaments,** Lights & Decorations, Vol. III, Johnson	$24.95
4649	Classic **Plastic Model Kits,** Polizzi	$24.95
4559	Collectible **Action Figures,** 2nd Ed., Manos	$17.95
2338	Collector's Encyclopedia of **Disneyana,** Longest/Stern	$24.95
4958	Collector's Guide to **Battery Toys,** Hultzman	$19.95
4639	Collector's Guide to **Diecast Toys** & Scale Models, Johnson	$19.95
4653	Collector's Guide to **T.V. Memorabilia,** Davis/Morgan	$24.95
4651	Collector's Guide to **Tinker Toys,** Strange	$18.95
4566	Collector's Guide to **Tootsietoys,** 2nd Ed., Richter	$19.95
4945	**G-Men & FBI Toys** & Collectibles, Whitworth	$18.95
4720	Golden Age of **Automotive Toys,** Hutchison/Johnson	$24.95
3436	Grist's Big Book of **Marbles**	$19.95
3970	Grist's Machine-Made & Contemporary **Marbles,** 2nd Ed.	$9.95
4755	Hake's Price Guide to **Character Toy Premiums**	$24.95
4723	**Matchbox Toys,** 2nd Ed., 1947 to 1996, Johnson	$18.95
4871	**McDonald's** Collectibles, Henriques/DuVall	$19.95
1540	**Modern Toys,** 1930–1980, Baker	$19.95
3888	**Motorcycle Toys,** Antique & Contemporary, Gentry/Downs	$18.95
4953	Schroeder's Collectible **Toys,** Antique to Modern Price Guide	$17.95
1886	Stern's Guide to **Disney** Collectibles	$14.95
2139	Stern's Guide to **Disney** Collectibles, 2nd Series	$14.95
3975	Stern's Guide to **Disney** Collectibles, 3rd Series	$18.95
2028	**Toys,** Antique & Collectible, Longest	$14.95